TWENTIETH-CENTURY
MURDER

TWENTIETH-CENTURY
MURDER

A YEAR-BY-YEAR ACCOUNT OF THE WORLD'S MOST PITILESS CRIMES

MARTIN FIDO

BRACKEN

THIS IS A CARLTON BOOK

For Roy and Glen

This 1995 edition distributed by Bracken Books,
an imprint of Studio Editions Ltd.,
Princess House, 50 Eastcastle Street,
London W1N 7AP, England.

Text and Design Copyright © Carlton Books Limited 1995

Project art direction: Russell Porter
Design: Paul Messam
Project editor: Liz Wheeler
Editor: Jim Davis
Picture research: Sharon Hutton, Charlotte Bush
Production: Sarah Schuman

ISBN 1-85891-390-X

Printed in the Slovak Republic

Author's Acknowledgements
This book could never have been completed in the time available with-
out the assistance of Causeway Resources Genealogical and Historical
Research, and my first debt of gratitude is to its founder and proprietor,
Keith Skinner. He and I are also very grateful for the help of the staffs of
the British Library, the British Newspaper Library, the Public Records
Office, the Metropolitan Police History Museum, and all in Room 216.
Karen Lynn Sandel has sent useful data from across the Atlantic. Glen
Taverner kindly made available an IBM compatible word processor.

Title page photographs: (top left) Peter Kürten; (top right) Ted Bundy;
(bottom left) Charles Manson; (bottom right) Henri Landru.

Contents

Introduction

ONE HUNDRED YEARS of murder seems a long time from close up; a time of great similarities from a distance. Seventeenth-century murder all looks of a piece to us today: treacherous poisonings and back-stabbings, motivated by political ambition or revenge or lust. We conduct our own power-hunting and sleaze with much more humanity if much less style.

But a gentleman of the reign of William III would not have seen it that way at all. The increasingly de facto near-union of England and Scotland was introducing ever more English manners to Scottish politics. Horror like the previous century's murders of Darnley and Rizzio, or the Gowrie conspiracy would not be likely to take place again. The nation had even managed to overthrow a second Stuart king in a Revolution that was Glorious because bloodless. Aristocratic murder in steamy Shakespearean plots like the Overbury affair were not likely to recur.

Yet it would have to be admitted that killing by duelling was ever more fashionable, if illegal. Rakehellishness was succeeding the riotous misconduct of Restored Charles II's mob of gentlemen, and the rakes with their swords were more dangerous to honest passers-by than late Elizabethan grandees. And highwaymen and footpads seemed to get more, not less dangerous. The streets of London were no safer – maybe a good deal more dangerous – than in the days of good Queen Bess.

Perhaps it is always so: always the best of times and the worst of times.

From our vantage point at the *fin de siècle*, it is easy to see good times lost. Sometimes we seem to be overwhelmed by the horrors of constant serial killings; paedophiles and child-murderers; dreadful and wanton cruelties practised by rootless and directionless young people.

Partly these crimes overwhelm us because they are the crimes we want to read about: the sales staffs of the tabloid newspapers will confirm that only a royal scandal will sell more copies than a truly horrific sequence of murders.

Partly they overwhelm us because we have grown in population. There are more of all kinds of us. And that includes murderers as well as caring daughters, child-molesters as well as conventional decent citizens.

And partly they overwhelm us because our interest in them drives out interest in the "good old-fashioned murder". Dr Crippen would be hard put to make the headlines now; an unsuccessful doctor with one lover and one dismembered wife. Only his neighbours would have been fascinated.

There are the pluses, too. Greater sexual freedom and honesty means far less murder to escape the scandal and responsibility of having impregnated a lady before matrimony. The end of the Victorian chivalric style means far less willingness to start a fight with a man whose remarks have "insulted my wife": and that also means less of the peculiar chivalric murders that could result from stiff middle-class English love affairs 50 years ago. There have been gains as well as losses.

Murder is never admirable; never glamorous. There will be as many murders in the next century as there have been in this. But if we study the cultural tendencies which have encouraged a particular type of murder in a particular decade, we may be able to avoid repeating a few unnecessary patterns.

Martin Fido, Heamoor, 1995

Swindler Arrested for Strangling Wife on Beach

AN ARREST has at last been made in the Yarmouth Beach Murder. On September 22, a woman's body was found lying on the sand, strangled with a bootlace. A courting couple passed the spot the previous night and saw a man and a woman lying there; but they interpreted the moans the woman emitted as an act of public indecency.

Over the last two-and-a-half months, police have identified the dead woman as Mrs Herbert Bennett, wife of a ne'er-do-well London clerk, who employed her in several nefarious schemes, including the sale of faked antique violins.

Further investigation showed that Bennett previously brought her to Yarmouth on August Bank Holiday, apparently testing the route and hotels he would use for his murder visit. On September 21 he came down from London alone, subsequently staying at another hotel, apparently wearing a false moustache. It seems certain that he inveigled his wife to the beach to murder her, especially as he was in possession of the gold chain she was seen wearing in her hotel on the night of the killing.

Observation of Bennett's movements in London prove that he was initiating a liaison with a young parlourmaid named Alice Meadows, and no doubt this explains his wish to detach himself from the wife who bore him a baby, yet whom he compelled to live in separate lodgings for the last few months of her tragically short life.

The case comes to trial early in the New Year.

Child-Killer is Century's First Woman on Gallows

LOUISE MASSET, hanged January 9, is the new century's first executed murderess. This merciless creature stripped and battered her son with a large stone from her garden in Stoke Newington, London, dumping the body in the ladies' lavatory at Dalston Junction Station.

Thirty-six-year-old piano teacher Louise bore Manfred out of wedlock four years ago and placed him in care at Tottenham. Recently, 19-year-old Eudore Lucas came to reside next door to her, and the woman immediately entered into an immoral relationship with him. In October last year, she arranged a weekend in Brighton with her paramour. On the 27th she collected Manfred, saying that his father was to take him over. The little boy showed signs of distress when seen with his mother at London Bridge Station around mid-day. His body was found at 6.30 pm. The murderess, meanwhile, went to Brighton and enjoyed her dalliance!

When Miss Masset was arrested, she told a story of having placed Manfred with two baby-farmers' from West London. She claimed to have handed the boy over at London Bridge, with £12 for his upkeep.

But before her execution, she confessed. She claimed she killed Manfred to spare him the abuse that all too often confronts the illegitimate.

But it is believed she really wished to rid herself of the obstacle to her vain ambition to captivate and hold young Eudore Lucas.

THE YEAR OF THREE ASSASSINS

In addition to Bresci's successful murder of "King Humbert the Good" the new century has seen two other attempts on royal lives.

In Paris, a young Belgian named Sipido fired on the Prince of Wales as he was arriving at the Gare du Nord in June. And in November an Algerian anarchist named Salsou fired at the Shah of Persia as he drove through the city in his carriage.

Fortunately neither of these did any harm. Sipido appears to be more of a pro-Boer than a true anarchist, and in any case has been found to be insane.

King of Italy Shot by Anarchist

The trial of King Umberto I's assassin

ON JULY 29TH, King Umberto I of Italy was assassinated as he travelled by carriage to a villa in Monza. An anarchist named Bresci pushed forward and fired three pistol shots into the king, who fell back on his cushions, saying: "I think it is nothing". By the time he reached the villa the King was dead.

" I THINK IT IS NOTHING "
King Umberto

Bresci planned his murder after a state of emergency in Milan led to artillery being turned on a crowd. He practised target shooting at Prato, and punctured the tips of his bullets with scissors to make them more deadly.

He has expressed no remorse and in August, a Milan court sentenced him to a life of penal servitude and solitary confinement.

President McKinley Assassinated in Buffalo, N.Y.

The late President McKinley, a safe conservative Republican

AFTER NINE DAYS, President McKinley has died from the anarchist's bullet that struck him in Buffalo, N.Y.

> ## I DONE MY DUTY!
> **Leon Czolgosz**

The President was busy shaking hands with visitors to the Pan-American Exposition on September 6, and smiled warmly as a dark-haired man with a bandaged hand reached the head of the line. When 28-year-old Leon Czolgosz was a few feet from the President, he pulled out the pistol his false dressing concealed, and fired twice at Mr McKinley.

"I done my duty!" was the killer's vainglorious cry as his victim staggered backwards. One of the President's guards immediately felled the assassin with a smashing blow to the face. The stricken President cried weakly: "Go easy with him, boys!" But the bullet had done its foul work, and Mr McKinley has succumbed to gangrene in the pancreas.

Secret Service investigations this spring followed rumours that anarchist gangs had decided to kill Mr McKinley. But all organized groups disavowed any such intent, warning however, that disaffected lone individuals might threaten the President's life. Czolgosz appears to be just such an individual, having been denounced in the anarchist journal *Free Society* as a dangerous crank who might even be a police spy. So the ominous warning that "only a single heartbeat separates Teddy Roosevelt from the White House" is entirely justified and Americans must come to terms with an intellectual aristocratic cowboy who knows how to "rough ride" as President.

> ## GO EASY WITH HIM, BOYS!
> **William McKinley**

The assassination of President McKinley at the Pan-American Exposition, Buffalo, N.Y.

Child Murdering Carpenter Caught by Chemist's Microscope

LUDWIG TESSNOW, accused of murdering four children, has been charged after a new scientific process establishes that blood on his clothes was definitely human, and not, as he claimed, animal.

Tessnow, a carpenter from the Baltic island of Rugen, was arrested in 1898 when the bodies of schoolgirls Hannelore Heidemann and Else Langemeier were found hacked to pieces near Osnabruck. He insisted that red marks on his clothing were wood dye stains, and this could not be disproved.

This July, the mangled bodies of the Stubbe children, Hermann (8) and Peter (6) were found on Rugen, shortly after they were seen talking to Tessnow. He again claimed that marks on his clothes were wood stains and cattle blood. But Dr Paul Uhlenhuth has found out how to identify blood with scientific certainty, even distinguishing human blood stains from animal blood stains, and Tessnow will go to trial.

IN BRIEF

HERBERT BENNETT, the Yarmouth beach murderer (*see* 1900), convicted and hanged on March 21.

Defence counsel Edward Marshall Hall cast grave doubt on the prosecution case. But Bennett insisted that he had not been to Yarmouth with his wife, despite clear witness identification. And this foolish lying persuaded the jury to convict him.

Hung Jury Leaves Peasenhall Murder A Great Mystery

SENSATIONAL CRIME IN SUFFOLK.
A VILLAGE GIRL'S MYSTERIOUS DEATH.

The front page of *Police News*, 1902, showing the sensation caused by The Peasenhall Murder

AROUND MIDNIGHT on June 1, a brutal murder was committed in the little Suffolk village of Peasenhall. Rose Harsent, resident domestic to the local Congregationalist deacon and his wife, was left lying in a pool of her own blood on the kitchen floor; a broken paraffin lamp dismantled around her. Her throat had been cut and an unsuccessful attempt was made to burn the body.

When she was found to be six months pregnant, and an anonymous note by her bed showed that some man had made a secret assignation with her that night, suspicion fell on local Methodist worthy William Gardiner, observed engaging in licentious familiarities with the 23-year-old the previous summer by two peeping toms.

A medicine bottle from Gardiner's house and a copy of the local paper to which he subscribed were discovered in the kitchen. And despite offering an alibi supported by his wife and next-door neighbour, Gardiner was put on trial.

The village has always been certain "Holy Willy" was guilty. He is a fine craftsman (a carpenter and wheelwright) but not especially popular as the foreman at the seed drill works which employs most villagers. Rose Harsent, by contrast, was a great favourite. A good-natured girl, much admired by the young men of Peasenhall, she was not severely criticized for her adulterous liaison.

Young barrister Ernest Wilde won great acclaim for his spirited defence of Gardiner. He roundly condemned the prurient curiosity of the young men who spied on Rose and Gardiner's naughty tryst, and established that another young man living next door to the girl pursued her with lascivious letters (which, it must be remarked, the unhappy young lady accepted in the lewd spirit in which they were offered).

But although Mr Wilde demonstrated a lamentably low state of morality in rural Suffolk, suggesting that more than one man may have wanted to father a child on Rose, he had not proved his client's innocence. The jury could not agree, and Gardiner is scheduled for re-trial early next year.

Mutiny and Murder on the *Veronica*

SEVERITIES INFLICTED on the largely foreign crew of the barque *Veronica* last December resulted in the deaths of seven men at sea and the execution of two more at Walton Prison, on June 7 this year.

A German seaman named Rau sparked off mutiny. He disliked the authoritarian discipline of First Mate Alexander MacLeod. Rau prided himself on his own seamanship and resented reproof.

When the ship was becalmed in the south Atlantic, Rau approached the youngest of the crew with his proposals. At midnight on the first Sunday in December the mutineers killed Mr MacLeod and two loyal seamen and threw them overboard. They locked Captain Alexander Shaw and the second mate in the cabin. They prepared a lifeboat. When all was ready the two captive officers were released. The mate sprang overboard and swam alongside the ship where the mutineers shot him. The captain was chased around the vessel with an axe, and finally shot. The seven survivors sank the *Veronica* and took to the lifeboat.

Rau prepared the story that a storm had injured one crewman and swept MacLeod overboard, whereupon the captain had promoted him to acting Second Officer. Then they were to say the ship caught fire and the entire crew took to the two lifeboats: Captain Shaw commanding one and Rau the other.

As the mutineers headed for the coast of Brazil, two of their number proved incapable of remembering the prepared story and were incompetent in handling the boat. So they, too, were murdered.

When the remaining five arrived in South America their story was accepted as a sea tragedy. Returning to England it became apparent that the negro sea-cook was afraid of his former shipmates, and eventually he confessed. Flohr, one of the two boys from the *Veronica*, gave way under interrogation and confirmed the cook's story. Rau and his co-conspirators, Smith and Monsson were put on trial in England. All were convicted, but Monsson was spared the gallows on account of his youth.

Many shipboard disturbances result from mutinous foreign seamen who fail to understand English orders. Perhaps it is time the merchant marine was crewed by Englishmen.

Seducer Lives Life of Orgiast on Spinster's Fortune

FOR FOUR YEARS, Samuel Dougal thought murder would never out, as he wrote cheques on his victim's bank account. This theft ultimately led police to arrest him, dig up Moat Farm near Saffron Walden and discover his terrible secret.

In 1898 the middle-aged, but virile, Dougal met 55-year-old spinster Miss Camille Holland. She was charmed by this twice-widowed ex-soldier. He was charmed by her possession of a fortune of £7,000 and cultivated her acquaintance.

The following year, disregarding propriety, the couple moved into the lonely farmhouse. Before long they quarrelled, as lusty Mr Dougal began to seduce the housemaids. Miss Holland ordered him to pack up and leave - yet it was she who disappeared from the neighbourhood.

For the next four years Dougal enjoyed himself in his remote sanctum. He returned enthusiastically to the practice of seducing the domestic staff, and took up the peculiar practice of bicycling with them in the nude.

A succession of strange women stayed at the farm and the neighbourhood was scandalized.

Then came the enquiry into Miss Holland's steadily diminishing bank account and Dougal fled to London.

After Dougal's arrest, police dug up the farm and uncovered Miss Holland's mouldering body wrapped in sacking and buried in a drainage ditch. She had been shot through the head.

Dougal was convicted at Chelmsford in June, and hanged on July 14, ridding the country of this deceitful felon.

Edwards launches his cowardly assault on Mrs Darby and child

Whole Family Killed and Buried: Shop Stolen

AT THE END of last year, neighbours in Camberwell were surprised when Mr William John Darby, his wife and baby disappeared from their grocery. True, the shop had been advertised for sale, but the Darbys had not said they had sold it before their disappearance on December 1.

On December 23rd, a grocer named Garland from Victoria Park, East London, went to see a man in Leyton calling himself Fox, who expressed an interest in buying Mr Garland's shop. Before the conversation had gone very far, Mr Fox attacked Mr Garland with a sash weight. The elderly grocer screamed and broke a glass panel in the front door, effectively summoning assistance.

Police examining Mr Fox's house found William Darby's business stationery, and when they dug up Mr Fox's garden, they found the entire Darby family buried there. Mr Fox had battered all three to death with his sash weight, and then carted them and their furniture back to Leyton.

Fox's real name was Edgar Edwards. He had a criminal record and had only recently come out of prison, when he began his short murderous career. There is evidence of insanity in his family, and his lawyers tried to exploit this in his defence, though their client refused to plead. After being convicted, Edwards said: "Let 'em get on with it as soon as they like," and on hearing the death sentence passed he burst into gales of laughter. Finally on the scaffold, his last words to the chaplain were:

> ## I'VE BEEN LOOKING FORWARD TO THIS LOT!
> **Edgar Edwards**

MISS HOLLAND AND DOUGAL MET THROUGH AN ADVERTISEMENT.

Samuel Dougal makes the acquaintance of Miss Holland

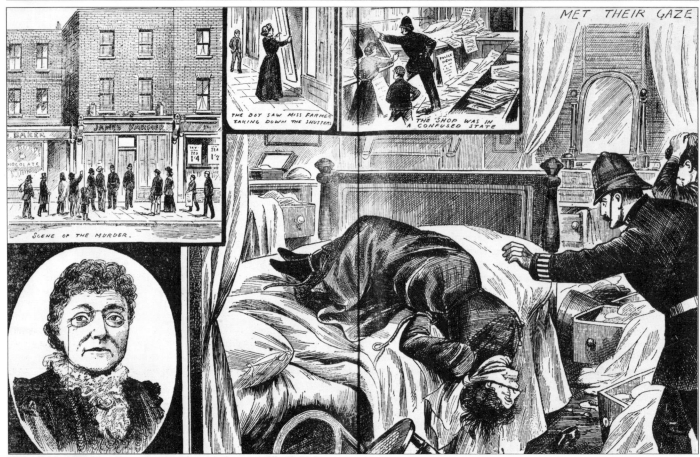

THE BOY SAW MISS FARMER TAKING DOWN THE SHUTTERS

THE SHOP WAS IN A CONFUSED STATE

MET THEIR GAZE

JAMES BARKER

BAKER

CHOCOLATE

TEA 1/4

TEA 1/2

SCENE OF THE MURDER.

The dreadful discovery of the robbery and murder of Stepney businesswoman Miss Matilda Farmer

London Robber Confesses Before Hanging

ANY DOUBTS about the conviction of Conrad Donovan and Charles Wade were resolved when, as they went to the scaffold, Donovan said he had not meant to kill the old lady.

Miss Matilda Emily Farmer, newsagent and tobacconist of 478 Commercial Road, Stepney, was found lying face-down on the floor of her premises with her hands tied on October 12. She had choked on a gag in her mouth. Her false teeth and one shoe were beside her, and her jewellery was missing.

Miss Farmer had been well known in the neighbourhood for owning and wearing jewels.

A Sunday school teacher subsequently identified Donovan and Wade as two men he had seen lurking suspiciously about the premises two nights prior to the crime.

Although there was probably no intention on their part to kill Miss Farmer, the law is quite clear that accidental killing in the course of committing a felony wherein the perpetrators predetermined to use force is murder. Donovan and Wade have now paid the supreme penalty.

Second Jury Deadlocks over Floradora Girl

NEW YORK is agog over Nan Patterson's trial. The 22-year-old chorus girl from Floradora divorced her husband and became the mistress of wealthy socialite gambler Frank "Caesar" Young. Their attempts to elope to Europe were foiled by Young's wife, and in June as the two were riding along Broadway in a hansom cab, bystanders heard a shot ring out, and, at the same time, Miss Patterson's voice exclaiming: "Look at me, Frank. Why did you do it?"

Miss Patterson thereupon directed the cab to a drugstore, and thence to Hudson Street Hospital. But Young proved dead on arrival. The two had been quarrelling over Young's agreement to go to Europe with his wife the following day, and Miss Patterson – either falsely or under a genuine misapprehension – told him she was pregnant. She claims that he committed suicide when she challenged his acceding to Mrs Young's request for a marital holiday.

Prosecutors allege that she shot him in sheer fury before he could frame an answer. Gunsmiths argue that he could not have held the pistol that killed him, given the position of the wound in his head.

Miss Patterson's first trial in November was broken off when a juror died. The December trial has now ended with the jury deadlocked, unwilling either to acquit her of the charge or find her guilty, although Miss Patterson has not changed her story to meet the evidence against her. It remains to be seen next year whether a third jury can survive the excitement and bring themselves to convict this very attractive young lady.

'Bluebeard' Bigamist Sets Record for Murdering Wives

GERMAN IMMIGRANT Johann Hoch, who lived well by marrying often, has been arrested in New York and sent back to Chicago for trial.

The "Stockyard Bluebeard" bigamously married at least 55 women, deserting his brides as soon as he had relieved them of their possessions. One woman testifies that he crept from her bed during the night, removing her gold false teeth from the glass of water on the bedside table!

But at least 15 of Herr Hoch's lady wives did not survive matrimony. These women's bodies have been exhumed and examined, and all contain arsenic.

The insouciant Mr Hoch expressed no surprise, pointing out that undertakers' embalming fluid is richly charged with the poison. His claim is true, but unfortunately for him, his penultimate "wife", Mrs Marie Walcker of Chicago, was embalmed and buried by an undertaker using a new technique and a fluid which contains no arsenic whatsoever! For this reason the "Stockyard Bluebeard" goes back to the city of the stockyards to face his trial and fate.

The great ladykiller offers all men a formula for success with women: "The average man can fool the average woman if only he will let her have her own way at the start" is his maxim.

> ## " THE AVERAGE MAN CAN FOOL THE AVERAGE WOMAN IF ONLY HE WILL LET HER HAVE HER OWN WAY AT THE START "
> **QUOTE** Johann Hoch

MAN COMBINES BIGAMY AND TRUNK MURDER

George Crossman combined bigamy with "trunk murder". When his tenant complained of the bad smell coming from a trunk under the stairs in his house in Queen's Park, London, Crossman agreed to remove the "box of size" that had "gone bad". When a policeman approached him as he removed it, he ran away and cut his throat. The box proved to contain Ellen Sampson, the fifth "Mrs Crossman", packed in cement.

Mystery of the Girl Found Dead in a Tunnel

COMPLETE MYSTERY surrounds the death of Sophia Mary Money, whose body was found in the Merstham Tunnel on the London to Brighton Railway line at 11.00 pm on Sunday, September 24.

Pretty Miss Money worked at a dairy on Lavender Hill, and was regarded by her employers as a reliable and respectable young woman with a good character and no followers. Yet her actions on the day of her death imply a secret life that confounds all who knew her.

Permitted the afternoon off work, Miss Money told a friend she was going for a walk. At a sweet-shop in Lavender Hill she remarked that she was going to walk to Victoria. Yet instead of doing so, she made her way to East Croydon, where she was seen furtively boarding the 9.33 train from London Bridge to Brighton. As this train passed the Purley Oaks signal box, the signalman was startled to see a man struggling with a woman in one of the compartments. And at 11.00 pm Miss Money's body was found.

It does not appear that she was pregnant, which might have provided a clue to the mystery. The police are completely baffled, and nobody has managed to put forward any helpful suggestion concerning Miss Money's last day on earth.

There was no evidence of immodest outrage on the girl, nor had she apparently been robbed. Her brother Robert, who identified the body, insists that the family have no suspicion of any sinister associates in her life.

IN BRIEF

Albert and Alfred Stratton of Deptford have been hanged for murdering local shopkeepers Mr and Mrs Farrow. Sole evidence against the burglar brothers — Albert's thumbmark on a cashbox! Never before has the novel "fingerprinting" technique led to the gallows.

Wife Murderer Hides Body in Trunk

CHEMIST'S ASSISTANT Arthur Devereux found that even if two can live as cheaply as one, three cannot ... and five certainly cannot! Life as a married man with three children entailed serious financial hardship. In January he bought a large trunk and some morphine and chloroform.

Somehow he persuaded his wife and their twin children to drink the poison. Then he sealed his three victims into the trunk with an airtight mixture of glue and boracic acid, and deposited them at a warehouse in Harrow, England, before moving to Coventry with his surviving son. Mrs Devereux's mother successfully traced her son-in-law's movements and tracked down the bodies to the warehouse. Police apprehended Devereux, who has been convicted and hanged.

Society Sex Scandals Behind New York Killing

Killer Drowns Pregnant Obstacle to His Engagement

WHILE NEW YORK reels at the impossibility of convicting Nan Patterson for the murder of her playboy lover (*see* 1904), yet another Floradora chorus girl features in a high society murder.

On June 25, the rich and famous sipped their bubbly in the roof restaurant of Madison Square Garden as the new musical *Mamzelle Champagne* unfolded before them. Suddenly, 34-year-old railway heir Harry Thaw walked over to where millionaire architect Stanford White was dining and shot him in cold blood, saying: "He deserved it. He ruined my wife."

Shocking facts emerged at Thaw's trial. In 1902, when Miss Evelyn Nesbit was 16, she was plucked from the chorus line by big, heavily-moustached Stanford White who took her to his apartment, plied her with drugged champagne, and seduced her.

> ## "HE DESERVED IT. HE RUINED MY WIFE."
> ### Harry Kendall Thaw
> *QUOTE*

After that she joined him in bizarre sexual pursuits: swinging high on a velvet swing with some of her clothing removed; dressing up as a little girl for him to fondle; letting him take indecent photographs of her. Nor was she the solitary victim of his lusts. White introduced other young chorus girls to his velvet swing.

Last year Miss Nesbit left White and married Thaw. Her new husband had peculiar tastes of his own, liking to tie her to the bed before thrashing her with a dog-whip. She found that she could escape his frenzy by telling him how White had abused her. Thereupon Thaw redirected his rage to the seducer, and insisted thenceforth that Evelyn should only refer to White as "The Beast", "The Bastard", or just "The B".

Thaw's millionaire mother is spending a fortune to denigrate White, and present her son as the eccentric defender of a maiden's honour. She says she will spend $1 million to save his life. Thaw faces trial next year.

FACTORY FOREMAN Chester Gillette (22) wanted to marry money. In Courtland, New York, the upper crust knew that Chester was the nephew of the prosperous skirt-manufacturer who employed him. So society ladies let the young man court their daughters, and Chester had every hope of seeing his ambitions realized.

Until Grace "Billie" Brown told him she was pregnant. Farm girl Billie came to Courtland to work as a secretary for $6 a week, and cheating Chester found her more accommodating than the beautiful socialite to whom he hoped to become engaged. When he declined to answer Miss Brown's letters, she became desperate and threatened to expose him. Whereupon Chester asked his uncle for a week off and took Miss Brown upstate to Utica, and thence to a hotel on Big Moose Lake.

On July 11 Chester hired a rowing-boat and took Miss Brown for a picnic lunch on the lake. That evening he was seen walking through the woods, dripping wet and carrying a suitcase. At 9.00 pm he registered as "Carl Graham" at another inn, where he asked whether there had been any report of a drowning in the lake.

The following day Miss Brown's body was found floating. She had been battered to death before being thrown in. The murder weapon – a tennis racquet – was found buried by the lake shore.

At his trial, Gillette claimed first that Miss Brown had attempted suicide and thrown herself into the lake, and then that the rowing boat had capsized and the lady struck her head against the hull. He could not explain his own failure to rescue her, although he is a competent swimmer.

The jury found him guilty, and he has been sentenced to death.

Harry Thaw, killer of his wife's former lover

Evelyn Nesbit Thaw, the girl who swapped a velvet swing for a dog-whip

Joy as Wood is Acquitted of Camden Town Murder

AFTER a tense trial, London is rejoicing that Mr Edward Marshall Hall has secured a young commercial artist's acquittal on the charge of murdering Phyllis Dimmock in September.

Railway dining-car attendant Bert Shaw returned to his flat in Camden Town on the morning of September 12, to find his common-law wife, Miss Dimmock, lying in bed with her throat cut.

Mr Shaw was apparently unaware that Miss Dimmock plied her trade as a prostitute around local public houses during his absence on night-trains.

A letter in the lodgings signed "Bert" invited Phyllis to meet the writer at the Eagle public house on September 11, and a postcard in the same writing signed "Alice" included a caricature of a winking sun to illustrate its invitation to a meeting at the Rising Sun.

When this was publicized, a young prostitute named Ruby Young recognized the drawing as the handiwork of one of her clients, Mr Robert Wood.

But Wood asked her to keep quiet about it. She, however, mentioned it to a journalist friend, and thus Wood was then traced.

Mr Marshall Hall succeeded in persuading the court that identifying witnesses, who recognized Wood's distinctive gait as that of a man leaving Miss Dimmock's house in the early hours of September 12, are unreliable since they saw their suspect under exceedingly dim street lighting.

And Wood himself made an excellent impression in the witness box, leading to his popularity throughout the metropolis.

The police have no further suggestions to offer as to the commission of the crime. Given the extent to which Wood has benefited by Mr Marshall Hall's famous eloquence and the jury's exercise of a very slender "reasonable doubt".

We should perhaps see him as an extraordinarily lucky young man to have escaped the gallows, rather than very unfortunate to have had his sordid love-life exposed in the harrowing circumstances of a murder trial.

Phyllis Dimmock, the murdered prostitute of Camden Town

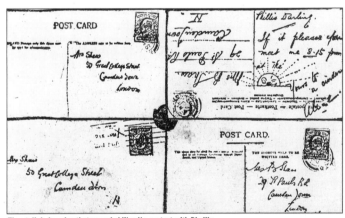

The stylish drawing that revealed Wood's contact with Phyllis

IN BRIEF

THE JURY in the Thaw case (*see* 1906) cannot agree, and he will stand trial again next year. His mother has said she will spend more than $1 million to secure her son's freedom.

Irish Swindlers Caught with Body in Trunk

VERE AND MARIA GOOLD, the Monte Carlo trunk murderers, have been arrested in Monte Carlo, despite the lady's attempt to bribe a police officer.

These seedy Irish adventurers have been living in Monaco using the assumed titles of Sir Vere and Lady Goold. (True, Goold is in line for a baronetcy, but he has not yet succeeded to it.) Not for the first time, "Lady" Goold has been living off her wits, while her (third) husband drifted in an alcoholic stupor.

The couple were close to penury at the beginning of this year. Then they met Madame Levin, a rich old Swedish lady, who lent Maria £40. No amount of wheedling, however, could persuade her to increase the loan, and by August she was pressing for repayment. Maria invited her to tea at the Goold's shabby lodgings, and while "Sir" Vere held their guest in conversation, "Lady" Goold crept up from behind and battered Madame Levin with a poker. Then she cut her throat, decapitated her and cut off her legs. The torso was packed into a trunk labelled for Charing Cross, London; the head and limbs into a carpet bag. A visitor that evening was told that gore all over the apartment was the result of Vere's being taken ill and vomiting blood.

The following day the Goolds fled the principality and deposited the trunk in Left Luggage at Marseilles. A clerk who noticed blood oozing from it sent to their hotel asking what it contained. "Lady" Goold haughtily responded that it was poultry, and ordered him to despatch it to London. The clerk went to the police instead, and Maria's offer of 10,000 francs to Inspector Pons ensured her arrest.

Widow Advertised for Husbands – Killed Forty

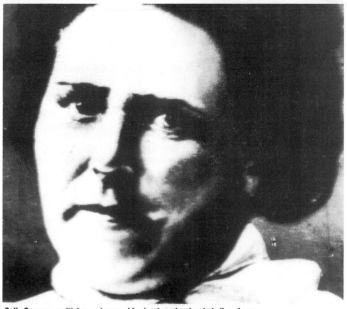

Belle Gunness, multiple murderess of husbands on her lonely Indiana farm

WHEN THE Gunness farm near La Porte, Indiana, burned down during the night of April 28, Joe Maxon, the hired hand, was apparently the only person to survive. The bodies of the widow Gunness's four children were found in the basement, together with a headless woman, presumed to be Mrs Gunness, since her false teeth lay alongside.

Suspecting arson, police arrested recently sacked hired hand, Ray L'Amphere, whose unrequited passion for Mrs Belle Gunness had led her to make several complaints about him. But once in custody L'Amphere's statements started police digging around Belle's pigsty.

They unearthed the remains of 14 men. And that was less than half of it! L'Amphere estimates that the widow murdered at least 42 people over the last four years, including her 14-year-old adopted daughter Jennie Olson, who told authorities back in 1904 that she saw Momma Gunness beat out Poppa Gunness's brains with a cleaver. At the time, Belle's alternative story was believed: that a meat grinder fell off a high shelf on to the unfortunate Peter Gunness's head.

Fat, ferocious and fiftyish, Widow Gunness advertised for matrimonially interested men willing to help her pay off the mortgage on the farm. They came with their savings. And Belle rapidly disposed of them. She drugged their coffee, or chloroformed them, and finished them off with her trusty cleaver.

Recently, she seems to have panicked when the brother of one of her missing suitors enquired about his disappearance. Belle drew up a will and paid off one of her mortgages. Then came the fire.

Did Belle perish in it? No part of the head except her false teeth has been located. The burned body appears to have stood five inches shorter and weighed fifty pounds less than Belle. Moreover it did not burn to death, but was poisoned before the fire consumed it .

It seems that Mrs Gunness lured some poor vagrant to her farm and killed her to conceal her own escape. The wicked widow is still at large, somewhere, in possession of a small fortune.

Recovering the bodies from the basement where Belle killed her children

Tragedy of a Retired Couple

ON AUGUST 24, Major General and Mrs Charles Luard set out at 2.30 from their home, Ightham Knoll in Kent, for an afternoon walk. The 69-year-old general proposed going a couple of miles to his golf club to fetch his clubs in preparation for a holiday. His wife was only accompanying him for half a mile, as she expected a visitor for tea. They strolled through Fishpond Woods to a summer-house known as the Casa, where Mrs Luard stopped and the general went on.

At 3.15, local people heard three shots. The general got home at 4.30, and was surprised to find his wife was not there. He entertained the visitor in her place, and then went back to the Casa to look for her. Mrs Luard lay on her face in the summerhouse. She had been struck on the head with a blunt instrument, and then shot twice. Her rings had been pulled off her fingers; a pocket cut away from her dress.

There can be little doubt that some vagrant or hop-picker committed this crime, but police have failed to link anyone known to be in the area with it.

Somewhat deplorably, local rumour suggested that the general himself destroyed his wife. Lonely and depressed by cruel anonymous letters, the general took his own life by lying in front of a train on September 18.

IN BRIEF

THE SECOND trial of Harry Thaw (*see* 1906) has produced a verdict of Not Guilty by Reason of Insanity, and Thaw has been sent to Matteawan Asylum for the Criminally Insane.

Did this Sinister German Really Kill?

OSCAR SLATER, the 37-year-old German Jew extradited from America and convicted of the murder of Miss Marion Gilchrist last December, has been reprieved.

On December 21, Miss Gilchrist's maid, Helen Lambie, returned from an errand to find a neighbour outside her mistress' apartment door, from where he had heard some commotion. As Miss Lambie entered the flat, a respectably dressed man walked calmly out and ran down the stairs.

Miss Gilchrist was found battered to death with a chair leg. Parts of the flat had been turned over, but the only item missing from Miss Gilchrist's extensive collection of jewellery was a crescent-shaped diamond brooch.

On Christmas Day, police learned that Slater had tried to sell a pawn ticket for just such a brooch. When they went to his lodgings on Boxing Day, they learned that he had just sailed for America.

Slater is a man with an infamous reputation who has, among other things, lived off the immoral earnings of women. Police followed him to New York where Helen Lambie and other witnesses, who had seen a man leaving or in the vicinity of the building, all more or less positively identified Slater.

Slater has consistently denied knowing anything about Miss Gilchrist, but his counsel dared not let him give evidence on his own behalf.

Nevertheless, sufficient doubt exists in this case that Slater's death sentence has been commuted to life imprisonment. Sir Arthur Conan Doyle, who is taking up the cudgels for Slater, observes that the brooch pawned by Slater has been traced: he pawned it a month before the murder, and it was not Miss Lambie's. Furthermore, his journey to America was long pre-arranged, and not, as police suggested, a guilty flight to evade the long arm of the law.

It is to be hoped there has been no miscarriage of justice.

Oscar Slater, a shady character dubiously convicted of murdering Miss Marion Gilchrist

Two Extortionist Pimps Murder Drunken Sailor

THE CONVICTION of Morris and Marks Reubens for the murder of William Sproull has clarified the law on premeditation in murder cases.

Second mate McEarchen of the freighter *Dorset* was found drunk and incapable in London's Whitechapel Road. When he reported that he and his friend, second engineer Sproull, had been attacked in a house in Rupert Street, Whitechapel constables repaired to that sordid alley of brick shacks, and found Sproull dying in a gutter.

A trail of bloodstained three-penny-bits from his pockets led back to the house used by prostitutes Ellen Stevens and Emily Allen, where they and their pimps, Morris and Marks Reubens were cowering.

The gang's claim to know nothing about Sproull collapsed when a search revealed Morris's bloodstained pocket-knife hidden behind the stove. McEarchen testified that after he and Sproull had gone to the house with the girls for an immoral purpose, the brothers sprang out to accuse them of molesting their "wives", and Marks threatened the seamen with a hippopotamus-hide whip. When McEarchen and Sproull fought back, Morris pulled his knife and stabbed the engineer.

The judge decided that this was premeditated murder, since the clasp-knife had to be opened before it could be used, and the short period of opening proved intent to injure.

Despite pleas from the dock in the name of their "poor old mother", the brothers will hang.

1910

Siege of Sidney Street – Robber-Murderers Die

Peter the Painter: escaped from the siege at Sidney Street, Stepney, in east London

Armed police marksmen take aim at No.100 Sidney Street

AN EXTRAORDINARY train of events led Home Secretary Winston Churchill and a company of guardsmen to the battle in Sidney Street, Stepney, in London which it is hoped, will end the depradations of the anarchist gangs associated with "Peter the Painter" and Fritz Svaars.

Earlier this year, Latvian anarchists led by George Gardstein planned a robbery at Harris's jeweller's shop in Houndsditch. They were overheard tunnelling their way into the shop by night from an empty house at the rear, and when police arrived, the foreign subversives shot their way out, killing three policemen and injuring two.

In this unspeakable violence, however, they also injured their leader fatally, and Gardstein died in hiding a few days later.

The remainder of the gang scattered. But it finally reached authority's ear, that two or three were holed up in 100 Sidney Street, and would probably resist arrest with more gunfighting.

Police surrounded the building under cover of darkness, and tried to evacuate all innocent tenants and neighbours. The two anarchists attempted to hold the landlady hostage, removing her skirt on the assumption that a devout Jewish lady would not face the public in her underclothes.

They were mistaken. She fled as soon as their attention was distracted, and the siege began. When Detective Sergeant Leeson was injured, the guardsmen were called in. Firing at and from the house continued for several hours, until it was seen to be ablaze

It is not certain whether the anarchists started this conflagration themselves. In any case, both men perished. One had been shot, and died well before the signs of their surrender. The other, believed to be Fritz Svaars, dodged from window to window, keeping up a fusillade of bullets singlehanded until he was overcome by smoke and fumes and had to surrender.

But "Peter the Painter" had escaped.

ANARCHISTS IN LONDON

Anarchists have been a serious social problem in Europe for the last 30 years, since many of them adopted the policy of haphazard terror and assassination to "destabilize bourgeois society".

No crowned head seems safe from their pistols and bombs, and no respite from their activities can be predicted until they have stirred some cataclysmic upheaval in Europe.

Technically the terrorist anarchists are a very small section of a minority group within the international revolutionary movement, which embraces constitutional "Fabian" socialists at one end, and the violent revolutionary extremist Social Democrats at the other. Russian political exiles and the immigrant Jewish community in the East End have introduced these doctrines to England, and special sections of the police keep a wary eye on the dangerous Social Democrats in Stepney.

Guardsmen take over from police to conclude the amazing gunfight in the East End

Steinie Morrison in the dock before magistrates as a Snelwar's Restaurant waiter (left) testifies to his carrying an iron bar on the night Beron was killed

Clapham Common Murderer to Live

HANDSOME BURGLAR Steinie Morrison will not hang. British Home Secretary Winston Churchill, has commuted his sentence for the murder of Leon Beron to life imprisonment.

Last New Year's Eve, Morrison spent the evening at a Polish cafe in Whitechapel, talking to Beron – a local slum landlord and, it is whispered, stolen-goods receiver's agent. A waiter at the cafe insists that a parcel Morrison left with him felt like an iron bar. Morrison swears it was a flute.

Subsequently Beron and Morrison were seen in Whitechapel Road, after which Morrison's landlady confirms he went home and retired to his room.

The following morning Beron's battered body was found miles away on Clapham Common, his face carved with waving lines that might imitate a letter "S". Three cabmen reported taking men answering the description of Morrison and Beron between Whitechapel and Clapham, and one who looked like Morrison, from south London to Finsbury Park.

Morrison disappeared from his lodgings and when arrested on January 8, said he had been spending the time with a new girlfriend – a lady of the streets – in Lambeth.

At his trial he persuaded another girlfriend, 16-year-old Jane Brodsky, whom he seduced last year (much to her own satisfaction), to provide him with a false alibi. This was exposed in court, and coupled with Morrison's criminal record swayed the jury against him.

Nevertherless, his conviction seems unsafe. He might merely have identified Beron to confederates who committed the actual murder: he might even, as he claims, have had nothing whatever to do with the man's removal to Clapham.

Although Morrison calls himself a socialist, the police do not endorse the popular belief that the murder is associated with recent anarchist outrages, or that the "S" on Beron's face accuses him of being a spy.

Steinie Morrison, fastidiously dressed burglar, in the dock at Bow Street

Doctor Deliberately Gave Patient Diphtheria

A DOCTOR HAS been exposed in Petrograd (the former St Petersburg) of using his skill to murder. Patrick O'Brien de Lacy, a resident of the city, divorced his wife in order to marry wealthy Mademoiselle Burturlin. It was Mademoiselle's fortune rather than her face which attracted him, however, and he planned to murder every member of her family who stood between him and his father-in-law's estate!

A Dr Panchenko accepted 360,000 roubles to inoculate members of the Burturlin family with poison. When Mrs O'Brien's brother died of blood-poisoning, suspicion was aroused, and at length Dr Panchenko confessed to substituting a preparation of diphtheria for the young man's anti-cholera medicine.

Although the moving force in the conspiracy was de Lacy, it seems that Dr Panchenko's is the name that will live in the annals of crime.

He is most unusual in abusing his skills murderously for a fee, instead of killing on his own account, as one would expect.

Dr Crippen: No escape for Wife-Murderer

Simpering Belle Elmore on the music-hall stage

A Second-Rate Soprano

CRIPPEN'S WIFE Cora was last seen on January 21, 1910 when she and Crippen entertained their friends, retired "musical acrobats" Mr and Mrs Martinetti. Mrs Crippen herself had attempted a singing career, appearing as one "Cora Motzki" in operetta, and as "Belle Elmore" in various music-halls. She was christened Kunigunde Mackamotzki, so she had every excuse for adopting a stage-name!)

Belle Elmore's singing career was a flop. Ultimately she restricted herself to serving as treasurer of the Music Hall Ladies' Guild, a charity which brought her into contact with great stars. The Guild's office in New Oxford Street also brought her into contact with the quiet typist Miss Ethel Le Neve, who worked for her husband. Crippen was hawking patent medicines and acting as a dentist's anaesthetist in the same building. As he qualified as a homeopath in his native America, the BMA would not license him to practise medicine in Britain.

Where's Belle?

Two days after the dinner with the Martinettis, Crippen brought the Ladies' Guild a note with Belle's resignation and apologies. She had to return to America to see a dying relative.

When friends asked how Belle was getting on, Crippen reported that she was ill, and finally, that she "passed on of pneumonia up high in the mountains of California".

Variety artistes were shocked, however, when the bereaved doctor brought his secretary to the Ladies' Guild Ball wearing Belle's diamond brooch. Neighbours in Hilldrop Crescent, North London, were shocked that Ethel had moved in with him. Friendly enquiries in California revealed that nobody knew anything about Belle's visit, illness and death. Gossip culminated in a tip-off to Scotland Yard, and Inspector Walter Dew went down to New Oxford Street to see the doctor.

Duping Dew

Crippen easily deceived the good-natured detective. He confessed that the story of Cora's death was false. He explained that she had run away with a younger man, and he felt so humiliated that he had put about the story of the sick relative and Cora's ultimate demise.

Dew accepted this story completely. Had he made enquiries, he might have found plausible support for it. For Cora frequently cuckolded her husband. (We do not say she "deceived" him, for she was contemptuously open about her liaisons with younger, stronger men from the music-hall world, and made the wretched Crippen clean their boots when they stayed at Hilldrop Crescent.)

At Crippen's invitation, Dew searched 39 Hilldrop Crescent. Apart from a litter of unwashed clothes in the kitchen, where Crippen and Ethel seemed to be living permanently, he saw nothing amiss. And the case would have been closed, had not

Ethel Le Neve in her shipboard disguise

Respectable Dr Crippen

Dew returned to New Oxford Street on July 11 to confirm the exact date of Belle's departure for his report.

Headlong Guilty Flight

Crippen had gone. Ethel had gone. They left no forwarding address and no explanation. Dew's suspicions were reawakened. For the next two days he searched the house from top to bottom. And at last he rapped his stick on the brick floor of the basement and heard it ring hollow. The floor was taken up and pieces of flesh were discovered, wrapped up in a pair of pyjamas.

Belle had been found. Crippen's flight was explained. The widely publicized man-hunt was on.

Dr Harvey Hawley Crippen, whose flight, arrest and trial have held the world spellbound since July, was hanged at London's Pentonville Prison on November 23. The previous week his lover, Ethel Le Neve, was acquitted of complicity in the murder of his wife. Crippen's last request was that a photograph of Ethel should accompany him in his coffin.

You're nicked: detectives escort the wanted man down the gangplank of the *Montrose*

FOOD FOR THOUGHT

The world is treating Captain Kendall as a hero: a real life Sherlock Holmes who spotted Crippen and confirmed his identification.

But just suppose ... he had been wrong ... Imagine that the Robinsons really were two unfortunate inverts with a taste for wearing ladies' underwear... would anyone ever again travel by a line that encourages its captain to snoop on people, and broadcasts the humiliating results of the spying in the popular press?

Immoderate Affection

As the papers reported the nationwide man-hunt, Captain Henry Kendall of the liner *Montrose* was perturbed by the appearance of unnatural passions between two of his passengers who claimed to be Mr John Philo Robinson and his 16-year-old son. As they stood behind a lifeboat, Captain Kendall saw what seemed a shocking display of homosexual ardour. "The younger one squeezed the other's hand immoderately. It seemed to me unnatural for two males, so I suspected them at once" said the good captain.

But on re-examining his newspaper the captain changed his mind. He whited out Crippen's spectacles and moustache in a newspaper photograph, and the likeness of Mr Robinson was before him. Captain Kendall tested his theory, inviting the Robinsons to dine at his table and observing Master Robinson's suspiciously feminine shape. He called, "Mr Robinson" to the pair on deck, and noted that the passenger made no immediate response to his name. And when Master Robinson's trousers split down the beam-end and the young man fastened them with a safety pin, the captain was positive.

The World Follows the Chase

The *Montrose* is one of the first vessels equipped with Marconi's radio-telegraph, and Captain Robinson used this equipment to tell his owners he believed Crippen and Le Neve were on board. The owners told the police and the press, so that the public knew all about the daring escape and the amateur detective captain. The public learned about Ethel's trousers, and heard when Captain Kendall found ladies' underwear in the Robinsons' cabin.

Scotland Yard immediately despatched Inspector Dew by the *Laurentic*, a faster vessel that would reach Montreal before the *Montrose*. And so when Crippen landed and was arrested, the world's press was there to witness this first murder case cracked by the Marconigram.

The Trial

Crippen's defence was a plea of complete ignorance of the flesh in his cellar. But young pathologist Bernard Spilsbury proved that a fringe of pubic hair matched Belle's known coloration, and a scar matched her operation wound from an illegal sterilization. Traces of hyoscine in the remains showed how she had been poisoned. And Crippen had recently bought an unusual quantity of the drug. No one knows how Crippen disposed of the rest of the body. But no one doubts his guilt.

A MURDERER EVERYONE LIKES

The meek and mild-mannered doctor has won the affection and, to some extent, admiration of his jailers. Unfailingly polite, he has also impressed them by his total devotion to Miss Le Neve and the courage with which he insists that, whatever the cost to himself, nothing in his defence must harm her.

By contrast, only the rather "brassy" artistes of the music-hall seem to have liked Cora, a vulgar, domineering, promiscuous woman.

1912

Open Murder Under Blazing Broadway Streetlamps

THE HEADLINE of the *New York World* for July 16 screamed: GAMBLER SAYS POLICE LIEUTENANT WAS HIS PARTNER.

At 1.00 am, that same gambler, Herman "Beans" Rosenthal bought a copy of the first edition and sat down to a steak in his favourite resturant, the Hotel Metropole on Broadway.

With his betting outfit on West 54th Street doing badly, and his corrupt political protector Tim Sullivan dying, Rosenthal found the greedy extortion of Police Lieutenant Charles Becker more than he could handle.

So he was exposing Becker to journalist Herbert Bayard Swope who, in turn, fed the information to District Attorney Charles Seymour Whitman. And the D.A.'s office hoped the revelations would enable them to crush corruption in New York.

In a secret meeting with Whitman, Rosenthal promised that he would testify before a Grand Jury, describing police collaboration with Manhattan gamblers and criminals. And he evidently calculated that his personal ties with leading gangster Jack Zelig (who has headed Monk Eastman's mob ever since Eastman's imprisonment in 1904), coupled with the publicity he was receiving in the press, would protect him from sudden death.

Rosenthal was wrong. As he left the Metropole at 2.00 am and walked into the brilliant lights and crowded pavement of Broadway, a voice cried, "Over here, Arnold."

With that four men sprang from the shadows, pistols blazing, and killed him at pointblank range.

They escaped in a Packard limousine that was easily traced, as it has often been hired by mobsters. Even so, a bystander who took the car's number had great difficulty in persuading police to accept it from him. It is clear that New York Police Department contains powerful officers who do not wish to see this crime properly solved.

As of December, the four young thugs who did the actual shooting – Harry "Gyp the Blood" Horowitz, "Lefty" Louie Rosenberg, Jacob "Whitey Lewis" Seidenschmer, and "Dago" Frank Cirofici - have been tried, convicted and sentenced to death. However, the District Attorney's office is still struggling to find evidence to bring to trial their commander-in-chief, Big Jack Zelig, and the crooked policeman Charlie Becker who, it is believed, is the one to have ordered the murder, with the words: "I want Rosenthal croaked!"

The Metropole Hotel, Broadway, where Herman Rosenthal (inset) had his last meal

Illicit Liaison Ends with Bullets in Taxicab

EDWARD HOPWOOD'S love affair with actress Florence Dudley ended twice over on September 28. In the morning the lady – real name Florence Alice Bernadette Silles – learned two unacceptable facts.

Hopwood was already married, and the police wanted him for passing bad cheques. Horrified at the notion of bad publicity and an uncertain future the actress, (appearing at the Tivoli Theatre), told Mr Hopwood their relationship was over.

In the afternoon Hopwood took a taxi with her to Fenchurch Street Station, London, pleading for forgiveness. When this was not forthcoming, he drew a pistol and shot her. Then he turned the gun on himself.

He did not die, however, but was nursed back to life to stand trial and die on the gallows in December

The Merstham Tunnel Murder: New Sensational Information

A SENSATIONAL SUICIDE and murder in the English seaside town of Brighton recalls the mysterious murder of Sophia Money in the Merstham Tunnel (*see 1905*).

A man calling himself C R. McKie shot his wife and three children in their boarding house; then set fire to his petrol drenched room before shooting himself. His sister-in-law escaped, screaming, just before the massacre began.

It turns out that McKie, who also passes himself off as "Captain Murray" and pretends to be a barrister's son, is actually Sophia's brother Robert, who identified her body when it was found. He had enjoyed liaisons with both Mrs McKie and her sister in Clapham, having children by each of them. Now financially at the end of his tether he decided to destroy himself and all his dependents.

Lovers Kill Their Spouses in Agra, India

F AMILY LIFE in the sub-tropical climate of Anglo-India may have all the fervid passion of Mr Rudyard Kipling's romances, it seems.

Illicit associations that cross racial boundaries and involve English women and Eurasian men may produce consequences as sinister as those depicted in the author's inappropriately named *Plain Tales from the Hills*.

In 1911, 42-year-old Eurasian Dr Henry William Clark of Agra in India formed a liaison with 35-year-old Augusta Fullam, wife of an army auditor. The guilty couple decided to get rid of their unwanted spouses. Clark sent Mrs Fullam arsenic for her husband's soup, but the dose proved ineffective. Clark then offered to treat his rival for "heatstroke", and injected him with the alkaloid poison gelsemine. When Fullam died in October 1911, Clark signed the death certificate and nobody suspected anything but heatstroke.

Last December the lovers rid themselves of Mrs Clark. Four native assassins broke into the house and hacked her to pieces. They were quickly caught and executed.

Clark drew attention to himself and his lover by explaining his absence from the house truthfully. He was dining with Mrs Fullam. A search of her house uncovered a tin box full of love letters from the doctor and a few abusive letters to Mrs Clark.

With the contents of this box and a little pressure applied in order to persuade Mrs Fullam to testify against her lover, the prosecution had no difficulty in securing a death sentence for Clark. He was executed on March 13. Mrs Fullam was saved from sharing his fate because she is pregnant. She has therefore been imprisoned.

Triple Killer Gives Himself Up to Save Father

G ANGSTER ORESTO Shillitoni, "The Paper Box Kid", gave himself up in June when he heard that his father had been arrested. On May 3, New York police officers Charles Teare and William Heaney moved in to stop two men fighting on the street. One of the combatants thereupon pulled a gun and shot both policemen and his antagonist, a well-known gangster named John Rizzo. All three died.

Over 100 policemen were assigned to the hunt for Oresto Shillitoni, but he successfully disappeared until, in June, an eyewitness suggested that Shillitoni's father had been implicated.

When the elder Shillitoni was arrested, "The Paper Box Kid" in fear for his father's life, turned himself in so he could make a statement clearing his father.

He now goes on trial for the murder of the policemen and his fellow criminal.

Oresto Shillitoni, "The Paper Box Kid" who murdered two policemen and a fellow gangster

Killer Caught by Lure of Soccer

W ANTED MURDERER George Ball was an anonymous figure until he went to watch his Merseyside team play. Then he was recognized from photographs that had been flashed across the city's cinema screens all week.

Ball worked at a tarpaulin shop, and resented the authority of 40-year-old manageress Miss Christine Bradfield. On December 10, Ball stayed late at work and indecently assaulted Miss Bradfield in the room behind the shop, before battering her with an iron pipe when she scratched his face severely in retaliation. The loathsome killer then sewed her body into a sack.

The night was windy, and at about 10.00 pm one of the shop's shutters blew down, denting the hat of a passing seaman walking his girl. Eighteen-year-old Samuel Eltoft came out of the shop to replace the shutter, and summoned Ball, who reimbursed the seaman. A few minutes later, the young couple watched Ball and Eltoft push a handcart bearing a heavy bundle away down the windy streets.

Miss Bradfield's body was found in the canal next day. Enquiries quickly indicated that only her shop clerks could have been responsible. Eltoft soon told the police what had happened. But Ball disappeared until his arrest outside the soccer ground.

The two men go on trial for murder next year.

Boy Strangled on London Train: Father Cleared

FIVE-YEAR-OLD Willie Starchfield's little body rolled up and down the railway carriage between Chalk Hill and Dalston all one afternoon, until a passenger noticed the child's hand under a seat.

Willie's mother left him in the care of a neighbour during the morning, but returned to find the babysitter distraught as the boy had not returned from a simple errand.

Two passers-by told police they had seen Willie in the company of a man, and one of them subsequently identified Willie's father, newspaper-seller John Starchfield, as the man in question.

Mr and Mrs Starchfield have been acrimoniously separated for some time, and the father's alibi for the day - that he had spent much of the time resting on the bed in his lodging-house - seemed inadequate.

Charges were brought, but Starchfield's solicitor mounted a vigorous defence before magistrates, presenting evidence that other witnesses had seen Willie unwillingly abducted by a woman, and persuading the witness who had identified Starchfield that she was not really sure of her identification at all.

The case has been dismissed, and it seems likely to remain a mystery.

John Starchfield (foreground) bows his head at the inquest on his son Willie

Murderer Preaches, Retracts, Confesses on Scaffold

HENRY SPENCER (34) aroused suspicion in Wheaton, Illinois, when he was seen withdrawing all his fiancée's savings from the bank. As he tried to leave the town by train, the local sheriff accosted him and took him away for questioning.

Spencer, who claimed to be a salesman, turned up in Wheaton earlier in the year, and paid assiduous court to Allison Rexroat, a woman much older as well as much richer than himself. After the couple announced their engagement, Spencer took her for a picnic in the country. And it was on his return - alone - from this pleasant outing that he was seen helping himself to the lady's savings.

Miss Rexroat was a respected local resident, so bank tellers and customers alike wondered why she had permitted a comparative stranger to the town such freedom with her assets. Some of them had already suspected the young man's motives.

Under questioning, he insisted that he did not know where Miss Rexroat was. But a farmer had seen the couple on a hillside, and a search in the area led to discovery of the lady, her head battered by a hammer. Shortly after, Spencer confessed.

At his trial, he alleged that the confession had been beaten out of him. The jury was unimpressed, and he was convicted and sentenced to death.

His execution was a remarkable occasion. Hangings are still open to the public in Wheaton, and a vast crowd came to see the murderer die. Spencer declared that he had embraced religion and was a reformed character. "I've joined the ranks of God's children," he averred, and springing up the scaffold, he cried: "This is the happiest day of my life!"

Finally, as the drop fell, he withdrew his confession with the words: "I never harmed a hair on her head. So help me God!"

IN BRIEF

ORESTO SHILLITONI has been found guilty of the New York triple murder (*see* 1913) and sentenced to death.

ESCAPED MILLIONAIRE lunatic killer Harry Thaw (*see* 1906, 1913) has been extradited from Canada and returned to New York. His mother's lawyers, however, have secured him a retrial which will take place next year.

GEORGE BALL has been convicted and executed for the murder of Christine Bradfield (*see* 1913). His young accomplice Samuel Eltoft has been imprisoned for 4 years.

Murdering Monster Dies a Coward's Death

GEORGE JOSEPH SMITH, the "Brides in the Bath" killer was dragged to the scaffold on August 15, wailing to the executioner: "I am in terror!"

Smith's career ended in January this year when Charles Burnham of Aston Clinton, England, spotted a news item describing the death of Mrs John Lloyd (née Margaret Lofty) in Highgate. The lady drowned in her bath only a few days after her marriage. Mr Burnham was interested, because his daughter Alice had died at Blackpool in exactly the same way. Her husband, a Mr Smith, had made life very unpleasant for the Burnhams as he tried to extract Alice's trust fund from them. Mr Burnham drew the attention of the police to the coincidentally similar deaths.

So too, did Alice Smith's Blackpool landlord, Mr Joseph Crossley.

Police quickly established that Smith had a long record as a petty thief, swindler, bigamist, and confidence trickster preying on lonely spinsters. They also discovered that Alice Burnham was not the first of his wives to end their lives drowned in a bath.

In 1912 Smith reunited with Beatrice (Bessie) Mundy, a respectable spinster whom he had married bigamously in 1910, and rapidly deserted when he believed he could only secure £138 of her £2,500 inheritance.

After the reunion, Smith and Bessie exchanged wills in each other's favour. Five days later Bessie was found drowned in her bath.

Smith profited by his three murders to the tune of about £3,800, and would have made a further £700 on Margaret Lofty's life insurance had not the company withheld payment.

He had invented a plausible accident, and found an almost perfect means of murder. He hanged himself by his greed.

> ## I AM IN TERROR!
> **George Joseph Smith**
> QUOTE

George Joseph Smith with Bessie Mundy, his first "bride in the bath"

One Month's Jail for Honeymoon Killer

EPILEPTIC PORTER CHARLTON has been released from custody after serving just 29 days in prison for the murder of his wife in 1910. Young Charlton, then 21, married fierce-tempered actress and heiress Mary Scott Castle and took his markedly older bride on holiday to Italy. The marriage was stormy, and Charlton soon battered Mary to death and disposed of her remains in a trunk in Como.

He confessed willingly on his return to America, and a three-year delay ensued while Italy and the USA wrangled over which should try him. In 1913 he was extradited to Italy, but further delays and the outbreak of war put off his trial until October 18 this year.

After all that waiting, with Charlton's epilepsy in evidence, he has served just one month for his murder.

Mob Kills Leo Frank in Georgia Prison

A LYNCH-MOB CALLING ITSELF "the Knights of Mary Phagan" broke into Milledgeville Prison Farm on August 17 and hanged 31-year-old Leo Frank, serving a life sentence for the murder of Mary Phagan (*see* 1913). State governor John Slaton commuted Frank's death sentence when new evidence suggested chief prosecution witness James Conley was the real murderer. Conley, a semi-literate black janitor, is known to have enjoyed sexual perversions of a kind he claimed to have witnessed Frank practising. His bad spelling makes him a probable author of the note accusing his co-worker Newt Lee found beside the body. And there are inconsistencies in his story of helping Frank hide the body.

Frank's protestations of innocence, by contrast, have been perfectly consistent. Slaton was convinced that Frank ought to be reprieved, but the mob resented being cheated of his execution.

Racist rednecks find Jewish Frank even more of an unwelcome exotic than black Conley. So Frank has been lynched before a blazing cross, and Governor Slaton's political career will probably end when he next runs for re-election.

Drama at Palace as Rasputin is Murdered

RASPUTIN, "the Mad Monk", who has been called the power behind the Russian throne, was brutally murdered by a group of aristocrats on December 15.

Gregoriy Efimovich Novikh "Rasputin" was an uneducated peasant holy man from Siberia. He preached, prophesied and practised faith healing. He is reputed to have enjoyed sexual orgies with female followers, saying that one must sin to be forgiven. His power lay in his charisma. He was introduced to the court when the Tsarina despaired over the haemophilia which threatened her son's life. Rasputin's hypnotic therapy proved effective in staunching any minor bleeding which might have proved lethal to the Tsarevich, and the empress demanded the constant presence of this healer.

Although Rasputin's personal corruption went no further than occasional drunkenness and sexual adventures, and his political influence never amounted to more than gaining petty posts for friends and clients, he was deeply resented by the aristocracy. Some blamed him for failures of imperial policy. At one point he was exiled, but the Tsarina demanded his return.

This December, a group of aristocratic thugs led by Prince Yussoupoff decided to rid the court of the contaminating peasant. They invited Rasputin to dinner, and discovered that he was so strong it was difficult to assassinate him. They gave him drugged and poisoned sweets. Rasputin ate them greedily and asked for more. They pulled a pistol and shot him. He advanced furiously on them. They bludgeoned him, and still he fought back. They dragged him to a car, drove him out to the frozen river, and forced him under the ice to drown. And with superstitious arrogance, they offered to the world their incompetence as proof that Rasputin was supernaturally evil!

He was not. He was not a monk. (He was married.) He was not mad. He was not the Romanoffs' *eminence grise*. He was simply a peasant faith healer, murdered by snobbish brutes who couldn't stand a common man outranking them at court.

Rasputin, the Siberian faith healer Gregoriy Efimovich Novikh

Thaw Again! Now He Ravishes a Boy

MAD, MURDEROUS, millionaire molester Harry Thaw, was back in the dock this year. He was finally acquitted last year of the murder of Stanford White (*see* 1906), following three trials, two sanity hearings and an escape to Canada, all financed by his doting mother.

Now this New York sadist, long known for the pleasure he takes in whipping young women, has changed the object of his lust. Early this year he kidnapped 19-year-old Frederick B. Gump, beat him, and sexually molested him.

He was tried, and once again found insane. But Mrs Thaw poured out her dollars and achieved another sanity hearing. This time Thaw was declared sane, and then it transpired the Gumps were now going to drop all charges.

Mrs Thaw is said to have paid them $500,000 to leave her loathsome offspring at large.

Meanwhile Evelyn Nesbit, the former Mrs Harry Thaw, on whose account the millionaire murdered Stanford White, has herself dipped into the Thaw millions again.

After some years appearing in vaudeville as "The Girl on the Red Velvet Swing" – the infamous sex-toy she sat in at Stanford White's apartment – she announced last year that she was expecting, and the father was … her ex-husband Harry Thaw! She claimed to have bribed guards to let her into Matteawan Asylum for a post-marital dalliance.

Highly improbable as Evelyn's story seems, Mamma Thaw has again handed over the cash to defence lawyers to keep her evil son out of trouble.

IN BRIEF

TRIPLE-MURDERER Oresto Shillitoni (*see* 1913) tried to escape death by shooting Sing Sing guard Daniel McCarthy one week before his execution date. He was electrocuted as scheduled on June 30.

French Butcher Hid His Mistress' Head and Hands

Voisin's basement kitchen: scene of butchery

BRILLIANT DETECTIVE work by Inspector Frederick Wensley of the CID has solved London's Regent Square mystery. On November 2, a road-sweeper found a sack containing a woman's headless, handless torso, wrapped in a sheet in Bloomsbury Square. Another bundle contained legs of the same woman, with some elegant French underwear. The sheet bore the laundrymark IIH, and a piece of paper with the torso had the words, "Blodie Belgiam" scrawled on it. Pathologists suggested that the dissection showed a degree of skill.

From the clue of the underwear, and the appearance that the scrawl misspelled the word "Belgium", Wensley directed his men to check laundries for one which had washed the sheet, asking especially about French or Belgian women. This identified the woman as 32-year-old Emilienne Gerard, in whose kitchen an IOU for £50 signed by Louis Voisin was found.

Voisin, a butcher, lived in nearby Cleveland Street. He had been Mme Gerard's lover, but also enjoyed the favours of Berthe Roche, who was with him when police came making enquiries.

Wensley then asked Voisin to write the phrase "Bloody Belgium". Voisin reproduced exactly the spelling errors left with the body.

The Inspector was now sure the paper had been left to mislead police into imagining that the murderer was some Englishman who resented our being dragged into a continental war on behalf of France and Belgium.

A search of Voisin's basement kitchen uncovered bloodstains and one of Mme Gerard's earrings, caught in a towel. A cask of alum in the coal cellar contained her head and hands.

Police deduce that Mme Gerard came round to Voison's rooms during the frightening Zeppelin raid of October 31, only to find him ensconced with Berthe Roche. A quarrel ensued and the two killed her. Both will be tried for her murder.

Man on Death Row Hugs Victim's Picture

DUTCHMAN PIET VAN DE CORPUT, awaiting execution in Sing Sing, has obtained a picture of the woman he killed, which he says he will take with him to the electric chair before he meets her again in heaven.

De Corput, a sailor, enjoyed a drunken leave in New York in the autumn of 1915. During this time, widowed Barbara Wright was suddenly attacked on the street by a man who stabbed her with a long-handled knife, and ran away.

Police investigation suggested the killer was John Hendricks, a Dutchman who roomed in the same house as Mrs Wright and pestered her. New York was plastered with pictures of his face, to no avail.

When they picked him up a year later, after he had reverted to his real name of Piet van de Corput, they discovered he had been in the city all the time, once complaining at a police station of being mugged.

Eye-witnesses easily identified de Corput, and he rejected his lawyers' suggestion that the identification parade had in any way been mishandled. The jury took only a few minutes to reach a guilty verdict.

Mad Scheme to Kill Lloyd George

A LUDICROUS PLOT to assassinate British Prime Minister Lloyd George has come to light. Mrs Wheeldon, a widow in Derby, holds strong Suffragette, Socialist and Pacifist beliefs. In her Suffra-gette days, she discussed the possibility of assassinating Mr Lloyd George by poisoning a nail in his boot. With the Prime Minister prosecuting the War energetically, she decided to move from theory to action.

Using a simple code based on the sentence, "We'll hang Lloyd George from a sour apple tree", she wrote to her son-in-law Arthur Mason, a chemist exempted from conscription as his work is of national importance. Mason willingly sent her phials of strychnine and curare. And Mrs Wheeldon turned to two supposed deserters she was hiding, apparently Bolshevik representatives of the International Workers of the World, for assistance in conveying the poison to the Prime Minister.

Unknown to her, the deserters, Alec Gordon and Herbert Booth were really government agents. Mrs Wheeldon and the Masons have been sentenced to varying periods of penal servitude.

Philandering Doctor's Wife Slain By His Playmate

> **" I DID NOT DECEIVE HER OR LEAD HER ON. OTHER WOMEN HAVE CARED FOR ME, BUT I WAS MARRIED AND THEY KNEW THEIR LIKING FOR ME WOULD COME TO NOTHING PERMANENT. SO THE AFFAIRS USUALLY FADED AWAY. "**
>
> QUOTE **Dr David Roberts**

The trial of Grace Lusk, Waukesha, Wisconsin, for the murder of Mrs David Roberts

NAUGHTY DR DAVID ROBERTS of Waukesha, Wisconsin, is a dangerous man in an illicit liaison. The married doctor plays around constantly, and never expects his playthings to ask for more than a little dalliance. When Grace Lusk pulled out a pistol and shot the doctor 's wife, he wept as he exonerated himself.

Mrs Roberts tried to hasten Grace Lusk's fading. She visited the lady and tendered the warning that one of the doctor's previous lovers had died in an attic after an operation. After this peculiar veiled threat, she expressed her own unfavorable opinion of Miss Lusk's value to the doctor as a mistress. When Miss Lusk found the personal observations unbearable, she shot Mrs Roberts dead with a .25 pistol. Her attempt to kill herself immediately failed.

She has been convicted of second degree homicide and sent to prison.

Grace Lusk

Double Murderer Caught on Second Insurance Claim

ARRESTED IN France on August 21, swindler Henri Girard must have believed he had long got away with murder. In 1909 he persuaded broker Louis Pernotte to give him power of attorney. He also insured Pernotte's life for 316,000 fr. In 1912 he put a culture of typhus bacilli in Pernotte's drinking water. And as Pernotte lay sick, he prepared a syringe of camphorated chamomile which he persuaded Mme Pernotte to inject into her husband. At the same time he remarked, like a conjuror: "You observe that I have nothing in my hands."

Even so, no suspicion was aroused, and Pernotte's death was attributed to an embolism.

After this, Girard tried unsuccessfully to poison M.Mimiche Duroux. He had better luck with widowed Mme Monin, who died fifteen minutes after eating a mushroom Girard gave her at a Paris Metro station. The Phoenix Insurance Company, with whom Girard had insured the lady's life, was suspicious. And M.Girard is now in custody trying to explain the fatalities to a *juge d'instruction*.

French Ladykiller Landru Killed 200 Ladies

Landru, the French Bluebeard

BALD-HEADED, bushy-browed and spiky-bearded, Henri Desiré Landru may yet be the world's greatest ladykiller. In both senses. Shortly before the war he discovered the lure of matrimony and thereafter he preyed on lonely, middle aged women, promising to marry them.

Landru entrapped his victims through advertisements in the newspapers. A typical Landru snare read: "Widower with two children, aged forty-three, with comfortable income, affectionate, serious and moving in good society, desires to meet widow with a view to matrimony."

Many women responded to such appeals and many were fascinated since Landru radiated a voracious sexual appetite.

Landru was caught this year because of his greed two years ago. After the disappearance of 47-year-old widower Mme Buisson on August 10, 1917, he turned up at her apartment with a forged note demanding her furniture. Mme Buisson's relatives knew she had been corresponding with this man for two years and intended to marry him. Since they heard no more from him after the lady disappeared, Mme Buisson's sister was interested when she saw Landru strolling down the Rue de Rivoli on April 11 this year, with a pretty young woman. She informed detectives, who trailed Landru to a villa in Gambais.

There they found a notebook with a classified list of 283 women and voluminous correspondence from these ladies – nearly all of whom have disappeared!

They also found a quantity of women's clothing and possessions, much of it identifiable as belonging to women last known as being "engaged" to this creature. In the stove, they found human bone ash.

It seems that Landru began his activities using a villa at Vernouillet as his base, moving to Gambais in 1916 when he felt he had killed two victims dangerously close to each other. Neighbours have commented on the number of women who visited him and the noxious smoke that poured from his chimneys after the visitors had "left".

CATEGORIES OF WOMEN CORRESPONDENTS

The French Bluebeard's notebooks listed his prospective victims under the following cynical headings:

1. To be answered poste restante.
2. Without money.
3. Without furniture.
4. No reply.
5. To be answered to initials poste restante.
6. Possible fortune.
7. In reserve. For further investigation.

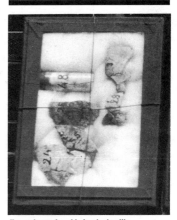

Human bones found in Landru's villa

Elderly Doctor Murders Wife: Hangs Himself

SIXTY-SEVEN-YEAR-OLD Dr Walter Keene Wilkins, convicted earlier this year of his wife's murder, has hanged himself in Mineola Jail.

The old couple lived on Long Beach, Long Island, and Mrs Wilkins died there on the night of February 27. Police found the doctor tending his dying wife in the driveway when they responded to his emergency call. He told them that he and Mrs Wilkins had surprised a gang of housebreakers when they returned home from New York City, and the lady had been attacked.

Shortly after that, Mrs Wilkins' lawyer received a copy of an invalid will, dated 1915, in which she left two bequests to her husband. Her previous will, of 1903, disposed of her assets so that the doctor gained nothing.

Meanwhile police were puzzled at finding Mrs Wilkins' false teeth and gloves inside the house. It seemed odd that she went to the city without them. It was further noted that Dr Wilkins' hat-brim was stained with blood, and the picture-wire binding the abandoned lead cosh which had been the murder weapon was identical with wire found in the house.

Dr Wilkins promptly disappeared. When he resurfaced in Baltimore, he was arrested. His fingerprints matched those on the lead cosh. A tie-pin he claimed the housebreakers had stolen was found in his overcoat pocket. And he was found guilty of first degree murder.

Ex-Officer Light Cleared: So Who Killed Bella?

THE ACQUITTAL of former British army officer Ronald Vivian Light on the charge of murdering 21-year-old factory worker Bella Wright is a triumph for the great defender, Sir Edward Marshall Hall.

Bella's body was found beside her bicycle in a Leicestershire lane last year. A bullet had passed cleanly through her head and lay nearby. She was not robbed or sexually assaulted.

Enquiries established that a man on a green bicycle rode with her when she visited her uncle at Gaulby, and went away with her, though she had only just met him. A search for this well-spoken squeaky-voiced man, in his thirties or forties was unsuccessful until, this February, a dismantled green bicycle was dragged up from a canal, and near it a pistol holster containing ammunition identical to the bullet beside Bella's body.

A serial number on the bicycle frame identified it as one bought in 1910 by Cheltenham schoolmaster Ronald Light. The holster, too, was identified as his army-issue property.

Light claimed to have sold the bicycle and to know nothing about the holster.

But in court he confessed that he had been lying. He had, he said, been panicked by newspaper assertions that the green bicycle's owner was the murderer. He had, indeed, met Bella and lent her a spanner. They parted before she went to the lane where the body was found.

Light gave his evidence clearly and cogently, persuading the jury, if not the judge. In addition, Sir Edward showed that the clean wound in Bella's head was not such as would be expected if she had been shot from close range. Marshall Hall suggested that a spent or riccocheting bullet from a rook-rifle fired at a distance had killed the girl.

But assuming Light to have been justly freed, considerable mystery still surrounds the girl's death.

Ronald Light in the dock: the bicyclist schoolmaster accused of killing Bella Wright

Man Shot: Is this the End of the Axeman?

MRS MIKE PEPITONE, who saw the mad axeman of New Orleans after he killed her husband, has shot dead Joseph Mumfre in Los Angeles, and declares that he was the monster.

The axeman's carnage raised terror to new levels last year. In March he injured Mr and Mrs Charles Cortimiglia and killed their two-year-old daughter. Mrs Cortimiglia claimed to recognize him – or rather, them: Iorlando and Frank Jordano, rival grocers from the same street. Both were convicted on Mrs Cortimiglia's sole testimony in May, and released in September when she confessed it was a pack of lies.

Three more people were attacked during 1919, the last being grocer Mike Pepitone whose wife found him dead in bed, and saw the axeman rush past her.

After their experience with Rose Cortimiglia, police are loath to accept Mrs Pepitone's identification of Mumfre, and she has been given ten years' imprisonment for homicide. But Mumfre spent time in prisons around New Orleans, and the axe murders always took place when he was free and his whereabouts couldn't be determined.

New Orleans hopes its panic is now over.

Daughter says She Also Drank the 'Poisoned Port'

IN HIS second triumph of the year Sir Edward Marshall Hall has won acquittal for Kidwelly solicitor Harold Greenwood. The Welshman was suspected of poisoning his middle-aged wife with weed killer.

Dr Willcox the pathologist testified that there was arsenic in Mrs Greenwood's remains. Parlourmaid Hannah Williams swore that Mrs Greenwood was the only person to drink from a bottle of port Greenwood fetched from the pantry for lunch.

But Sir Edward easily established that a barely competent local GP prescribed a morphine and arsenic tonic to Mrs Greenwood, poorly labelled and in dangerous quantities, so that she might have taken it in mistake for a sedative or digestion mixture. Mrs Greenwood's daughter swore under oath that she too had drunk port from the suspect bottle, which has not been recovered.

Greenwood seems to have been the victim of tattling neighbours who resented his marrying a pretty young woman soon after he was widowed.

Second Welsh Solicitor Accused of Poisoning Wife

Pathologist Dr Webster (left) and Armstrong's family doctor, Dr Hinks

MAJOR HERBERT ROWSE ARMSTRONG (52), solicitor and clerk to the court at Hay-on-Wye, will pass through the dock of his own court in the New Year, charged with murder.

Earlier this year the major was unable to return moneys held in escrow for a client of rival Hay-on-Wye solicitor, Oswald Martin. While Mr Martin was pressing the major for restoration of these funds, he received a box of chocolates anonymously through the post. A friend who ate one was sick, and Mr Martin threw the remainder away.

Shortly after this, the major invited his rival to tea, ostensibly to discuss their business differences. When his housekeeper brought in a plate of scones, the major selected one and passed it to his guest, with the words: "Excuse my fingers, Mr Martin!"

Mr Martin ate the scone, and was extremely ill. His doctor analysed his urine, and it contained arsenic.

When the police were informed, they noted that Mrs Armstrong, a dominating woman who henpecked, and humiliated her tiny husband, died suddenly last year after an illness which always improved when she was in residential care, but worsened when she returned to her husband for nursing. Arrangements were made to exhume her body and analyse the contents.

In the meantime, the unfortunate Mr Martin had to fob off a positive barrage of invitations to tea from the major!

Finally, on New Year's Eve, the major was arrested as there were large quantities of arsenic in Mrs Armstrong's body. At the time of his arrest, the major had a little packet of arsenic in his pocket and 19 more have been found distributed around his house. He claims that he prepares individual doses of poison to kill individual dandelions on his lawn, and finds it handy to carry them around with him in case a weed suddenly catches his attention.

Local opinion is that the major was inspired by the acquittal of brother-solicitor Harold Greenwood (*see* 1920).

IN BRIEF

HENRI GIRARD (*see* 1918) still awaiting trial for the murders of Louis Pernotte and Madame Monin, has swallowed a germ culture and died in prison. He told his guards, "I will always be misunderstood - abnormal, as I have been called - and for all that, I am good, with a warm heart."

US Anarchists Murder Two in Wage-Snatch

IN A CASE reminiscent of Britain's Tottenham outrage, robbers at Braintree, Massachusetts on April 15 killed a cashier and guard at the Slater and Morrill Shoe Company, and made off with a $16,000 pay-roll.

The villains escaped in a car, which police believe they recognized a month later. The men in charge of it, Nicola Sacco and Bartolomeo Vanzetti, were arrested and found to

Bartolomeo Vanzetti and Nicola Sacco between guards

be illegally in possession of firearms. They also turned out to be anarchist immigrants and members of a group of subversives already viewed with suspicion by police. Vanzetti has been charged with another robbery in the vicinity, and both men go on trial for the Braintree shootings next year.

There is considerable hostility to the anarchists in New England, as law-abiding citizens hoped the anarchist outrages of the years before the Great War had been brought to an end by that carnage.

Surburban Stabbing After Letters of Passion and Poison

> **HE NEVER ACTED LIKE A MAN TO HIS WIFE. HE ALWAYS SEEMED SEVERAL DEGREES LOWER THAN A SNAKE.**
> QUOTE **Frederick Bywaters**

Edith and Percy Thompson on holiday, in happier days before her love for Bywaters led to his death

ON OCTOBER 3, Percy and Edith Thompson were returning home in Ilford, Essex, after the theatre, when a young man rushed out and stabbed Mr Thompson. Mrs Thompson, hysterically distressed, said she had no idea who the assailant could have been.

But when Chief Inspector Frederick Wensley learned that neighbours were scandalized by 29-year-old Mrs Thompson's liaison with 22-year-old ship's clerk Frederick Bywaters, he arranged to have Bywaters arrested and Mrs Thompson brought to a police station where she could glimpse her lover in another room. Immediately Mrs Thompson betrayed her complicity by crying: "Oh, why did he do it? I did not want him to do it!"

Bywaters' lodgings contained scores of letters Mrs Thompson had written to him. Many discussed poisoning Percy, and even claimed that Edith had put ground-up light bulbs in his food.

The two stood trial in December. Mr Justice Shearman, expressed the strongest distaste for their adulterous liaison.

After two hours deliberation, the jury convicted both. Bywaters is justly found guilty; he told police he attacked Thompson because: "He never acted like a man to his wife. He always seemed several degrees lower than a snake."

But Mrs Thompson, who moaned, "I am innocent! I am innocent!" on hearing the verdict, may be correct in strict law. Even Lord Chancellor Birkenhead notes that, while she undoubtedly willed her husband's death and probably conspired to bring it about, the assault which killed Percy – the actual murder with which she was charged – was unplanned, unpremeditated, and an unwelcome suprise to her.

Unless there is a reprieve, the two will be executed in the New Year.

> **OH, WHY DID HE DO IT? I DID NOT WANT HIM TO DO IT!**
> QUOTE **Edith Thompson**

Prostitute Killer, True, Goes to Broadmoor

THERE IS public disquiet over the reprieve of Ronald True, convicted of murdering prostitute Gertrude Yates (who operated under the name "Olive Young") in her basement flat in Fulham, London.

Miss Yates' maid saw True when she came to work on the morning of March 6, and accepted his story that he had taken Miss Yates a cup of tea in bed. Shortly after True left, the maid discovered that the bed contained pillows, and Miss Yates' body lay in the bathroom. She had been battered with a rolling pin and strangled with her dressing-gown cord.

True left a visiting card in the flat, and was easily traced to a music-hall that evening. *En route* he had pawned some of Miss Yates' jewellery and changed his bloodstained clothing.

He offered the extraordinary defence that he has a "double" named "Ronald Trew", who goes around London bouncing cheques and committing petty frauds and thefts for which True is held responsible. True says Trew killed Miss Yates.

The universal conclusion is: "Not true. Not Trew. True."

But True's conduct had been unbalanced for years. He was thrown out of the Royal Flying Corps during the War because of his eccentric behaviour. His estranged wife found him too mad to live with. The Home Secretary has therefore reprieved him, and sent him to Broadmoor.

Still, many people wrongly suspect that he escaped the noose because he is the black sheep of a middle-class family, and his victim was a humble prostitute; whereas Henry Jacoby was hanged as a working-class boy who impertinently murdered a lady.

Ronald True, mad murderer of Gertrude Yates

Madame Fahmy Freed: Shocking Story of Perversions

A T THE height of a thunderstorm during the night of July 10, shots rang out from a luxury suite in the Savoy Hotel, London. Servants found Madame Marguerite Laurent Fahmy standing over the body of her husband, Prince Ali Fahmy Bey, a smoking pistol in her hand.

The marriage had been unhappy. Mme Fahmy is a Parisian adventuress, who won wealth and status when she captivated the young Egyptian millionaire diplomatist. But life in romantic Egypt proved frightening and sordid. The prince bullied her. He was more interested in men friends than his wife. It was widely believed that he enjoyed an unnatural relationship with his sinister secretary, Said Enani. She feared for her life when forced to travel up the Nile with the prince's devoted and gigantic black bodyguard. The prince used Madame Fahmy sexually as though she were an unnatural male lover: an abuse which gave her distressing ailments in an embarrassing place.

It was Mme Fahmy's hope that their visit to Europe might result in a separation, and she could return to Paris for surgery on her injured fundament. But quarrels continued, culminating in the prince's death in their hotel.

Sir Edward Marshall Hall triumphantly secured the lady's acquittal. He demonstrated that her Browning pistol was so complicated that her story of accidentally firing it under the impression that she was removing the bullet from the chamber could easily be true.

Unfortunately, he also laid great stress on Mme Fahmy's marrying an Egyptian pervert, and seemed to suggest that all Egyptians subject their wives to "oriental" vices. This has resulted in a strong diplomatic protest from the Egyptian Embassy.

But Madame Fahmy at last walks free.

Inspector Crosse at Fahmy's inquest

Woman Kills Boy: Uses Daughter to Conceal Body

M YSTERY SHROUDS 30-year-old Susan Newell's murder of a Glasgow newspaper boy. Nobody doubts that she was justly hanged on October 10 for killing 13-year-old John Johnston. Nobody can imagine why she did it.

Mrs Newell and her 8-year-old daughter Janet were given lifts by a lorry and a car whose drivers saw them pushing a heavy handcart carrying a bundle. As they left the car, a passer-by saw a head and hand loll out of the bundle, and called the police.

Mrs Newell tried to blame her husband, with whom she had quarrelled. When that failed she made no further useful statement. Janet testified to helping her mother put the boy in the bag.

Mme Fahmy, Parisian adventuress

1924

Millionaires' Sons Kill 14-year-old Boy for Fun

THRILL-KILLERS Nathan Leopold and Richard Loeb have been saved from execution. In a brilliant display of trial tactics, Chicago lawyer Clarence Darrow pleaded the two boys guilty to avoid having their crime described to a jury, and in a two-day hearing before Judge John Calverley persuaded him that the boys were emotionally retarded and disturbed, and it would be barbaric to execute them. While his clients smirked and giggled, Darrow's eloquence and humanity won the day against all odds.

Leopold and Loeb, respectively 18 and 19 years old, are the brilliant homosexual sons of millionaires. University of Chicago students, they have been influenced by Nietzsche's philosophy and think themselves "supermen". They planned to demonstrate their superiority by committing the perfect crime.

In May this year they kidnapped 14-year-old Bobby Franks. They gagged him, and killed him with four blows of a chisel to the head. Then they left the body in their unlocked hire-car while they ate a five-course meal in an exclusive restaurant.

Replete, they poured hydrochloric acid over Bobby's face to impede identification and hid the body in a lonely culvert. They typed a ransom note demanding $10,000 which they posted to Bobby's father, and followed it up with another signed "George Johnson" which they left on a train. But by the time this one was delivered, Bobby's body had been found.

They were easily caught. Leopold's spectacles slipped out of his breast pocket at the culvert. The frames were a specially crafted horn-rim design

Nathan Leopold (*left*) and Richard Loeb, rich spoiled and brilliant students who murdered Bobby Franks to prove their cleverness

only supplied to three customers. A stolen typewriter was recovered from the lake where they had thrown it, and proved to be the one which typed the ransom notes. District Attorney Richard Crowe was sure he would send these boys to their death, and public opinion had no sympathy for the self-important spoiled brats.

This letter, written by Leopold after his arrest, is unlikely to sway public opinion

Hangover Cure Proves Deadly

MRS MABEL JONES met red-bearded radio technician Jean Pierre Vaquier in Biarritz last summer, and enjoyed a holiday dalliance with the 46-year-old Frenchman.

This February Vaquier turned up on St Valentine's Day at the Joneses' Blue Anchor Hotel in Byfleet, Surrey, to resume the relationship. Mrs Jones was no longer so keen, and Vaquier decided to get rid of her husband. He bought strychnine in London, claiming it was for wireless experiments. He signed the poisons book as "J.Wanker", and returned to Byfleet to administer his poison.

Mr Jones drank the strychnine in his bromo salts to cure a hangover on March 29. The doctor who attended his last moments spotted strychnine crystals by the bar and had them analysed.

Vaquier was convicted and hanged in August.

Jean-Pierre Vaquier, self-styled "Mr Wanker"

Popular 'Public Enemy No.1' Charged with Murder

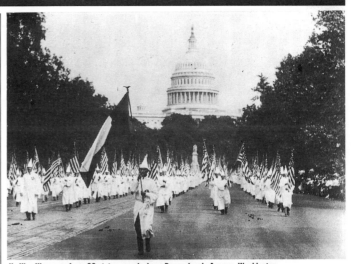

Ku Klux Klansmen from 22 states parade down Pennsylvania Avenue, Washington

IN AN ATTEMPT to undo the popularity they were giving a criminal, the newspapers began labelling Gerald Chapman "Public Enemy Number One".

> ## DEATH ITSELF ISN'T DREADFUL BUT HANGING SEEMS AN AWKWARD WAY OF ENTERING THE ADVENTURE. "
>
> QUOTE
> ## Gerald Chapman

Like many popular villains, Chapman wins admiration for his daring and athletic escapes. In 1921 he robbed a mail truck in New York City by leaping from a moving car on to the truck's running board, and holding a gun to the driver's head. (That venture netted $1,424,129, the largest haul on record.)

He took an up-market apartment in New York, and became known as "the Count of Gramercy Park". When he was betrayed by an informer, he flabbergasted in-terrogators by saying, "Sorry, gentlemen", and diving out of a 75ft high window. He was swiftly recaptured, however, when a cleaning woman signalled that he had wriggled down a ledge to another open window.

He escaped from Atlanta penitentiary after feigning illness by drinking disinfectant. Retaken and shot in the process, he none the less escaped again within six days.

But on October 12 last year he participated in a robbery in Connecticut accompanying an inexperienced criminal who shot a policeman as they made their getaway. Taken and held under tight security, Chapman has been charged with murder, and seems likely to be executed.

In his cell he has composed epigrams, including the remark: "Death itself isn't dreadful but hanging seems an awkward way of entering the adventure."

PUBLIC ENEMIES

Chicago has adopted this term for its Crime Commission's list of "Persons who are constantly in conflict with the law."

The first, published in 1923, led off with Al Capone, followed immediately by one of his bodyguards, and his brother Ralph.

KKK Grand Wizard Rape Leads to Woman's Suicide

D.C. STEVENSON, charismatic Ku Klux Klan "Grand Wizard" of Indiana, has been convicted of murdering 28-year-old Madge Oberholtzer whom he kidnapped, stripped, beat and raped in the private berth of a railway sleeping-car last year.

Miss Oberholtzer was permitted by her captor to buy some medication to alleviate her pain, but actually bought six bismuth of mercury tablets which she took in an attempt to commit suicide.

When she became extremely ill, the Klansmen returned her to her parents, explaining her injuries as the result of a road accident.

Miss Oberholtzer died this year, and the courts have made a landmark decision that death following a suicide attempt may be charged as murder against the person whose felonious conduct brought about the suicidal impulse.

Stevenson's abominable action has halted the growth of the murderous Klan, which had hitherto passed itself off as an organization for the best in white Protestant manhood.

Teeth and Ear Betray the Wrong Corpse

FRAUDSTER CHARLES SCHWARTZ decided to fake his own death in the destruction by arson of his Berkeley, California chemistry laboratory. With this in mind, he murdered evangelist Warren Gilbert Barbe and doctored the body to resemble his own.

He burned off part of Barbe's chest where he himself had a scar, punctured the different coloured eyeballs and extracted two teeth where he had lost two.

After the building exploded, investigators swiftly observed that "Schwartz's" corpse was different in a number of small but significant ways. The corpse had a mole on the ear which the fraudulent chemist did not have, and its missing teeth had been recently extracted.

Finding himself hunted for murder, Schwartz committed suicide in the Oakland boarding-house where he was hiding.

Murder of Minister and Chorister Still a Mystery

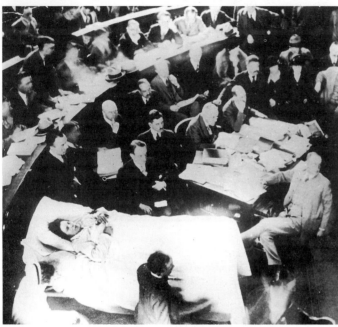

Mrs Jane Gibson, "the Pig Woman", testifies from her sickbed at the Hall-Mills trial

ON SEPTEMBER 16, 1922, the bodies of the Rev. Edward Wheeler Hall (42) of St John's Episcopal church, New Brunswick, New Jersey, and choir singer Mrs Eleanor Mills (34) were found under a crab-apple tree in lonely De Russey's Lane. Both had been shot through the head, and Mrs Mills' throat had been cut. Love letters from the singer to the minister were scattered around.

This year, the Halls' maid told police that Mr Hall had said he intended to elope with Mrs Mills. The authorities, accused in the popular press of letting the minister's widow and her family buy off witnesses, finally decided to prosecute Mrs Eleanor Hall (53), her two brothers Willie and Henry Stevens, and her cousin Henry Carpender.

Star prosecution witness was Mrs Jane Gibson (56), the "Pig Woman", who raised pigs around her dilapidated shack at the bottom of the lane. On the night of the murder she rode her mule up and down the lane, first looking for suspected predators, then looking for a moccasin she dropped on her first sally. She said she saw four people around the tree, threatening and beating Mr Hall and Mrs Mills. She heard one call another, "Henry".

Unimpeachable witnesses proved that Henry Stevens was away on a fishing trip that weekend. Mrs Gibson's mother sat in front of her, muttering, "She's a liar! She's a liar!" Mrs Hall gave calm and dignified evidence on her own behalf, though her icy disbelief that there could have been any impropriety between her husband and Mrs Mills strained credulity. And Willie Stevens, though eccentric, was sufficiently definite in his account of his movements that night to satisfy the court that he had no hand in the murders. All four defendants were cleared.

Since Mrs Mills' husband, the church sexton, was decisively cleared in the original investigation, it is very hard to imagine who wanted to execute the guilty couple.

Fingerprint expert Fred Drewer studies Willie Stevens' fingerprints

Tragedy of Respectable Inscrutable Immigrant

A RESPECTED LEADER of the Chinese community in Liverpool has been hanged for the wilful murder of his wife and two daughters last December. Lock Ah Tam (53) came to Britain as a seaman and opened a club in Liverpool. He was successful, generous and good-natured, and the authorities used him as a mediator with the immigrant community.

In 1918 he was struck on the head with a billiard cue while stopping a brawl. After that his character changed. He became morose and took to drink. His business deteriorated, and last year he was bankrupted.

On December 1 he hosted a birthday party for his son, behaving graciously while guests were present. But once the family were alone, Lock went into a blinding rage. His son hurried away to fetch the police, but in his absence Lock deliberately shot dead his wife Catherine and their daughters Cecilia (18) and Dorothy (20). Then he calmly telephoned the police and told them what he had done, waiting patiently for them to come and arrest him.

Sir Edward Marshall Hall argued movingly for temporary insanity. But the jury could not believe that the oriental stoicism with which Lock summoned his own arrest was the act of a lunatic and they found him guilty.

Woman Steals Worthless Junk: Then Kills Owner

LEEDS PROSTITUTE Louie Jackson persuaded nightwatchman Arthur Calvert to marry her in 1924 by pretending to be pregnant. In March this year the baby still had not arrived, and Louie told Arthur she was going to stay with her sister in Dewsbury, Yorkshire, for her confinement.

In fact she lodged in Leeds with eccentric widow Mrs Lily Waterhouse. While there she adopted the baby of an unmarried teenage mother, and took it to Arthur in triumph. She also took some worthless cutlery and household items.

Mrs Waterhouse had already notified the police that she thought her lodger was stealing from her. When they found the landlady battered to death in her home, they arrested Louie, who confessed to having previously killed another man for whom she worked as housekeeper. She was hanged at Strangeways in June.

Gorilla Killer Caught and Convicted in Canada

AFTER A YEAR'S reign of terror, the "Gorilla murderer" has been caught in Canada. In February last year, Mrs Clara Newman of San Francisco was strangled by a man with a monkey-face and ape-like arms to whom she let a room. Over the next six months he killed four more middle-aged California landladies. All were stripped and raped after they had been killed.

In October three landladies died in Portland, Oregon. In November he killed one in San Francisco and another back in Portland. In December the attack moved to Council Bluffs, Iowa, and then on to Kansas City where both Mrs Germania Harpin and her 8-month-old daughter were strangled.

A woman was killed in Philadelphia in April: another in Buffalo in May. Two sisters (raped together) died in Detroit in June, and then Mary Sietsome of Chicago became the last victim in the USA.

On June 8, flower girl Lola Cowan disappeared in Winnipeg. On June 9 Mrs William Patterson was raped and killed in her home in that city. While the Winnipeg victims were not landladies, the pattern of strangulation and a ravished corpse matched the American Gorilla murders.

In Regina, 200 miles from Winnipeg, the killer attacked a woman in a rooming-house who screamed and escaped. The police were informed, and the Gorilla murderer was seized at the edge of town.

The police had in custody 30-year-old Earle Nelson, a man who vanished for seven years after raping his estranged wife in a hospital ward in 1919. He was tried and convicted promptly, and will be executed in the New Year.

New York Mobster Shot Dead, Bodyguard injured

GANGSTER Jacob "Little Augie" Orgen was shot dead in New York in October. His bodyguard, Jack "Legs" Diamond, was injured.

Augen was a labour racketeer, offering thugs to employers or unions to beat up strikers or blacklegs. His lieutenant Louis "Lepke" Buchalter urged him to infiltrate union locals, so as to control their subscriptions and pension funds. But Orgen was not interested.

Since Buchalter associates with the new generation of hoodlums like "Lucky" Luciano and Meyer Lansky, who co-operate across ethnic boundaries that have hitherto separated mobs, it may be that Augen's labour interests will now gain some Italian input. His bootlegging and narcotics trade is inherited by Diamond.

Woman's Body in Charing Cross Trunk Identified

SKILLED DETECTION solved London's Charing Cross trunk murder this summer. The malodorous deposit in Left Luggage contained a butchered woman's body wrapped in pieces of cloth. One bore a laundry mark; another an embroidered greyhound. The first led to a Mrs Holt, who employed a succession of maids over the last few years; the other to the Greyhound Hotel, where one of Mrs Holt's former maids, Minnie Bonati, worked. And Minnie had disappeared.

Meanwhile, a taxi-driver reported taking a man with a trunk to Charing Cross from an office in Rochester Row. When police visited the office it was deserted. The tenant, Mr John Robinson, had left no forwarding address. But his waste paper basket contained a bloodstained split matchstick. And a woman came forward saying that she was meeting Robinson at the Greyhound Hotel.

The matchstick and the cloth from the Greyhound cracked Robinson's claim to know nothing of Minnie Bonati. He finally claimed that she had approached him at Victoria station, come to his office, and tried to extort money. When she attacked him he pushed her away, and she fell, striking her head.

But pathologist Bernard Spilsbury established that Minnie was suffocated as well as struck over the back of the head. Robinson was convicted and hanged in August.

The trunk left at Charing Cross station, containing the body of Minnie Bonati

1928

Essex Policeman With Eyes Shot Out, Villain Arrested

THE HORRIFYING murder of village bobby PC Gutteridge may be solved. His body was found in a country road between Ongar and Romford in September. He had been shot twice, and then his eyes had been shot out. (It seems the killer believes the legend that a dead man's eyes retain the reflection of the last person they saw.)

Tyre marks and scraping on the grass verge indicated that Gutteridge had stopped a car when he was murdered. And the car itself soon turned up, abandoned in Brixton. It was the property of Dr Lovell of Billericay, stolen from his garage during the night. There was blood on the driver's side and an empty cartridge case on the floor. But not a single fingerprint.

Since the car was abandoned in South London, police suspicions quickly fastened on Guy Browne, a Clapham garage owner with a long record of convictions for housebreaking, car theft and general thuggery. But there was no evidence to link him with the crime.

Then, at the end of the year, a robbery took place in Sheffield, and a witness took the getaway car's number. It belonged to a known Sheffield criminal, and on being apprehended he admitted his responsibility, and told police that Browne had been his confederate. He also revealed that Browne had confessed to him that he and a villain named William Kennedy murdered Gutteridge.

With that statement on record, the police had the necessary evidence for a warrant to search Browne's premises. In the garage they found a box of old-fashioned black powder cartridges – just the unusual type that had been found in Dr Lovell's car. A Webley revolver belonging to Browne proved to be the weapon that fired it. Browne has been arrested.

An intensive search is under way for Kennedy, a petty criminal who also has convictions for indecent exposure. The authorities hope to secure an early arrest so that the two men may be tried together early next year.

The body of murdered Police Constable Gutteridge was found on the left of this stretch of road between Ongar and Romford

Guy Browne

William Kennedy

Youth Murders his Employer the Priest's Housekeeper in Ireland

FATHER JAMES MCKEOWN, an Irish country village priest, employs a housekeeper and a handyman-chauffeur. Last year he had servants who disliked each other. When 36-year-old Mary Callan, the housekeeper, disappeared with her bicycle on May 16, Gerard Toal the chauffeur expressed no concern.

It was thought she had visited her mother, but the old lady had not seen her. Chauffeur Toal claimed she left the house after giving him dinner.

Mary seemed to have absconded permanently, and Fr. McKeown hired another housekeeper. Then, early this year, parts of a woman's bicycle, which Toal confessed he had stolen, were found in his room.

In April Fr. McKeown sacked the young man. Toal announced that he was going to Canada, but was in fact arrested for theft in Dundalk 10 days later.

At this point police made a thorough search of the presbytery and garden, and found women's clothing and more bicycle parts in the ash-pit. Finally Mary Callan's decomposed body was found in an abandoned water-filled quarry nearby.

Toal confessed that there had been a violent quarrel between the two in May 1927, but swore that her death was accidental. The trial judge advised the jury against bringing in a verdict of manslaughter, however, and the 18-year-old was hanged in Dublin on August 28.

Crook Slays Garage Manager after Frauds

THE MURDER OF Southampton garage manager Vivian Messiter was finally wrapped up in December with a guilty verdict passed on prime suspect William Podmore.

Messiter had been brutally battered about the head and his body concealed behind oil drums in the Wolf's Head Oil Company Garage for two months before it was discovered in January. The police also found in the garage an accounts book with pencil indentations from ripped-out pages showing false sales and commission credited to one "W.F.Thomas". This individual, a recent employee of the garage, had not been seen in Southampton since the disappearance of Messiter late last year. Investigations revealed that he was actually a man called Podmore with a substantial criminal record.

Podmore was charged with fraud and convicted; then, when the details of the fraud had been more fully established from the accounts book, he was tried for and convicted of the additional charge of murder. He will be hanged in the New Year.

The garage in Southampton where Mr Vivian Messiter's body lay for two months

Hundreds Attend Open-Air Trial in California

THE TRIAL of Eva Rablen for poisoning her deaf husband Carroll aroused so much interest in Columbia, California, that hundreds swarmed to the trial. The little town is not accustomed to receiving so many visitors, and the tiny courtroom was bulging at the seams just with the news hounds wanting a sniff of the case. Deciding that justice must be seen to be done, Judge J.W.Pitts adjourned to a large open-air pavilion in the town centre.

The defendant was a glamorous and outgoing young woman who enjoyed a lively social life. She adored partying and especially dancing. Not so her older husband Carroll, who was as unsociable and withdrawn as she was gregarious and fun-loving. He did not try to curb her activities, however, and tolerated her dancing with other men. At a dance in Tuttletown this April, Eva fetched her husband a cup of coffee as he stood on the sidelines. He had hardly time to say that it tasted bitter before he fell writhing to the floor, and died soon after.

Carroll's father believed Eva had poisoned her husband for his $30,000 insurance policy, and when a strychnine bottle was found in a cupboard in her house, she was arrested. The bottle had been sold to a woman calling herself Mrs Jo Williams who said she wanted it to poison gophers. But an autopsy turned up no trace of poison in the body. Judge Pitts sent the case on to a higher court.

Before Eva could come to trial, she learned that another pathologist had succeeded in tracing strychnine in Carroll's stomach as well as on the dress of a woman she had passed while coffee spilled from the cup. She changed her plea to guilty and entered San Quentin Prison in June.

Respectable Surburban Family Deaths from Arsenic

WITHIN THE space of a year, three members of the same family from Croydon in Surrey, England, have died of arsenic poisoning.

In April 1928, retired colonial officer Edward Creighton Duff took to his bed on returning from a fishing trip, and died shortly after. His death was ascribed to a weak heart. His wife brightly suggested that a bottle of beer he "snaffled" from the larder might have gone bad and strained his system.

In February this year, Mr Duff's unmarried sister-in-law, Vera Sidney, also died suddenly. She, too, was believed to have strained her heart – by cranking her car with a starting handle. This was surprising because Miss Vera was a hearty and sporty spinster, a masseuse by profession, well up to the exertion of cranking her car.

But when Miss Sidney's widowed mother Violet died the following month, there was no mistaking the signs of arsenic poisoning. Exhumation and analysis proved that Mr Duff and Miss Sidney had died of the same cause. Mrs Duff and Miss Sidney's brother Tom, a concert entertainer, live in the same neighbourhood, but have not been affected.

Nobody has any grudge against the family, and they do not share servants. Suspicion falls on Mr Tom Sidney and Mrs Duff, both of whom use arsenical weedkillers and are known to have been in and out of their relatives' houses. Yet the authorities cannot discover a likely motive for either to murder their blood relatives. Unless some striking new evidence emerges, it seems unlikely that charges will be brought against anyone, and this curious case will remain open.

IN BRIEF

GUY BROWNE and **WILLIAM KENNEDY** were convicted and executed in April for the murder of PC Gutteridge (*see* 1928).

1930

Monster Longs to Hear His Own Blood Gushing

PETER KÜRTEN, the Düsseldorf monster, ended his life with a grisly ambition. Facing beheading in Cologne, he asked the executioner: "After my head has been chopped off, will I still be able to hear at least for a moment the sound of my own blood gushing from the stump of my neck? That would be the pleasure to end all pleasures." All Kürten's pleasures ended on July 2.

In August 1929 Düsseldorf realized it had a murdering maniac in its midst. A 26-year-old housemaid escaped from being stabbed with scissors by a man whose advances she refused, shortly after the bodies of a 14-year-old girl and her 5-year-old sister were found. Citizens then recalled that another housemaid, a 9-year-old girl, and a drunken man had all been found stabbed to death with scissors earlier in the year.

Before long, Kürten had killed two more young women and an-

other child, changing his weapon to a hammer.

These were not his first murders. By his own account, he deliberately drowned a child when he was six, and almost strangled his girlfriend when he was 14, discovering in the process that it was even more satisfying than the cruelties he loved to inflict on animals.

He spent half his adult years in prison for theft and arson. In 1913 he killed a 13-year-old girl in her home. He dropped his initialled handkerchief on that occasion, but suspicion fell on the child's father, Peter Klein.

He was caught on May 14. He offered to see 21-year-old Maria Budlick home, and took her to his flat where he gave her a meal. Then he led her to a public park and tried to rape her. Failing in this, he asked if she remembered how to reach his home, and released her when she claimed to have forgotten.

Maria led police there, and to

the amazement of Kürten's wife, who had never suspected him, he was arrested.

Kürten killed at least 23 people in the course of his murderous career. He was charged with the murders of nine

Peter Kürten, the monster of Düsseldorf

> ## "AFTER MY HEAD HAS BEEN CHOPPED OFF, WILL I STILL BE ABLE TO HEAR AT LEAST FOR A MOMENT THE SOUND OF MY OWN BLOOD GUSHING FROM THE STUMP OF MY NECK? THAT WOULD BE THE PLEASURE TO END ALL PLEASURES. "
>
> **Peter Kürten**

The crowd at Maidstone jail for the execution of Sidney Fox

Homosexual Ex-Gigolo Murders Mother for Insurance

SIDNEY FOX and his 61-year-old mother were swindlers. They travelled around hotels in England, passing dud cheques and flitting off without paying their bills. At 31, Sidney was past working as a gigolo or a rent-boy.

In April last year he insured Mrs Fox's life for £3,000. In October, just as the second premium was due, the pair were staying in the Hotel Metropole at Brighton. Guests were astonished when the trouserless Sidney ran downstairs screaming that his mother's room was on fire and she was in danger.

Mrs Fox was dead in her badly charred armchair before the gas fire. But there were signs that the conflagration had been deliberately started with old magazines.

And at his trial in March, Fox could not explain why he closed the door to shut the smoke (and his mother) in, rather than dragging her out.

This nasty perverted individual at last got his just deserts in April, when he was hanged at Maidstone jail .

Murder Mystery: Are You Mr Qualtrough, Mr Wallace?

William Herbert Wallace — innocent man or clever murderer?

TRIED FOR the murder of his wife, convicted, and freed by the Court of Appeal, William Herbert Wallace (52) features in one of the most puzzling mysteries outside the pages of detective fiction.

He arrived at his chess club in Liverpool on January 19 to receive the previously telephoned message that a Mr R.M. Qualtrough of 25 Menlove Gardens West wanted to see him the following night on business. Wallace, an insurance salesman, spent the early evening of 20 January fruitlessly searching the Menlove Gardens development, only to find there was no such address. (Menlove Gardens North, South and East all exist, but there is no Menlove Gardens West.) When he crossed the city and returned home, his wife lay battered to death in the front room. A small sum of money had been taken.

Police discovered that "Mr Qualtrough's" call to the club was made from a public kiosk outside Wallace's house when he left home. They speculated that Wallace set up the false appointment to give himself an alibi. They over-ruled a milkboy who claimed to have seen Mrs Wallace alive after Wallace had left the house. They thought Wallace had stripped and worn only an old macintosh (which lay under Mrs Wallace's head) to avoid bloodstains. But they were unable to suggest a motive for Wallace.

Despite the jury's verdict, the Court of Appeal has freed Wallace, declaring, uniquely, that the verdict ignored the facts in the case. So did chess player Wallace craftily plan his moves ahead? Or did some intruder come in and murder the lady?

'Legs' Diamond Shot in Lover's Apartment

LEGS DIAMOND, the gangster they couldn't nail, has been gunned down in hiding. Killers caught him at the apartment of his girl-friend, Kiki Roberts, in Albany, New York.

The gangster's troubles began after he took over "Little Augie" Orgen's rackets in 1927. He opened the Hotsy Totsy Club on Broadway, where he openly killed rival Red Cassidy in 1929. Before evidence could be given, the barman and three customers were murdered, and four more people, including the hat-check girl, disappeared. Diamond was not charged with the killing.

In 1930 he declared war on "Dutch" Schultz, who had tried to acquire some of his interests. This year he declared that he wanted some of Joey Fay's nightclubs and some of "Waxey" Gordon's boot-legging contracts. "Legs" was personally at war with some of New York's biggest criminals.

Yet he feared nothing. Bullets injured him in 1924, 1927, 1930, and last April. He survived every time, and came to believe he was truly invincible.

On 18 December, unknown killers proved him wrong.

"Legs" Diamond, after a bootlegging conviction

OBITUARY

JACK 'LEGS' DIAMOND (1896-1931)

Legs Diamond earned his nickname as a youthful and nimble smash-and-grab thief. Soon after the end of prohibition, Diamond went to work for racketeer "Little Augie" Orgen, and ran some small bootlegging operations. After Orgen's death (see 1927), Diamond took over his bootlegging and narcotics.

Spruce, slim and good-looking, double-crossing Jack Diamond is mourned by no men, but many women, including his wife and showgirl Kiki Roberts.

1932

Sir Patrick Saves Socialite with His Trigger Finger

Michael Scott Stephen, murdered lover of Elvira Barney

SOCIETY LAWYER Sir Patrick Hastings has saved drunken socialite Mrs Elvira Barney from the gallows. In the small hours of May 31, neighbours in classy Williams Mews, in London's Belgravia, heard a shot, and then Mrs Barney's voice sobbing: "Don't die, chicken, don't die!"

(That's what they they *thought* they heard. Mrs Barney's actual words were: "Don't die, Mickey!")

A doctor arrived at the flat to find 24-year-old Michael Scott Stephen dead and fully clothed in the bedroom. He could see from the bed, however, that Stephen and the rather blowzy 27-year-old Elvira had been sleeping together earlier.

Mrs Barney, daughter of government auditor Sir John Mullins, reacted with contemptuous hauteur when police arrived, and were unconvinced by her story. She said that she and Stephen had been to a night-club with guests from a cocktail party the previous evening. On their return a quarrel began, and Stephen picked up her pistol to shoot himself. As she struggled to stop him, the gun went off and Stephen fell, mortally wounded.

"I'll teach you to arrest me, you bloody swine!" screamed the "bright young thing" as she realized she was going to be charged with murder or manslaughter.

Neighbours described an occasion when Mrs Barney appeared naked in her bedroom window and fired her pistol at Stephen in the mews below, crying: "Laugh, baby, laugh for the last time!"

But she never changed her story one iota. And Sir Patrick, exercising great stamina, clicked her pistol's trigger repeatedly at the court ceiling after a gun-smith testified that it took a 14lb pull, languidly remarking that it didn't seem difficult to him. So, at the cost of a sore finger, the great advocate persuaded the jury that his client was innocent. And Mrs Barney continues on her merry boozy way.

Mrs Elvira Barney, enjoying an outing after her acquittal

Woman Kills Two Husbands, One Son

NURSE DAISY DE MELKER, hanged in South Africa this December for three murders, almost got away with two of her crimes. In 1923 her first husband, William Cowle, died after 14 years of matrimony. His doctor diagnosed a stroke, and Mrs Cowle inherited the bulk of his estate and £1,700 insurance.

In 1927 she married again. Robert Sproat did not last the year. He died leaving his widow £4500. Again, a stroke was diagnosed.

In 1931 Daisy married former rugby star Clarence de Melker. The following year, her step-son Rhodes Cowle was approaching his 21st birthday and looking forward to receiving an inheritance left by his father. Daisy bought some arsenic and gave him that instead.

His sudden death aroused suspicion at last. The chemist from whom a "Mrs Sproat" had bought arsenic recognized her as Daisy de Melker. Exhumation of her husbands showed they had died of strychnine poisoning.

Mrs de Melker did not confess before dying, but her guilt is not in doubt.

Two Trunk Murders Found in Brighton by Police

Tony Mancini, the London gangster

Blazing Shed Suicide Murderer's Suicide

A FIRE IN HAWLEY STREET, Camden Town, this January, appeared to be the last suicidal gesture of builder Samuel Furnace. The blaze was in the shed he used as an office, and the body sitting at his desk had apparently left a note reading, "Good-bye to all. No work. No money. Sam J.Furnace."

Investigation proved the lament to be true. Furnace's business was failing, and it seemed that melancholia and a fondness for drink were handicapping his attempts to find any work. Police and firemen were ready to close the case.

But before the body was prepared for burial, it was suddenly noticed that a bullet had caused death. And since the bullet was in the back and the pistol was not lying beside the body, it could not be self-inflicted.

Was the body even Furnace? Examination proved that it was not. The corpse was twenty years younger, and its wallet and watch were missing. This appeared to be a robbery and murder with the victim disguised as his own killer. Police soon discovered that the unknown young man was Walter Spatchett, a rent-collector who often played billiards with Furnace.

Now the search was on for the lethally treacherous builder. Reports of his moves through London reached the police too late for him to be caught in the capital. After

briefly staying at a friend's house near Regent's Park, Furnace disappeared, as the press burst into shrieking headlined pursuit of him.

All investigations proved fruitless until Furnace incautiously broke cover. He had run out of clean clothes, and wrote to his brother-in-law asking for some clean shirts to be sent to him. He explained the grisly discovery in Hawley Street with the claim that he had been quarrelling with Spatchett and foolishly brandished a pistol which went off accidentally. Since this had been the termination of a heated dispute, he feared he would not be believed in saying it was unintended. And so he had fled in panic.

Police observed quietly that Furnace did not explain why panic led him to abstract Spatchett's watch and wallet. And they believed his failure to sell or pawn the watch had more to do with a wish to cover his traces than any concern for seeing that it went to Spatchett's proper heirs. Happily for the authorities, Furnace gave the address where he wanted his clean shirts sent: a Southend boarding house.

Taking Furnace's brother-in-law with them, armed police surrounded the house and secured Furnace's arrest without further violence. The landlady revealed that he had been a strange tenant, refusing to go out, and constantly watching the road from his window.

Few doubt that Furnace would have been found guilty had he come to trial. But the wretched man hid poison while in custody, and achieved a genuine suicide in his cell.

The failure of the authorities to recognize the body as that of a murder victim gave Furnace time to escape. It was Furnace's carelessness, not police efficiency, that led to his capture.

IN JUNE, someone in Brighton deposited a woman's torso in a trunk at the station. To date she has not been identified and her killer has not been traced.

But while searching the town, police found another body in another trunk, abandoned by Tony Mancini, a London gangster, who frequently changed rooms over the previous weeks, taking his increasingly smelly trunk with him.

The body was quickly identified as Violette Kaye (real name Violet Saunders), a London exotic dancer and prostitute, who accompanied Mancini to Brighton. Although he worked as a waiter, he was essentially living off her immoral earnings.

On May 10, Violette turned up drunk at the Skylark Cafe and accused him of having other women. That was the last time she was seen.

Mancini says he arrived home and found her battered to death. He assumes she was murdered by a client. But he was sure that his record for violence would count against him, and so he travelled with her body for the next two months.

Mr Norman Birkett, defending

Mancini, made an impassioned plea to the jury not to judge his villainous criminal record, but to look at the facts of the case, which fitted Mancini's story.

The jury obliged, and a flabbergasted Mancini greeted his acquittal with the words:

The trunk containing Miss Kaye, as Mancini abandoned it

The bullet-riddled car in which Bonnie Parker and Clyde Barrow died

Texas Rangers Gun Down Bonnie and Clyde

KINKY, BLUNDERING, vicious, folksy, greedy, sentimental and murderous – Bonnie Parker and Clyde Barrow were all these things. The Texas robbers never hit anything bigger than grocery stores and the smallest small-town banks. Yet they killed 13 people in their clumsy getaways over the last four years. Ace getaway driver Clyde was forever piling into ditches and hitting lampposts.

They snapped each other obsessively with their Kodak Brownie, and Bonnie wrote greetings-card doggerel about their love: yet young William Daniel Jones who travelled with them for a bit was sexually abused by both poofter Clyde and nympho Bonnie.

It was Jones's successor, Henry Methvin, who finally had enough and turned them in to the Texas Rangers. After the Barrow gang was surrounded in July last year at Dexter, Iowa, and Clyde's brother Buck was killed, Methvin and his family arranged to betray Bonnie and Clyde's movements.

At Gibland, Louisiana, Texas Ranger Frank Hamer led the ambush party which trapped the pair on May 23, and Bonnie and Clyde perished in a hail of bullets.

Mother-in-Law is No Joke

DR ALICE WYNEKOOP (62) is a well-known Chicago physician and philanthropist. But her adored son Earle is a disappointment: a tipsy womanizer.

Some years ago Earle married violinist Rheta Gardner. A neurotic hypochondriac, she did little to stabilize him and resented his obsessive attachment to his mother, with whom the couple lived.

On November 21, Dr Wynekoop called a hospital to say something terrible had happened to Rheta. Police found the young woman's naked body on Dr Wynekoop's examination table, a bullet through her breast and chloroform burns around her mouth.

Dr Wynekoop lamely suggested that intruders had killed Rheta, but after taking a lie detector test confessed that she had done it. She claims that hypochondriac Rheta asked for an anaesthetic, and she administered chloroform, realizing suddenly that she had accidentally given an overdose. So she shot her daughter-in-law to put her out of her misery.

Earle has tried to save his mother by confessing to the murder, but there is no doubt that he was on a train travelling west at the time.

Flippin' Kid: Murdering Neighbour Fakes Child's Rape

ABERDEEN HOUSEWIFE Jeannie Donald was annoyed by 8-year-old Helen Priestley from upstairs in her tenement. The child would ring her doorbell and run away shouting, "Coconut!" when Jeannie's permanent wave frizzed badly.

On April 20 the child disappeared. After a wild goose chase involving a man in a car, said by a mischievous little boy to have abducted her, Helen's body was found next day in a sack under the tenement stairs. She appeared to have been raped. But pathologists determined she had been suffocated and then assaulted with a stick to simulate rape. Hairs and cinders in the sack could be traced to the Donald kitchen.

Helen's heart condition means she might have died accidentally if Jeannie had caught her and given her a good shaking. But deciding to plead Not Guilty to murder rather than Guilty of manslaughter, Mrs Donald has said nothing about what really happened, and stoically accepted the life sentence she has been doled out.

Preserved Skin of Flayed hand Gives Print

THE GRUESOME discovery of the glove-like skin of a dead man's hand led to the conviction of Edward Morey for murdering vagrant Percy Smith.

Smith's body, flayed by five weeks' immersion in the Murrumbidgee River near Wagga Wagga, Australia on Christmas Day last year, is quite unidentifiable. The "glove", from which prints could taken, was discovered on the river bank.

Smith was seen in Morey's company. When Morey's property yielded a bloodstained axe and clothing, he was arrested.

During the trial, prosecution witness Moncrieff Anderson was shot by his retarded wife, who had fallen in love with Morey and pretended that her husband had really killed Smith; then himself been shot by intruders.

Both Morey and Lillian Anderson have been convicted of their respective killings, and they face life imprisonment.

Alma Rattenbury Kills Herself: Stoner Reprieved

THREE DAYS after escaping conviction for murdering her husband, Alma Rattenbury has killed herself. Her sacrifice wins a reprieve for her lover, George Stoner.

Alma, a talented musician, married middle-aged Francis Rattenbury in 1928. They had two children. Their marriage became shaky after they moved to Madeira Villa, Bournemouth, where Rattenbury started drinking and the two slept in separate bedrooms. Last year they advertised for a chauffeur-handyman. They had difficulty retaining men in service, since 31-year-old Alma made improper suggestions to them.

Eighteen-year-old George Stoner was open to such suggestions, however, and was soon coming to Alma's bedroom at night where, as a shocked court heard, they made love while Alma's little boy slept in the same room.

On March 24 police were summoned to Madeira Villa, where Rattenbury was in his armchair, streaming blood from a battered head. Alma was extremely drunk.

She confessed confusedly to having killed her husband. But as she was also trying to kiss a policeman, her statements seemed worthless.

At 8.00 am, after a fitful night's sedated sleep, she made a confession which was accepted. She was charged with attempted murder: a charge which changed to murder when Rattenbury died in hospital.

Meanwhile Stoner told Alma's maid that he was responsible, and indicated where he had abandoned the murder weapon – a mallet. She told the police, and Stoner joined his lover in prison.

The two shielded each other, until Mrs Rattenbury allowed her defence to tell what seems to be the true story: that Stoner came up to her bedroom after she had retired and told her he had battered her husband.

Stoner was sentenced to death. Mrs Rattenbury was acquitted, but severely reprimanded for her immorality. Now she has walked into a river and stabbed herself. And the Home Secretary has ended this tragic bloodbath by reprieving Stoner.

Why Schultz Had to Die

The body of "Abbadabba" Berman

DURING PROHIBITION "Dutch" Schultz held the Bronx beer monopoly: then branched out into the profitable "policy" or "numbers" racket – a street betting operation in which punters venture almost impossible odds to predict a random combination of three digits that changes daily. Jacob "Abbadabba" Berman has found ways of fixing the odds to give the gangs even more of the takings, and is said to be the only man Schultz paid well.

"Dutch" only became violent over money, lethally so as fellow mobsters "Legs" Diamond and Vincent "Mad Dog" McColl found to their cost.

When "Lucky" Luciano and Meyer Lansky put together the "Syndicate" which has governed organized crime ever since Joe Masseria and Salvatore Maranzano died, Schultz was too powerful to be left out. He never accepted Luciano's view that leading criminals should keep a low profile.

This year he crossed the syndicate. Special Prosecutor Thomas Dewey has been appointed to crush organized crime. Schultz's Democrat friends in Tammany Hall could not protect him when Republican Dewey bit into his profits. The Syndicate categorically refused to assassinate Dewey. So "Dutch" insisted he would do it himself, planning to shoot him in a callbox he habitually uses on his way to work.

The Syndicate saved Dewey by killing Schultz and Berman. Arthur Flegenheimer died in hospital on 25 October, after being gunned down while using the urinal at a restaurant in Newark, New Jersey. What a way to go!

Shark Spits Out Murder Victim's Arm

AUSTRALIAN DRUG-SMUGGLERS, forgers and extortionists Patrick Brady, Reg Holmes and James Smith have been busy trying to murder each other this year.

In April, Smith's unmistakeable tattooed arm, was spat out by a recently captured shark in an aquarium. Smith had last been seen in company with Patrick Brady, who denied killing him, but implicated Smith's employer, Holmes.

Holmes denied knowing Brady, let alone having criminal dealings with him and Smith. But two days later police caught him trying to escape from Sydney in a speedboat. There was a bullet wound in his head, and now he confessed to knowing Brady whom he accused of murdering Smith.

Brady was arrested. But two days before Smith's inquest opened, Holmes was found shot dead in his car. With the star witness gone, Brady's prosecution failed.

Sydney, Australia starts to look like Chicago, Illinois!

Parsi Doctor Kills Wife and Maid

WHEN PARSI Dr Buck Ruxton's (or Bikhtyar Rustomji's) American common-law wife Isabella Van Ess disappeared in September last year, along with the family nursemaid Mary Rogerson, the doctor reported that she had deserted him and taken the pregnant maid for an illegal abortion.

Since the Ruxtons' relationship had been passionate but stormy, no one was particularly surprised, although Miss Rogerson's parents protested that he must be lying about their daughter.

At the end of the month, pieces of two human bodies were found wrapped in newspapers beside a Scottish river when floodwaters receded.

One piece of paper was a special Morecombe and Lancaster edition of the *Daily Graphic*. Lancaster police knew of the two missing women.

Pathologists proved that one body was Isabella's by superimposing an old photograph of her head upon a picture of a skull taken from the same distance, and angle. It was evident, too, that the murderer had destroyed separately identifiable parts of the body like Isabella's thick ankles.

Neighbours now recalled Ruxton's giving away bloodstained clothing and carpets after frenzied house-cleaning at the time of the disappearances.

His denials in the witness-box made no impact on the powerful circumstantial evidence against him, and the murderous Dr Ruxton confessed to the murders before he was hanged in April.

Love and Murder in Rustic Slum Setting

SEMI-LITERATE Charlotte Bryant enjoyed coarse couplings with bucolic lovers at her slummy farm in Dorset, England. Her husband Frederick seemed unconcerned, even when married gypsy Leonard Parsons moved in with the Bryants.

But Charlotte wanted more room for Parsons, and gave her husband arsenic weedkiller. The gormless woman was surprised to be charged with murder when Frederick died as a result of her ministrations

She seemed incapable of understanding the proceedings against her. Parsons was little better. Nor was he much concerned, as he caroused cheerfully in a pub while Charlotte awaited hanging on July 15.

Dead Pimp Found in St Albans

IN JANUARY a man's bullet-ridden body was found dumped by the roadside near St Albans in England. His fingerprints identified him as "Red Max" Kassell, a Latvian pimp active in England since the trial of his fellow-countrymen Cellio and Berard. Recently he had been using a Canadian passport and passing himself off as "Emil Allard".

Chief Inspector Richard "Nutty" Sharpe, Scotland Yard's expert on racetrack gangs and white slavers, picked up rumours that Kassell had actually died in Little Newport Street, Soho. A piece of broken window-glass led him to no. 36 where the removal of a bobbled fringe from Suzanne Bertron's curtain caught his eye, and the curtain was found to contain traces of blood.

Despite claims that Kassell is "the Vice Czar of London", the middle-aged pimp was probably dependent on one elderly prostitute at the time of his death. He borrowed money from Suzanne Bertron's pimp, Roger Vernon (aka Georges LaCroix), and the two men quarrelled in Bertron's room when Vernon tried to reclaim it. On realizing he had killed Kassell, Vernon telephoned a friend, Pierre Alexandre, who helped him drive the body to St Albans while Bertron and her maid cleaned up the room.

Vernon and Bertron fled to Paris, where the authorities refused to return them to England. Vernon was sent to Devil's Island from which he escaped: Mme Bertron was acquitted. Alexandre, who, like Kassell and Vernon uses a Canadian passport, was tried in England and sent to prison.

Self-Styled Nurse Kills Mother and Daughter

DOROTHY WADDINGHAM, a former infirmary ward maid, called herself a nurse, and falsely claimed that her house in Nottingham was a registered nursing home.

Last year, the County Nursing Association sent "Nurse" Waddingham and her paramour, Ronald Sullivan, 89-year-old Mrs Louisa Baguley and her paralysed 50-year-old daughter Ada as patients. The Baguleys were to pay the "nursing home" 30 shillings a week, though as Nurse Waddingham rightly remarked, the age of the one and the disseminated sclerosis of the other meant that they really required the care of a five guinea-a-week hospital.

Nobody was surprised when Mrs Baguley died of old age. Nor did the doctor hesitate to issue a certificate when her daughter followed her, apparently having suffered a stroke. But a peculiar note, purportedly signed by Ada Baguley, and asking for cremation rather than interment, aroused the suspicions of the crematorium medical referee. When it was found she had left all her money to Nurse Waddingham, she was autopsied, and found to have been poisoned with morphine. So had old Mrs Baguley, whose body was exhumed.

Nurse Waddingham went to the gallows this year.

Children's 'Uncle Fred' Kills Mona

Frederick Nodder, the children's "Uncle Fred"

On January 5, 10-year-old Mona Tinsley of Newark, England, failed to arrive home from school. Reports of a man taking her on a Retford bus led back to lorry driver Frederick Nodder, who once lodged with the Tinsleys and was known to their children as "Uncle Fred".

He had called himself Frederick Hudson when living with the Tinsleys, who were quite unaware that under his real name he had a police record, dating back to the search for him to enforce a paternity order for his illegitimate child.

Nodder was blessed with rather prominent "staring" eyes, which made his identification easy when a schoolboy reported seeing such a man waiting at a Newark bus stop with a little girl, and a passenger remembered seeing the pair on the bus.

Under interrogation he admitted to accompanying the child on the bus, and claimed that she had asked him to take her to her aunt in Sheffield. He said he put her off at Worksop with her fare money and instructions on how to reach Sheffield.

She never got there.

In March, Nodder was sentenced to seven years' imprisonment for abduction, the judge commenting severely that Nodder alone knew what he had done with the little girl, but time might reveal the truth. This seemed unlikely because an extensive search, in which rivers and canals had been dragged and dumps sifted, had yielded no clues.

In June, Mona's strangled body floated to the surface of the River Idle. The same judge passed the death sentence, saying, "Justice has slowly but surely overtaken you."

IN JANUARY, Frederick Nodder killed. In April, he seemed to have got away with it. In June, Nemesis at last caught up with him. In December, he was hanged.

Murderer's Scheme to Incriminate His Landlord

ARTHUR PERRY, convicted of murdering his wife and sentenced to death this November, has had his trial overturned. Perry now goes for re-trial next year. It seems that when Perry decided to kill his 20-year-old wife Phennie, he plotted that 39-year-old Arthur Palm, who sublet a room to the Perrys, should be incriminated.

He acquired samples of Palm's handwriting, and wrote a letter to Phennie in which Palm appeared to say he would kill the girl if she refused to let him have sex with her. Since Palm is a responsible chainstore salesman, and deacon at a Black Baptist church, Phennie was astonished. She showed the letter to her husband, who said he would deal with the problem.

On July 1, Phennie Perry took her baby with her to a bingo hall in Jamaica, New York. From there she should have gone to her sister's. But Perry waylaid her and battered her to death with an iron purloined from Palm's apartment. Beside the body he also left papers from Palm's dresser, a shirt-pocket ripped from one of Palm's garments, and a left shoe with a hole in it.

The papers led police straight to Palm's apartment, and the torn shirt and matching right shoe were found there. But Perry was taken into custody as well, since Palm had an unshakeable alibi for the previous night.

A handwriting expert declared that the threatening letter from "Palm" to Phennie had actually been written by Perry. Forensic tests found that one of Perry's socks was stained with mud and blood in exactly the position of the hole in Palm's shoe. And Perry found himself in the dock where he belonged.

Doctor, Witch and Actor Team Up To Kill

AN ASTONISHING gang of insurance-scam murderers has been caught in Philadelphia. Over the last five years, the Bolber-Petrillo ring has probably killed at least 50 people.

Dr Morris Bolber and his cousin Paul Petrillo stumbled into lucrative murder when Mrs Antony Giscobbe, one of Bolber's patients, complained of her husband's infidelities. Bolber sent Petrillo to seduce her, and propose that they murder Tony for his $10,000 life insurance.

A natural death was easily arranged. When Tony staggered home drunk for a good night's sleep, his wife left the window over his bed open to admit the rain. Soon Tony was dead of pneumonia, and Dr Bolber and Mrs Giscobbe were each the richer by $5,000.

Bolber and Paul now put their scheme on a regular business footing, and recruited another cousin, amateur thespian Hermann Petrillo. His job was to impersonate each uninsured victim and take out a policy. The gang's subtlety was best shown in the "on-the-job" accident (with double indemnity) arranged for a roofer. Before pushing him off a roof, they put filthy postcards in his hands, to suggest that he was carelessly distracted by the luscious naked lovelies.

Carino Favato, "the Witch of Philadelphia," was the gang's next recruit. This sinister "faith healer" had poisoned three of her own husbands, and sold poison to other women. She helped identify clients. The gang was caught when an ex-convict approached Hermann Petrillo with a proposal. Hermann was not impressed, and said: "Dig up somebody we can murder for some insurance and you can make some dough with us." The humble villain was appalled, and went to the police. Under arrest, the gang all informed on each other. The Petrillos have been executed for their crimes; the Doctor and the Witch sentenced to life imprisonment.

Man Says He Killed Blackmailing Prostitute Unwittingly

TWENTY-SEVEN-YEAR-OLD George Brain borrowed his firm's green Morris Eight van on July 13. Near Wimbledon Common, London, he was distracted by 30-year-old prostitute "Irish Rose" Atkins and offered her a lift.

George couldn't remember exactly why he did this, for almost immediately (he said) he suffered a blackout, prompted by fury when Rose demanded money from him, saying she would tell the St Pancras boot wholesalers for whom he worked that he had been out pleasure-driving in their van.

The police filled in the blanks for him: he had stabbed Rose, battered her over the head with a starting handle and then run the van over her body. He had also taken four shillings from her bag.

Two days later George's employers reported his disappearance with £32. His van, left in a workmate's garage, was bloodstained. Its tyres fitted the marks on Rose's body and its colour matched witness descriptions of a vehicle seen in the area of the murder.

After his photograph was published, George Brain was spotted by a schoolboy at Sheerness. He went on trial in November, and was hanged in December.

Prostitute "Irish Rose" Atkins, one of George Brain's victims

A Miscarriage of Justice Feared

MRS MARGARET DOBSON (67) was found, stabbed, on a cart track on January 18. For 30 years she and her husband have farmed near Wolviston, Durham, England.

Suspicion fastened on 21-year-old Robert Hoolhouse, who fitted a vague description of a loiterer seen near the scene of the crime. Hoolhouse's face and hands were scratched; his coat had blood and hair on it.

Five years ago his family quarrelled with Mr and Mrs Dobson, and were evicted from their tied cottage. The labouring family had to move to a village four miles away, and Robert, 16 at the time, did not pretend to have loved the Dobsons.

His legal advisers felt there was no case against him. Farm workers' faces and hands are scratched by briars: their clothing picks up blood and hairs in animal husbandry. Resentment of a high-handed landlord in 1933 was a thin motive for murder in 1938. A footprint near the body was definitely not Hoolhouse's.

For these reasons, counsel called no witnesses in Hoolhouse's defence. It seemed better to have the last word with the jury – something only permitted if no defence witnesses are called.

The strategy failed, and despite a petition with over 14,000 signatures, Hoolhouse has been hanged. But the public is not satisfied that justice has been done

Kidnapper Trailed from Wisconsin to Los Angeles

BURGLAR John Henry Seadlund turned his incompetent hand to kidnapping last year, and wound up a double-murderer with FBI chief J.Edgar Hoover flying to California for his arrest.

With accomplice James Gray, Seadlund picked an expensive-looking car in Illinois, swerved his own vehicle in front of it, and ejected the owner at gunpoint, leaving the chauffeur to raise the alarm.

Charles P.Ross, a Chicago businessman, was taken to Wisconsin and forced to write a note asking for a $50,000 ransom to be raised. This note, and one that succeeded it, were passed to the FBI.

The Bureau gave their usual advice: meet the demand first; let them try to catch the criminals after the victim was secure. But the notes yielded fingerprints. The typewriter on which they had been written was new, and the store which sold it gave a description of the as-yet unidentified Seadlund.

The ransom was delivered in marked bills, and these started turning up in a trail that led to Los Angeles.

On January 14 the FBI surrounded Santa Anita racetrack, where Seadlund was arrested. He then broke down and confessed to having murdered both Mr Ross and James Gray, and directed officers to the buried bodies in Wisconsin, where he had hidden them

Seadlund went to the electric chair in the spring.

Mad Butcher' is Dead, says Top Policeman

CLEVELAND POLICE chief Eliott Ness believes that the "Mad Butcher of Kingsbury Run", who has terrorized the city or four years, is now dead.

Ness was originally head of he group of prohibition enorcement agents known as "the ntouchables". Cleveland apointed him Director of Public afety in 1935.

In September that year, two ecapitated men were found ear ramshackle Kingsbury Run. our months later a headless rostitute was found hacked to ieces in the same neighbourood.

Three more headless and mangled men were found in 1936. In 1937 a headless, dismembered black woman was dumped under a bridge in a sack. A man killed later in the year was hacked to pieces.

Last year saw three more murders: two men and a woman.

In August last year, Mr Ness made a bold decision. Nearly all the victims were prostitutes or vagrants from the East 45th Street and Kingsbury Run warren of shacks and shanties. Mr Ness cleared the inhabitants out and burned the slum to the ground. And with his hunting-ground obliterated, the mad butcher stopped killing.

Ness didn't stop hunting him, however. He deduced from the number of male victims that the murderer was probably homo-sexual. He had to be big and strong enough to overpower his victims. He had to have a car to transport their bodies. He had to live on his own in a house clear of inquisitive neighbours. And he had to have sufficient money to maintain his house and car.

Investigations ultimately uncovered a man who fitted the model: a big, sullen, withdrawn and hostile homosexual. Mr Ness interviewed him repeatedly, hinting that he was trapped. The suspect, in turn, nursed his feeling of superiority to the investigators by almost admitting the offences.

Until he cracked – but not to the police. He committed himself to a mental home, where he died this year.

Eliott Ness, Cleveland police chief

'Brick Moron' Kills in LA: Executed in Chicago

THE MYSTERIOUS "Brick Moron", caught and executed in Chicago this year, rampaged pointlessly through two cities, using a different name in each.

The first brick killing took place in Chicago in 1936, when a young cocktail waitress was beaten in the hotel room where she lived with her 7-year-old son. The killer scrawled, "Black Legion Game" in lipstick on the dressing-table mirror. And he left a beautiful set of his fingerprints which showed that he was Robert Nixon, an 18-year-old black delinquent. But Nixon vanished.

In Los Angeles, a young black man called Thomas Crosby started amassing a record, with arrests for purse-snatching and suspicion of auto theft. A brick-murderer also began working in the city. He killed twice in March, and again in April. All victims were women killed in their own homes, with the last victim's 12-year-old daughter also battered to death. The clumsy stupidity of these pointless killings led to the assassin being dubbed "The Brick Moron".

In May last year, Mrs Florence May Johnson, a fireman's wife in Chicago, was killed with a brick. Soon after that, Chicago police picked up Nixon, and it was not long before he had confessed. Then the Los Angeles Police Department spotted the similarity between the Chicago brick murders and the killings in their own city. Exchanged fingerprints confirmed that Robert Nixon and Thomas Crosby were one and the same. Chicago tried the young man and electrocuted him this June.

Robert Nixon (aka Thomas Crosby), the moronic brick killer of Chicago and Los Angeles

New York Crime Investigations Uncover Murder Inc.!

Louis "Lepke" Buchalter, boss and racketeer

SPECIAL PROSECUTOR Thomas Dewey's work against organized crime in New York has been taken over by Burton Turkus. Spectacular results are coming from informer Abe "Kid Twist" Reles.

To escape conviction for the 1938 murder of informer "Whitey" Rudnick, Reles is informing on all and sundry – "singing like a canary" in underworld parlance. And he knows what he's talking about!

Reles was one of a gang of professional killers who met at Matilda's Cafe in Brooklyn. Run by Brooklyn crime boss Albert Anastasia, these men took contracts to kill dispensable villains and informers in other parts of New York city and the USA.

Learning of this assassination by outside contract (an old underworld method of keeping "the home team" out of trouble with safe alibis), the press have dubbed Anastasia's mob "Murder Inc."

Reles' revelations go back a long way. It seems that Bugsy Siegel, Vito Genovese, Joe Adonis and Albert Anastasia shot Joe "the Boss" Masseria (fingered by his lieutenant "Lucky" Luciano) in 1931, and four Jewish gangsters "rubbed out" his successor, Salvatore Maranzano shortly after this.

New York Special Prosecutor Tom Dewey (second from right) gives a press conference on his recent crime-busting activities

These two murders enabled Luciano and Meyer Lansky to divide up New York's crime operations between them, their gangs co-operating and so eliminating the murderous rivalry that was such a feature of underworld life in the Prohibition period.

Most sensationally of all, Reles ties crime boss and labour racketeer Louis "Lepke" Buchalter to the 1936 murder of one-time trucker Joe Rosen.

Lepke is already in secure custody for narcotics offences (*see* 1939). For the first time ever, one of the true heads of organized crime faces capital charges and the very real possibility of being sent to the electric chair for his many crimes.

English "Lady" Takes off Glove to Shoot Lover

FLORENCE RANSOM is an English lady who was caught because an English lady should never be seen without her gloves – even if she's gone out to murder. Florence became the lover of Lawrence Fisher of Matfield in Kent some time ago, and was delighted when he left his wife and family to move in with her at Piddington, near Bicester in Oxfordshire. But on July 9 she decided that Mrs Fisher's survival was inconvenient, and went down to Kent to pay a social call. She persuaded Mrs Fisher and her 19-year-old daughter to come out into the garden, where she shot them. When the housemaid came out to see what was going on, Florence shot her, too. Then she returned to Piddington. But she had dropped one of her kid gloves, which was traced. Adjudged guilty but insane, Florence was spared the hangman and transferred to Broadmoor after her trial.

Who Dropped the Canary Out of His Cage?

ABE "KID TWIST" RELES is dead. The 34-year-old killer whose testimony has blown the roof off organized crime in New York fell 75 feet from his window in the Half Moon Hotel, Coney Island, where a constant guard of six policemen watched him night and day.

Stoney-faced, the guards say they just weren't looking when it happened. Stoney-faced, the NYPD says it was either suicide or an escape attempt, pointing to a couple of sheets tied together. Stoney-faced, Mayor William O'Dwyer says that the capital case assembled against "Lord High Executioner" Albert Anastasia, head of Brooklyn's crime family, has died with Reles, and the promising murder charges in preparation for "Bugsy" Siegel must be dropped as well.

It is whispered that crime syndicate "Prime Minister" Frank Costello shelled out $50,000 in bribes to ensure that Reles died before Anastasia and Siegel could tread the path of Louis "Lepke" Buchalter.

For the crime family boss and labour racketeer has been sentenced to death on Reles' testimony. Never before has one of the top gang leaders faced the electric chair. It remains to be seen whether Lepke's money, friends and influence will somehow intercede with appeals and delays, or whether he will die with his shoes on, like so many of his enemies

Abe "Kid Twist" Reles

Kiwi Farmer Shoots Six Before Being Shot

NEW ZEALAND'S biggest manhunt has ended with seven people dead, one of whom was dangerous killer Eric George Graham. Graham's dairy farm started to fail last year, and the more he lost money, the more he withdrew into himself and blamed his neighbours. On October 7 he threatened two of them with a rifle, and they informed the police.

Constable Best went to re-monstrate with Graham, and was verbally abused. When Best returned with a sergeant and two other constables, Graham shot all four. (He has always been an expert deer-stalker and marksman). Best still lived, though mortally wounded and Mrs Graham ran out of the house to fetch him a doctor. Two strangers she met came to the farm to see if they could help. Graham killed them. Then he took off for the bush, returning at night to find the Home Guard occupying his home. He was wounded in an exchange of fire, and headed for the bush again. Five days later, man-hunters spotted him, and he was wounded for a second time, but escaped yet again.

Finally, on October 15, a police officer found Graham hiding in farm outbuildings and shot him without warning. This prompt action was commended by the coroner.

'DO SOMETHING ABOUT SOLDIERS KILLING KIDS'

Twentieth-century Murder is unwilling to recommend the Hunnish provision of field brothels for British fighting men. But as the country is turned into a stronghold with black-outs, the Army must take full responsibility for the armed and fit young men it draws out of homes and families and deposits in alien places.

We feel compelled to demand action in the light of three murders over the last twelve months.

Samuel Morgan used weekend leave from Seaforth Barracks to rape and strangle Mary Hagan in an empty Liverpool blockhouse last November. He was caught because he dropped an army thumbstall by the body and the bandaging and acriflavine exactly matched field dressings issued to Morgan's unit, which Morgan used when he cut his thumb on barbed wire.

Morgan was hanged in April. Harold Hill awaits trial for the murder in November of 8-year-old Doreen Hearne and 6-year-old Kathleen Trendle. They were stabbed in the throat and chest and dumped in Rough Wood, about four miles from their homes in Penn, Buckinghamshire. Hill picked them up in his army truck, which he then drove back to base in Yoxford, Suffolk. Only a laundry-marked handkerchief dropped near the bodies, and a schoolboy's observation of the truck's markings, traced this mobile military murderer.

These boys in uniform should be our heroes. Is the army doing enough? Should they provide something more than chaplains and bromide in the tea for soldiers' morals?

Since the South African War, British soldiers have mastered their libidinous desires with the true Englishman's gentlemanly self-control, assisted by unobtrusive doses of a depressant drug in their tea. The term "the licentious soldiery" has not been applied to our brave boys since Queen Victoria's day.

Black-Out Ripper: Young Killer Airman

Fire-Watcher Convicted for London Blitz Killing

ON FEBRUARY 13, a good-looking young airman in a Piccadilly brasserie in central London offered Mrs Greta Haywood a drink at the nearby Captain's Cabin. There, in the darkness of the blackout he attacked her, but ran off when she screamed, leaving his gas-mask behind.

It yielded the fingerprints of a ruthless killer who had already struck that night, strangling Mrs Doris Jouannet at her flat in Paddington, and savagely mutilating her abdomen and breasts with a tin-opener.

The night before he had done the same to prostitute Margaret Lowe. Two days before that, ex-Windmill dancer Evelyn Oatley was his victim. On February 9, respectable chemist Margaret Hamilton was attacked in Montague Square and robbed of her handbag after being strangled with the scarf she was wearing.

The man committing these crimes had no convictions, so his fingerprints were not on file. Now the police know he was Aircraftsman 525987 Gordon Frederick Cummins, a 25-year-old trainee pilot.

After leaving Mrs Heywood, Cummins made another attack on a woman: Katherine Mulcahy (aka Kathleen King), who took him back to her Paddington flat.

Cummins used the cash he stole from his murder victims to support a fanstasy image of himself as a well-heeled man about town. His pretence of noble birth and good education made him unpopular with his fellows in the Air Force and earned him the nickname "the Duke".

Cummins offered no defence at his trial except a denial, and was convicted and hanged.

HARRY DOBKIN'S trial this November 1942 brought the Russian-born Jewish fire-watcher a death sentence. Dobkin's marriage to Rachel Karpinski was arranged by a broker in 1920, and lasted three days! But in that time a son was conceived, and for the next 20 years Dobkin was harried for maintenance. When the child reached adulthood, Rachel's sister encouraged her to continue to press for support.

In April 1941, when he started fire-watching, Dobkin invited Rachel to meet him at a cafe. She was never seen again. Her sister had a premonition that Dobkin had murdered her, and wrote a long letter to the police.

On April 15 Dobkin reported a small fire in the vestry of the chapel in St Oswald's Place, Kennington Road. No serious damage clearance was done at the site until July 1942, when a burned human skeleton was found under a flagstone. Rachel Dobkin had been reported missing just three days before the fire in the chapel.

Mrs Dobkin's dentist identified the skull positively. Dobkin's persistent claim to know nothing about Rachel's disappearance, did not convince the jury, and he was convicted.

Harry Dobkin and Rachel Karpinski on their wedding day in 1920

Victim: Evelyn Oatley

Victim: Margaret Hamilton

Victim: Doris Jouannet

Black Magic Suspected in Murder of Nassau Millionaire

THE DUKE OF WINDSOR'S bomb-free sinecure as Governor of the Bahamas has been troubled by a murder, and HRH has dirtied his fingers trying to help solve it.

Millionaire Sir Harry Oakes was found dead in bed on July 8. White feathers all over the place coupled with an unsuccessful attempt to burn the body suggested at first that this was a native killing with "obeah" (black magic) overtones, carried out in the course of a robbery.

But Sir Harry had been killed by a blow to the head while he was facing downward, and blood had trickled from behind his ear to his cheek. Yet the body was found lying on its back, and the blood couldn't have run uphill! Native robbers seemed unlikely to have gone to the trouble of moving the body back to the bed.

The Duke called in two Miami detectives, who concluded that Sir Harry's French son-in-law, playboy yachtsman and chicken farmer Comte Alfred de Marigny, was responsible. They found one of his fingerprints on a screen near the bed, and the Comte was arrested and put on trial.

Alas, the Duke's detectives

Nassau police pull Gallic playboy Alfred de Marigny on suspicion of murder

Comte Alfred de Marigny, "undesirable alien" in the Bahamas

were incompetent. Marigny's was one among a multitude of fingerprints found in the room, yet all the others had been cleaned-off without being examined! And Marigny's dinner guests gave their host a pretty good alibi for the night. Not surprisingly, The Comte was acquitted.

Strange rumours are circulating in Nassau: that Sir Harry was seen during the night being driven to the harbour by his friend Harold Christie, who discovered the body; that Christie, Oakes and the Duke of Windsor have shared mysterious business deals.

But His Excellency the Governor, wanting his own way as ever, has used his powers with petty vindictiveness, and deported Alfred de Marigny as "an undesirable alien". What, we wonder, is our ex-King covering up?

Son Blows Up Father in Wheelchair with Mine

ARCHIBALD BROWN was a tyrant. His treatment of his wife niggled his 19-year-old son, Eric, but neither the lad nor his older brother could stand up to the bullying bank clerk.

Mr Brown's conduct was not made sweeter by paralysis of the spine, a disability which ultimately confined him to a wheelchair. On July 23, Nurse Mitchell was out with her patient near his home in Rayleigh, England, when Mr Brown demanded a cigarette. As she walked around the chair after lighting it for him, she was suddenly thrown to the ground by a mighty explosion. The wheelchair and Mr Brown were blown to bits.

Eric, it transpired, had got hold of a Hawkins Grenade Mine, capable of destroying a tank, and booby-trapped the wheelchair with it!

A court in Chelmsford this November learned that his sole motive was to ease his mother's life. He has been found guilty but insane.

Crime King Goes to the Electric Chair

Louis "Lepke" Buchalter, the infamous boss of Murder Inc

LOUIS "LEPKE" BUCHALTER has been electrocuted. The boss of the infamous "Murder Inc" murder squad was convicted in 1941 of ordering the killing of candy-store owner Jacob Rosen, who threatened to expose Buchalter's activities to the District Attorney.

Mindy Weiss and Louis Capone (no relations to Hymie or Al) carried out the actual killing, along with "Pittsburgh Phil" Strauss; they preceded their boss to the chair. Pittsburgh Phil was the most prolific killer in organized crime. Estimates of his murders range from 50+ to 100+. His girlfriend, Evelyn Mittleman, was known as the "Kiss of Death Girl", because of Phil's lethal response to men who made a play for her. But this is the first time that the head of a crime family has paid the law's penalty for ordering a killing.

To the end, Buchalter hoped that threats and blackmail would save him. He suggested to Governor Tom Dewey that he could ensure his victory over Mr Roosevelt in the November presidential elections. This was ironical, as the governor's political career took off from his successful prosecution of mobsters, which put "Lepke" in jail for narcotics dealing, making him liable for new charges when squealer "Kid Twist" Reles broke the "Murder Inc" story. But Republicans ignored hints that President Roosevelt's labour advisor Sidney Hillman is up to his neck in crime.

"Lepke's" final public statement that he has not talked to anyone was intended to secure his family against gangland retribution. While in Leavenworth Prison, Buchalter was astonished to encounter conscientious objectors serving sentences, and made a classic outsider's comment on the immorality of compulsory military conscription: "You mean they put you in here for not killing people?"

> ❝ **YOU MEAN THEY PUT YOU IN HERE FOR NOT KILLING PEOPLE?** ❞
> QUOTE **Louis 'Lepke' Buchalter**

SICILIAN 'MAFIOSI' HEAD NEW YORK MOBS

Buchalter's crime "family", with important labour racketeering interests and its lethal "enforcement" role, now passes to Albert Anastasia, "Lord High Executioner" of the so-called "Murder Inc". All New York's crime families are now under Sicilian leadership. In 1931 "Lucky" Luciano killed and replaced the elderly "Mustache Petes" who were warring for control of the old-style Sicilian Mafia. Luciano's new-style was coloured by experience with the inter-ethnic "Broadway Mob" of rum-runners Joe Adonis, Frank Costello, Meyer Lansky, Bugsy Siegel and Luciano himself. "Dutch" Schultz was a force to be reckoned with and Louis Buchalter had inherited "Little Augie" Orgen's labour rackets. The five "families" now are: Luciano's (with Vito Genovese managing on the outside for him while "Lucky" issues orders from Dannemora prison); Anastasia's; Joe Profaci's; Tommy Lucchese's (formerly Tom Gagliano's); and the slightly maverick but deadly efficient Joe Bonnano's. These men, with Joe Adonis and the relatively non-violent manipulators, Frank Costello and Meyer Lansky, are the all-important bosses whose agreement makes their policies law.

Heroic Ex-Naval Man Dragged to Death

SMASH AND GRAB raiders from south London became murderers when a retired naval commander bravely tried to stop their car.

Thomas Jenkins and Ronald Hedley tried unsuccessfully to rob a jeweller's shop in Birchin Lane in the City. As they rushed their getaway car through the tight right-angle turn into Lombard Street, Commander Ralph Binney tried to halt their progress. They drove ruthlessly over him, and his body was caught on the car bumper and dragged down Gracechurch Street and over London Bridge, to fall off, dead, in Tooley Street.

Hedley has been hanged for this hideous crime, and Jenkins is serving a very long prison sentence.

Improved store security may soon bring an end to "smash and grab" raiding.

Evil Doctor Killed Jewish Refugees from Paris

Dr Marcel Petiot

THE AUTHORITIES in Paris are nearly ready to go to trial with their case against Dr Marcel Petiot. In March last year, police and firemen called to investigate foul smoke and odours from the doctor's house in Rue Lesueur, were appalled to find 27 dismembered and decomposing bodies in the cellar. Petiot explained that these were collaborators killed by the Resistance. The patriotic officials winked at his activities, but suspicion was aroused when the doctor and his family suddenly left Paris. Those who knew of the bodies in Rue Lesueur started to wonder whether Petiot had really been collaborating with the Germans and using his killing chamber on their behalf.

With the Nazi scourge swept out of Paris, Petiot surfaced as "Captain Valery" of the Free French, and claimed that the Gestapo had framed him. The bodies in the cellar, he told the newspaper *Resistance*, were actually German soldiers, of whom he had killed 63 during the course of the war.

But records showed that "Captain Valery" had been a patriotic soldier for a mere six weeks; that Dr Marcel Petiot had a criminal record going back to the War of 1914-18 , when he was convicted of black marketeering. In 1928, as Mayor of Villeneuve, he was convicted of drug-trafficking. He was also suspected of murdering a woman patient, but the case was dropped when an important witness died suddenly.

It is now clear that Petiot's appalling scheme was the deception and murder of wealthy Jews trying to escape from occupied France. He offered, for a fee, to smuggle them abroad, and then killed them and stole their valuables. 47 suitcases whose owners thought the doctor was helping them to safety have been found in his possession. And he is believed to have stolen more than £1 million from his victims. If the case is proved, Dr Petiot will go down in history as an evil war profiteer.

Black Marketeers Start Killing Each Other

REUBEN MARTIROSSOFF was known to villains all over Europe as "Russian Robert". On November 1, his body was found covered by a blanket in the back of his small car parked in Chepstow Place, off Notting Hill in west London.

Through informants, police learned that Martirossoff had been telephoned by a Polish friend the night before, who arranged a meeting. From the limited information that the Pole was called Marian and had been a naval officer, police deduced that this must be Polish deserter Marian Grondkowski. When he was traced, Martirossoff's wallet and cigarette lighter were found in his possession.

Grondkowski blamed another Pole, Henry Malinowski. He said the two had met Martirossoff and gone with him to a pub to discuss their black market business. Afterwards, Martirossoff's car wouldn't start, and while the two were pushing it, Malinowski decided to kill and rob him after leaping into the back of the car when the engine turned over. Grondkowski helped him take the car and corpse to Chepstow Place.

Malinowski confirmed this story, except that he said Grondkowski was the killer. Both men have been found guilty of the murder and sentenced to death.

Police believe these two are also responsible for killing black marketeering taxi driver Frank "the Duke" Everitt, whose body was found in similar circumstances on Lambeth Bridge, and whose taxi was also abandoned in Notting Hill. It is hoped the opportunistic nature of Martirossoff's murder means it will not find imitators. Otherwise, rationing bodes ill for the murder rate in the capital.

1946

Sadistic Killer Inflicts Appalling Injuries on Women

NEVILLE GEORGE CLEVELY HEATH was handsome and charming: a perfect escort for ladies. His long record of petty criminality included housebreaking and jewellery theft. He habitually passed bad cheques and used false identities. During the war he claimed ranks and decorations to which he was not entitled, yet was so good a flying instructor that the South African Air Force continued to use his services, even when they knew he was not, as he claimed, "Lt. Col. Armstrong".

After his demob he led a raffish life in London, and met "Ocelot Margie" at the Panama Club in Knightsbridge. The two seemed perfectly suited, as she was a masochist and he had sadistic inclinations. They enjoyed at least one date on which the binding and beating was satisfactory to both parties.

On July 21, 32-year-old Margery Gardner's body was found in the Pembridge Court Hotel, Notting Hill. She had been tied up and gagged with a scarf. She had been savagely beaten with a riding whip: the lattice pattern of its weave had left clear marks on her body. Her breasts had been bitten till they bled. And some strong instrument – possibly a poker – had been forced into her vagina.

The room had been booked by "Lt. Col. and Mrs Heath". There was no sign of the colonel. He wrote to the police, however, disclaiming responsibility for the murder, and pretending that he had gone out so that Margery could sleep with another friend.

As "Group Captain Rupert Brooke", Heath turned up in Bournemouth. There he met 21-year-old Doreen Marshall who was convalescing at the Norfolk Hotel. She had tea and dinner with "Group Captain Brooke" on July 3, and then disappeared. On July 8, her strangled and mutilated body was found in Branksome Chine.

As "Brooke", Heath went to the police to make a statement about Miss Marshall. He was immediately recognized as Neville Heath, wanted in connection with Margery Gardner's murder.

At his trial he pleaded insanity. But an extraordinary impulse to do bizarre and wicked things is no defence in law if the defendant knows that what he is doing is wrong. Heath was convicted and hanged in October, going jauntily to the gallows with the springy manner of the habitual charming confidence trickster.

Twenty-one-year-old Doreen Marshall, Heath's second victim

Neville Clevely Heath, handsome con-man and sadistic killer of Margery Gardner

Shady Ladies Come to Sticky End

TWO UNCONNECTED murders of London women this year seem likely to remain unsolved mysteries. Efficient 36-year-old Dorothy Wallis ran an employment agency in High Holborn. Her secretary was shocked when she came in for work at 9.00 am and found Miss Wallis's battered body lying in a pool of blood.

A witness who rang the office shortly before 6.00 pm the night before, heard the telephone answered by a man with an educated voice, who gently put the caller off. And neighbours heard screams around 6.30.

Miss Wallis's diaries contained a clue and a shock. The respectable spinster businesswoman habitually went out alone to bars and picked up strange men for sexual recreation. It seems her sins have caught up with her. But police have little hope of tracing her killer among London's army of discreet promiscuous men.

Margaret Cook, on the other hand, always seemed poised for trouble. The 26-year-old ex-Borstal girl had become an "exotic dancer" and exhibited her charms, shielded only by a g-string, in Carnaby Street's Blue Lagoon Club; Elizabeth Jones had also undressed to music here.

Margaret is known to have been warned that a new boyfriend had a gun. Unfortunately it is not clear who the boyfriend was, or who gave her the warning: only that Margaret dismissed the idea. This was unwise – Margaret was found shot dead in an alley outside the club. There seems no way of tracing her murderer. Although this is being called "the Blue Lagoon murder", one thing the police have ascertained is that it has nothing to do with the club staff or patrons.

Two Reprieved in Chalk-Pit Murder

FORMER NEW SOUTH WALES Minister of Justice Thomas Ley fled Australian corruption charges in the 1920s. He settled in London with his mistress, good-natured Mrs Maggie Brook.

But paranoid jealousy possessed Ley as he approached 60. Last year he formed the delusion that bartender John Mudie enjoyed Mrs Brook's favours. In November he hired car-rental manager John Buckingham to abduct Mudie to Ley's house in Knightsbridge, where Ley and a builder called Smith beat and strangled Mudie, dumping his body in a chalkpit near Woldingham.

At their trial this year, Buckingham (who turned King's

Evidence) and Smith admitted bringing Mudie to the house and tying him up, but swore he was still alive when they left separately. Ley pompously professed ignorance of the whole thing, and bribed a petty criminal to appear with a preposterous story of having broken into the house to rob it, and tentatively pulled at the bonds of the still-living Mudie in such a way that it just might have strangled him!

Ley and Smith were both condemned to death. But as Ley has been found quite mad and transferred to Broadmoor, Smith, too, has been reprieved.

Thomas Ley

One Murder: Two Doctors' Suicides

FIFTY-SEVEN-YEAR-OLD Dr Robert Clements of England, killed himself after his fourth wife died. Not from grief at his bereavement, but because he could not face enquiry into whether he killed her. And his previous three!

Dr Clements normally married well and inherited largely when widowed. It happened again this year, when Mrs Clements died of what was diagnosed as mycloid leukemia. The doctor made the

diagnosis and suggested it to an inexperienced young colleague, Dr James Houston, who willingly signed the death certificate.

But suspicious tongues wagged; the corpse's eyes were noted to have pin-point pupils; an autopsy showed she died of morphine poisoning.

So did Dr Clements, anticipating his arrest and trial for murder. And so, alas, did young Dr Houston, horrified at his own error.

Actress Pushed Out of Porthole at Sea

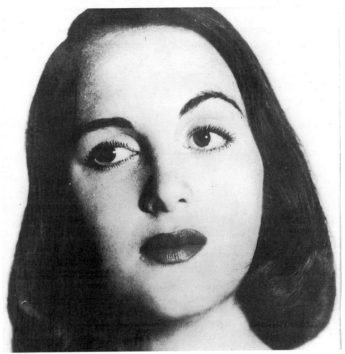

Gay Gibson: porthole murder victim

SHIPBOARD LOTHARIO James Camb is to be tried for the murder of actress Gay Gibson, missing at sea from the liner *Durban Castle*. The handsome 31-year-old deck steward enjoyed offering his sexual services to good-looking lady passengers, although company rules forbade him to enter their cabins.

At 3.00 am on October 18, the bell in the cabin-stewards' quarters summoned the night steward to Miss Gibson's first-class cabin. When he arrived, Camb half-opened the door and sent him away. In the morning, Miss Gibson was nowhere to be found, though marks on her bunk showed that she could have been strangled there or had some sort of seizure. After a good deal of hopeless lying about not being in the cabin at all, Camb has finally admitted that she died in his presence and that he callously disposed of the body by pushing it through the porthole.

He says she died of a seizure while making love. Police think he killed Miss Gibson while attempting to rape her. A jury will be left to decide the truth, next year.

IN BRIEF

BEN "BUGSY" SEAGEL, the hood who took big crime to Hollywood, shot dead by unknown hit-men in his mistress's plush Beverley Hills home.

CHARLES JENKINS (brother of reprieved smash-and-grab killer Thomas Jenkins – *see* 1944), Christopher Geraghty and Thomas Rolt, vicious south London thugs, violently robbed a Charlotte Street jeweller; shot brave motorcyclist father of six, Alex de Antiquis who tried to block their escape. Jenkins and Geraghty hanged; Rolt under-age so imprisoned.

1948

Thief Kills Policeman and Escapes Hanging

PC Nat Edgar, murder victim

Thomas's hideout with Mrs Winkless in Stockwell lodgings

ARMY DESERTER Donald George Thomas is a lucky man. Police-killers are always caught; police-killers never escape the gallows. Police and the courts see to that.

But Thomas, who killed Constable Nat Edgar early this year, timed his conviction to coincide with the temporary suspension of capital punishment this spring, while Parliament debated its abolition. Thomas has been convicted, but lives to tell the tale.

PC Edgar spotted Thomas loitering outside 112 Wades Hill, Southgate in London, England, on February 13. There had been several burglaries in the area, so he questioned the 23-year-old and noted his name and address before arresting him. Whereupon Thomas pulled a Luger pistol and shot him.

Thomas was not to be found at the Enfield address he had given Edgar, but police traced him to Stockwell in south London, where he and his mistress, Mrs Winkless, were lodging with a Mrs Smeed. As officers burst into his room, he reached under the pillow for his gun, but was overpowered before he could reach it. The habitual criminal remarked coolly: "You were lucky. I might as well be hung for a sheep as a lamb."

In the event it is Thomas who has proved lucky. Concealed in his room were 17lbs of ammunition, a rubber cosh, and a book entitled *Shooting to Live with the One-Hand Gun.* It is to be hoped that this lethal young thug is not given any future opportunity to practice its evil and sinister agenda.

> **YOU WERE LUCKY. I MIGHT AS WELL BE HUNG FOR A SHEEP AS A LAMB.**
> QUOTE **Donald George Thomas**

Old Lady Beaten, Tied: Put in Trunk to Die

HOUSEBREAKER George Russell has a long record of petty offences. But carelessness in leaving his fingerprints in the dusty house of reclusive widow Mrs Freeman Lee has brought him to the gallows.

Mrs Lee's body was found in her home in Maidenhead, England, at the beginning of June, when the milkman realized that she was not taking in her milk. The old lady was 93, so the house was quickly searched.

In the hall stood a large black trunk, with a woman's shoe beside it. Inside the trunk was Mrs Lee. She had been hit over the head and her hands were tied behind her back. Cause of death was asphyxiation, so she had apparently been bundled into the trunk alive, and died there for lack of air.

The neglected and cobwebby house had been ransacked, and Russell's fingerprints were on a cardboard box. Arrested in St Albans, he denied everything until a scarf of Mrs Lee's was found in his possession, and he was confronted with the fingerprint evidence. Then he broke down, and sobbed: "I was told she had a lot of money by another man. Did I murder this poor woman for something she was supposed to have, and had not?"

Apparently he did. He was hanged for it on December 2.

Police fetching the trunk with the body of 89-year-old Mrs Freeman Lee, to put in the ambulance

Lovers Prey on Lonely-Heart Widows and Spinsters

TWENTY-STONE Martha Beck met seedy Latin lover Raymond Fernandez through a Lonely Hearts Club in 1947. She fell for him, in his ill-fitting black wig, and he reciprocated her ungainly passion. Nor was Martha dismayed when Raymond revealed that he made his living by swindling and stealing from lonely widows he met through commercial introduction agencies. Martha went into the business with him, passing herself off as his sister.

And she added a new crime to the dodge of seduction and bigamous marriage. Murder.

Murder when Martha got jealous of her lover-boy tucked up in

Martha Beck (right) and Raymond Fernadez (middle) at a bench conference in court

" YOU ARE A DOUBLE-CROSSING TWO-TIMING SKUNK. "
Martha Beck

bed with younger, better-looking, thinner women.

In Michigan this January, Martha dosed 28-year-old Mrs Delphine Dowling with sleeping pills, and then Raymond shot her in the head. Delphine's 2-year-old daughter Rainelle was an additional problem. They bought her a dog when she cried for her mother. Then Martha drowned her in the bath.

When neighbours reported the

Dowlings' disappearance, police quickly spotted a grave-sized patch of wet cement in the basement, which yielded the missing couple. Michigan has abolished capital punishment for murder, so Beck and Fernandez cheerfully boasted about their many slayings.

But they certainly did not anticipate being extradited to New York to face trial for the murder of Alice Fay.

They have been convicted and

sentenced to death, and the love-letters exchanged between their cells have grown sour. Martha heard that Raymond has been joking about her size and blaming her for his fate, and she has written to him: "You are a double-crossing two-timing skunk."

Naughty Raymond was booked to accompany his fat vamp to the electric chair on August 20, but the pair have won a stay of execution pending their appeals.

Young Advertising Executive Kills Wife's Parents

TO ALL APPEARANCES, Danny Raven is a nice young Jewish boy, with a good job, and a sweet wife and baby. But on October 10 he had an altercation with his parents-in-law after the family went to

see Danny's wife and newborn son in the nursing-home at Muswell Hill, London.

When police visited Danny to tell him his parents-in-law had been found battered to death with a television aerial, they were surprised to find the young man spick and span in clean clothes late at night. On further investigation they found his half-burned bloodstained suit and shoes in the boiler. It didn't take much to guess why.

Twenty-three-year-old Danny is now in prison awaiting trial for the murder of Leopold and Esther Goodman.

Coarse Lesbian Cross-Dresser Batters Tramp-Woman to Death

THE MOST obvious trouble with "Bill" Allen was that she was still really Margaret. Dressing in men's clothes and swilling pints of beer in pubs didn't change this, and her one woman friend Mrs

Annie Cook broke off with her when "Bill" proposed a sexual relationship.

None of which explains why Margaret Allen killed bag-woman Mrs Nancy Chadwick, who came begging at her door in August last year. "I was in a funny mood," she told police when charged. "I just happened to look round and saw a hammer in the kitchen. On the spur of the moment I hit her."

And up to the point when she was hanged in January, she gave no further explanation of this motiveless murder. It will remain a gallows' mystery for all time.

1950

Pieces of Black Marketeer Washed up in Essex

Donald Hume, spiv acquitted of murdering Stanley Setty

BRIAN DONALD HUME has been acquitted in a London court of murdering fellow racketeer, Stanley Setty. But, as accessory after the fact he goes to Dartmoor for 12 years.

Levantine "car dealer" Setty's headless, legless torso was washed up on Tillingham marshes in October last year. A stab wound in the chest showed how he died. Fingerprints showed who he was.

Trained pilot Hume was one of Setty's known associates, handling stolen cars. Police found that Hume had hired a light aircraft on October 5 and boarded it with two parcels. The shady crook claimed that the parcels contained parts of a printing press for counterfeiting ration books.

He now says that three powerful gangsters, known to him only as "Greenie", "Mac" and "the Boy" forced him to dump the parcels a sea for them. He concedes that a "gurgling noise" from one of them suggested that he was perhaps disposing of a dismembered Stanley Setty, whose disappearance wa the subject of intense speculation in the underworld.

The jury at Hume's trial in January could not agree. With a new jury empanelled, the judge ordered a verdict of Not Guilty to the murder charge, and accepted Hume's plea of Guilty to the accessory charge.

It is understood that, the police are not making any particular efforts to trace "Greenie", "Mac" or "the Boy", who are more likely to be the creation of Hume's fertile imagination than genuine denizens of his slimy spiv world.

Van Driver Makes Impossible Confession to Murder

Timothy John Evans, brought to Paddington from Wales by detectives

WELSH POLICE In Merthyr Tydfil were astonished when 24-year-old Timothy John Evans turned up unannounced, and confessed to "disposing of" his wife Beryl down the manhole outside his London home, 10 Rillington Place.

Evans is a tiny man, and the solid iron manhole cover required a special key and three strong policemen to raise it! Needless to say, no trace of Beryl was evident in the shaft. But a search of the couple's flat in the end-of-terrace house yielded the gruesome discovery of Beryl and her baby daughter, both of whom had been strangled and their bodies left in the small wash-house at the rear. Confronted with his own tie, used to murder baby Geraldine, Evans confessed.

By the time Evans came to trial this February, he had withdrawn his full confession, and, to the acute embarrassment of his legal advisers, made an unwarranted attack on his downstairs neighbour, Mr John Christie, accusing him of killing Beryl in the course of performing an illegal abortion.

Christie, a temporary special policeman during the second World War, and a World War I veteran whose voice carries permanent damage from mustard gas, made an excellent impression on the court. His evident unwillingness to expose his unhappy young neighbour's mendacity was particularly affecting. As a simple warehouse clerk, Christie would, of course, have no capability of performing an illegal operation, and Evans's desperate lies were an outrageous injustice to a middle-aged man in poor health who has served his country well.

They did not save the educationally backward van-driver, who has been hanged for the murder of his nearest and dearest.

Pretentious Would-be Poet Planned Perfect Murder

HERBERT LEONARD MILLS, a 19-year-old of Nottingham, England, telephoned the *News of the World* on August 9 to say he had found a body. He told them, too, that his reaction on finding 48-year-old housewife Mabel Tattershaw strangled in Sherwood Vale was to read a poem. Finally he asked the paper to pay him for a literary composition, which turned out to be a confession. He decided to commit a perfect murder.

He had met Emily in a cinema, flattered her by his "educated" attentions, and arranged a meeting. Then he strangled her. He goes to the gallows in December.

Herbert Leonard Mills points to the spot where he found the body

Collaborateuse Stands Trial for Shooting Lover

AS A TEENAGER in occupied France, Pauline Dubuisson disgusted neighbours by her affair with a Wehrmacht colonel. After the war she suffered the public humiliation awarded *les maitresses des Boches*; then went to Lille University, where she had many liaisons, and kept a secret journal describing her lovers' sexual quirks.

Handsome student Felix Bailly realized his mistake in time, and broke off an engagement to her, proposing to marry a Paris girl. Pauline brooded for 18 months; then, in March, bought a gun and uttered threats. Bailly hired bodyguards, but she got past them into his flat and shot him. Then she tried to gas herself. She is still in a serious condition and will not face trial until November. Most inhabitants of the land of love feel no great affection for this *traitresse sexuelle*.

Murderous English Robbers Give Themselves Away

SEVENTY-NINE-YEAR-OLD Frederick "Gossy" Gosling was believed to keep £1,000 in his little home above the shop in Clay Corner, Surrey. Brothers Joseph and Fred Brown, broke in and tried to rob him on January 11.

The following day, two men broke in again. This time Mr Gosling was tied up and gagged, and bruising over his face showed he had been beaten to make him talk. Mr Gosling choked to death on his gag. The robbers killed him for a mere £60 loot.

In a couple of days the police picked up the Browns, but quickly freed Frederick and charged third man, Edward Smith as Joe Brown's accomplice. On hearing that Gossy had choked to death, Smith said defensively, "If I wanted to hurt him I could have hit him or something."

Since someone had done just that, the remark hanged Smith and Brown.

> ❝ **IF I'D WANTED TO HURT HIM I COULD HAVE HIT HIM OR SOMETHING.** ❞
>
> QUOTE **Edward Smith**

1952

Child-Killer Escapes Broadmoor, Strikes Again

THE ENGLISH public's fears were realized this March, when murderer John Straffen escaped from Broadmoor Criminal Lunatic Asylum and, in a bare three hours of freedom, slew another little girl.

Twenty-two-year-old Straffen was committed to Broadmoor last year after killing two small girls near Bath. He said he did it to annoy the police. As he is a known child-molester, it is more likely that he committed his crimes from perverse sexual desire. Doctors who had found him mentally defective in 1947 testified to his continuing state of near-imbecility. As a result, he was found unfit to plead, since he would not be able to understand the circumstances and procedure of a trial.

His escape was a consequence of extraordinarily lax security at Broadmoor. Straffen was left sweeping a yard beside an unlocked gate while guards attended to the exercise of other prisoners. Staff have complained for many years that the institution is dangerously undermanned.

Public horror at this incident was such that Straffen was put on trial again, with Broadmoor doctors testifying that their treatment had improved his understanding

John Straffen taken by police to Reading Magistrates's Court, charged with murdering 5-year-old Linda Bowyer

to the extent that he could now follow the case in court. Straffen was convicted and sentenced to death.

Loathsome though this defective is, we must concur with the Home Secretary's view that it would be uncivilized to hang a man whose mental grasp is so feeble. Our relief at his reprieve is only tempered by anxiety that there be no further failure in keeping this creature immured and away from the public until the end of his natural life.

Wastrel Kills Parents: Tips them off Cornish Cliff

YOUNG MILES GIFFORD was an idle and irresponsible worry to his Cornish solicitor father. Psychiatric treatment when Miles was 14 suggested that he was responding badly to his father's attempts to instill discipline into him. Since serving in the Merchant Navy during the War, Gifford junior has done nothing but scrounge off his parents.

In August this year 27-year-old Miles met 19-year-old Gabriel Vallance in Chelsea and decided to marry her. When his father pointed out that he could not marry until he could support himself, Miles wrote to Gabriel, "Short of doing him in, I see no future in the world at all."

On November 7, Miles battered his parents to death in their home near St Austell, probably killing his mother only because he saw no alternative after having killed his father. He took the bodies in a wheelbarrow to nearby cliffs and dumped them into the sea. Then, purloining some of his mother's jewellery, he drove his father's car to London and met up with Gabriel. She thought he was joking when he said he had killed his parents, and happily went with him to the cinema and on to the Prospect of Whitby pub at Wapping .

But as a taxi returned them to Gabriel's Tite Street home, police cars surrounded the vehicle. Miles was arrested and charged immediately with stealing his father's car; subsequently with murder.

He goes on trial in the New Year, and it seems unlikely that a bucolic and conservative Cornish jury will pay much attention to medical evidence that this young man was disturbed and ruined at an early age by his stiff-necked upper-class father's unbending severity.

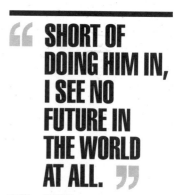

"SHORT OF DOING HIM IN, I SEE NO FUTURE IN THE WORLD AT ALL."

QUOTE

Miles Gifford

Corpses in Necrophile Christie's Ghastly Kitchen

Reg Christie poses in his graveyard garden

J AMAICAN Beresford Brown had a nasty shock when he tore away a puzzling piece of wallpaper covering an alcove in the ground floor flat he'd just rented at 10 Rillington Place. Concealed in his kitchen were the half-naked corpses of three strangled streetwalkers!

Police started an urgent hunt for the flat's previous occupant, 55-year-old clerk John Reginald Halliday Christie – especially when they found Mrs Christie mouldering under the sitting room floorboards! And the garden yielded the skeletal remains of two more women (the thighbone of one having been incorporated as a strut in the fence!)

Picked up by an alert policeman on Putney Bridge, Christie confessed to killing women by offering them a Friars' Balsam inhalant into which he introduced household gas. When they were dead, he ravished their bodies. For this repulsive lecher, who collected pubic hairs in an old tobacco tin, couldn't function properly with real, living lovers.

Worst of all, Christie admits to murdering his upstairs neighbour Mrs Beryl Evans in 1949; a crime for which her husband, retarded van-driver Timothy John Evans, was hanged (*see* 1950).

Christie has now been hanged himself. But the case of Timothy Evans will have to be reopened to satisfy public concern.

Police recovering the skeletons of Christie's victims Ruth Fuerst and Muriel Eady

London 'Cosh Boys' Fight Ends in Murder

T EENAGERS Fred Chandler and John Beckley were ready for a fight when they jeered at the sharp drape suits worn by "The Plough Boys" – a gang of yobs from Clapham Common. What they didn't expect was that knives would be pulled on them.

The two were chased to Clapham Common North Side, where they flagged down a bus in which Chandler escaped. But Beckley was hauled off the platform, and stabbed to death before the eyes of horrified commuters.

Six youths were identified as participating, but in the end all but one escaped with common assault convictions. On the testimony of one commuter, and one commuter only, 20-year-old John Michael Davies was accused of delivering the fatal blow. He denies this, and states firmly that he does not own and was not carrying a knife.

His denial is supported by his own gang, and even by Fred Chandler. So the Home Secretary has commuted his death sentence. Derek Bentley has sated the establishment's lust for cosh boys' blood this year.

Lancashire Jury find Housekeeper Guilty of Murder

L OUISA MERRIFIELD, 46-year-old housekeeper-cum-companion of elderly widow Sarah Ricketts, is to hang for poisoning the old lady. Louisa's nasty 70-year-old husband Alfred has been released after the jury could not agree on his guilt.

The Merrifields went to work as resident companions to Mrs Ricketts in March. Within a week Mrs Merrifield told friends that she was being left Mrs Ricketts' house. Within two weeks she called in a doctor to confirm that Mrs Ricketts was mentally fit to write a will. Within three weeks Mrs Ricketts was preparing to sack the Merrifields. Within four weeks, Mrs Ricketts was dead by poisoning.

It was proved in court that a Manchester chemist had sold the poison to the Merrifields. Proved, too, that its acrid taste is effectively disguised by rum, which Mrs Ricketts took as a nightcap. Proved that Mrs Merrifield's handbag contained a spoon, still dirty with a mixture of Rodine and rum.

So this squalid woman, who falsely accused her husband of a liaison with aged invalid Mrs Ricketts, will hang at Strangeways in September.

1954

Lesbian New Zealand Schoolgirls Murder Mother

NEW ZEALAND schoolgirls Pauline Parker and Juliet Hulme (16 and 15) were due to be separated when Dr Hulme, Juliet's father, decided to emigrate to South Africa; partly because of marital difficulties, but partly also to separate Juliet from Pauline – the latter's mother had alerted him to the way the girls bathed, slept and talked sex together obsessively, activities which he regarded as not healthy.

Pauline immediately declared her intention of accompanying her friend and lover, but Mrs Honora Mary Parker flatly forbade her to do so. Whereupon the adolescent lesbians determined to eliminate this obstacle to their furtive passion.

On June 22 the girls went for a walk together in Victoria Park, Christchurch with Mrs Parker. As Pauline and her mother argued, the girl persuaded the older woman to bend down, whereupon she hit her over the head with a brick stuffed in a stocking. Mrs Parker did not die instantly, so first Pauline then Juliet went on and on hitting her until, after 45 separate blows, the unfortunate woman finally expired.

The girls told a cock-and-bull story to police of Mrs Parker's slipping and hitting her head on a brick, against which it "kept bumping and banging" as they tried in vain to help her. The pathologist's report stopped that idea from gaining credence with the police authorities and they were charged with murder.

Their attempt to plead not guilty by reason of insanity collapsed when Pauline (said by psychiatrists to consider herself a genius and above the law) uttered coldly, "I knew it was wrong to murder and I knew at the time I was murdering somebody. You would have to be an absolute moron not to know murder was against the law."

The two teenagers have been found both sane and guilty, and detained at Her Majesty's pleasure.

> ## " I KNEW IT WAS WRONG TO MURDER AND I KNEW AT THE TIME I WAS MURDERING SOMEBODY. YOU WOULD HAVE TO BE AN ABSOLUTE MORON NOT TO KNOW MURDER WAS AGAINST THE LAW. "
>
> QUOTE **Pauline Parker**

Pauline Parker (left) and Juliet Hulme, lesbian schoolgirl murderesses

French Girl Made to 'Sacrifice' Her Child

VILLAGE POSTMASTER'S daughter Denise Labbé had a lot of lovers after she went to work in Paris, and bore an illegitimate daughter. But she was a nice simple girl, and adored little Cathy, whom she placed at her own expense in foster-care and regularly visited. Until she fell in love with St Cyr officer cadet Jacques Algarron.

This Mephistophelean would-be *übermensch* dazzled her with his self-aggrandizing satanical philosophy. He forced her to make love to other men; then plead for his forgiveness. He scratched and bit scars on her back, and got her to parade them at the beach. He openly slept with other women. And he promised they two should be the "exceptional couple"; hinted he would marry her, but on one condition – that she murder her own daughter!

Pressed by his threats and cajolements, Denise tried three times to do as he said. She could not bring herself to drop little Cathy from a high window. She threw her into a canal, but screamed for help in time to have her saved. Finally she drowned the child in a washtub. And the evil Algarron casually says it means nothing to him, now, and he would never marry her!

The two go on trial at Blois next year: Denise facing the death sentence; Algarron an inadequate maximum 20 years' hard labour.

Agreement with Germans Saves BAOR Sergeant-Major

Sergeant-Major Frederick Emmett-Dunne (right) on his way to court-martial in West Germany

A QUIET WEDDING in Taunton last year prompted whisperings among former NCOs in the BAOR. When REME Sergeant-Major Frederick Emmett-Dunne married pretty blonde widow Mia Watters, the late Sergeant Watters' mess-mates began whispering about his suicide by hanging at the barracks in Duisberg. And the whispers reached Scotland Yard.

Home Office pathologist Dr Francis Camps flew out to Germany and examined Reginald Watters' exhumed remains. His report? "This man never died from hanging… he died from a severe blow across the front of the throat." Just such a blow as a sergeant-major trained in unarmed combat might inflict, in fact!

Emmett-Dunne was taken back to Düsseldorf to stand trial for murder. His original story of leaving Watters earlier in the evening before his body was found was now changed. He claimed that Watters had threatened him with a pistol, knowing (as the trial fully proved) that he was having an affair with German-born Mrs Watters. He had accidentally killed Watters in self-defence, and staged the suicide in panic.

The story didn't ring true at all, and Emmett-Dunne was convicted and sentenced to death. But Germany has witnessed a lot more state executions than anybody thinks reasonable during the last 20 years, and the West German government has no wish to continue a tradition of murderous authoritarianism. So the accord between the Bonn government and Britain stipulates that there shall be no executions on federal territory leased to British military authorities.

Emmett-Dunne is lucky. He has been brought home to serve a life sentence.

IN BRIEF

Houseboy Fires his Counsel and Proves his Guilt!

DISSATISFIED with the conduct of his defence, Bart Caritativo, on trial this January for the murder of wealthy Joseph and Camille Banks at Stinson Beach, San Francisco, fired his lawyers, writing, "I have lost the trust to my attorneys."

Prosecuting counsel were delighted. For Caritativo's memo reproduced the solecistic use of "to" also found in a suicide note that appeared to be signed by Joseph Banks, saying: "I am responsible to what you see and find."

Philippino houseboy Caritativo (49) became friendly with a compatriot who was housekeeper next-door to his employers some years ago. When she had the good fortune to marry her boss and become wealthy, Camille Malmgren remained a friend of Bart's. And their shared literary aspirations kept them close after Mr Malmgren died, and throughout Camille's relatively short-lived marriage to English alcoholic Joseph Banks.

A good-natured lady, Camille allowed Joseph to go on living in her house when the relationship was clearly dead. It came as a shock, therefore, when an estate agent, coming to survey the property before Camille moved abroad, found Mrs Banks in the bedroom with her skull split, and Mr Banks surrounded by whisky bottles in the living room. A knife was in his chest, and his suicide note apparently explained something of the tragedy.

But Banks would not have misused the preposition. Mrs Banks's will proved equally full of solecisms and spelling mistakes. And it left all her property to Caritativo. Handwriting experts believe he forged it. Pathologists say Joseph Banks was too drunk to have stabbed himself as the note implied. Caritativo went on trial. And ensured his conviction when he fired his counsel.

Finger-Printing Potters Bar Catches Teenage Killer

WHEN MRS CURRELL'S battered and strangled body was found by the 17th tee on Potters Bar golf course in Hertfordshire on April 30, the only clue to her murderer was a bloody palmprint on the iron tee-marker that had been used to assault her. Mr Currell was in the clear. He had reported his wife's failure to return from walking the dog the previous night.

The print did not show up on police files, so 9,000 Potters Bar men were laboriously fingerprinted. And 17-year-old local government clerk Michael Queripel was charged with the murder.

Queripel admitted seeing Mrs Currell and seizing her with the intention of rape. When she struggled, he struck her repeatedly with the marker. Then he tied her stocking round her neck. Finally he ran home, and cut his arm with a razor blade to explain the blood on his clothes.

His guilty plea cannot lead to a death sentence as, at 18, he is under-age, and he has been sentenced to detention at Her Majesty's pleasure.

Killing Mom – And a Plane-Load with Her

John Graham — matricide plus

The failing Denver drive-in restaurant Mrs Daisy King bought for her son, John, to manage

CREW-CUT 24-year-old American Jack Graham seems the perfect momma's boy. The mechanic's mother, Daisy King, rescued him after his conviction for embezzlement five years ago. She paid back $2,000, and arranged for him to repay another $2,000 from his earnings. She opened a drive-in restaurant for him to manage. By this year, Graham's debt was down to $100.

Graham seemed devastated when his mom died in the United Airlines Flight 629 disaster at Denver last year. But FBI men made some surprising discoveries. Traces of dynamite in the baggage hold showed that the plane had been bombed. The only passenger whose luggage had disintegrated was Mrs King. Her life had been insured for a staggering $62,500 in Jack's favour.

After hours of questioning last December, Graham confessed. He fell out with his mother when the drive-in stopped paying. He tried unsuccessfully to burn it down for the insurance. He wrecked a car for insurance. And finally he killed his mother (and the other 44 passengers and crew on Flight 629) to receive the pay-out on her life.

Graham withdrew and reinstated his confession several times before his trial this February, and tried to kill himself once. But his guilt was clear and his appeal has been rejected. He is scheduled to be executed in the New Year.

Cop Killer Took Family Hostage, Goes to Chair

PETTY THIEF Richard Carpenter lived by demanding the takings of small Chicago bars and grocery stores, using a pair of six guns as persuasion. In August last year, however, detective Bill Murphy recognized him on the subway and arrested him.

As they left the train, 26-year-old Carpenter shot Murphy dead and escaped. On the street he forced a driver to take him to central Chicago's Loop district, and disappeared among the crowds of shoppers and workers.

Now the city's most wanted man, he had to sleep on the run. He was spotted snoozing in the back row of a cinema by off-duty policeman Clarence Kerr. When Kerr tried to arrest him, Carpenter shot his second cop. But Kerr did not die and another policeman came to his aid, shooting Carpenter in the leg as the killer raced from the cinema.

That night, Carpenter forced his way into the home of truck-driver Leonard Powell, forcing him and Mrs Powell to go about their business at gunpoint. The Powells did not alarm their children by explaining his presence, and Powell went to work the following day as normal. When he came home that evening, Powell suggested that suspicion would be aroused if the family did not make their regular visit to his wife's mother. Amazingly, this ruse worked – Carpenter let them go and within minutes the house was surrounded by cops.

Carpenter could not escape. At his trial he could not exculpate his wanton murder resisting arrest. He died in the electric chair at Joliet prison this year.

Gangland Slaying of Albert, the Lord High Executioner

THE LORD HIGH EXECUTIONER is dead, executed in his barber's chair at the Park Sheraton Hotel, New York City. No sooner had Brooklyn crime tsar Albert Anastasia settled himself with hot towels for a haircut and manicure than his bodyguard innocently left the room and two gunmen with scarves over their faces marched in to blast away the man who has blasted so many in his time.

A devoted follower of "Lucky" Luciano and Frank Costello, Anastasia seized headship of the Brooklyn "family" in 1951 by eliminating Phil and Vincent Mangano. He went too far the following year, killing non-Mafioso Arnold Schuster for betraying the non-Mafia burglar Willie Sutton. But for the time, Luciano, Costello and Meyer Lansky needed him to ward off rival Vito Genovese's retrograde attempt to make himself "Boss of all Bosses". Now, perhaps, they don't.

Albert Anastasia's body is taken from a Brooklyn funeral parlour for interment

OBITUARY

ALBERT ANASTASIA (1903-1957)

Albert Anastasia and his brother "Tough Tony" became prominent in labour racketeering soon after they entered the USA as immigrants in 1920. Albert quickly became known as a hit man. He spent 18 months in Sing Sing awaiting trial for killing a long-shoreman. He was acquitted because the key prosecution witness disappeared – something that often happened to potential witnesses against Albert.

His love of being present at killings rather than leaving them to sub-contracted gunmen earned him the nickname "the Mad Hatter". Later he became the "Lord High Executioner" when he oversaw the work of Abe "Kid Twist" Reles and his "Murder Inc." group (see 1940).

Mafia Bosses Caught Out at Upstate New York Convention

IT MIGHT HAVE been a scene from the Keystone Kops! New York State police investigating a mysteriously large gathering of out-of-state cars parked near an isolated mansion in Appalachin on November 14 flushed out 58 of the nation's top Mafia bosses, gathered for a conference on Joe Babara's estate. Vito Genovese, Santo Trafficante, Joe Profaci, Joe Bonnano and Carlo Gambino were prominent among the elegantly dressed town-ees whose pointy-toed patent-leather shoes tripped away so unfittingly over the rough country ground. And as one by one they were hauled in by chortling cops, their reiterated explanation, "Just happened to be passing and dropped in to visit an old pal", made even the hoods realize they were looking particularly dumb.

The purpose of the meeting was to crown Vito Genovese "Capo di Tutti Capi"; a mighty chieftaincy that has been in abeyance since "Lucky" Luciano and Meyer Lansky firmly terminated the silly rivalry among ancient "Mustache Petes" for anointed headship (see 1931). But maybe Vito was set up. Too bad, so soon after he hired "Crazy Joe" Gallo and his brothers to murder rival Albert Anastasia!

Circumstantial Evidence Convicts 61-year-old Man

SOME CIRCUMSTANTIAL evidence is strong and some is weak. Sixty-one-year-old Leonard Scott Ewing of Bel Air, California has been convicted of his wife's murder although there is no real proof of his guilt, just a strong motive.

Leonard married wealthy widow Evelyn in 1949. Two years ago he cancelled premiums on her jewellery insurance and explained her sudden absence by saying she had gone away, but he knew not where. He declared that if she did not return after seven years he would begin a new life.

He waited one year before proposing marriage to another woman. Then Evelyn's spectacles and false teeth were dug up in a neighbour's garden. Scott, his finances under scrutiny, fled to Canada, where he was arrested.

Scott refused to testify and was found guilty of first-degree murder. Now in prison, he still asserts his innocence.

IN BRIEF

CLARENCE VAN BUUREN hanged for the murder of Joy Aken.

DR JOHN BODKIN ADAMS, acquitted of murdering Mrs Morrell after defence counsel Geoffrey Lawrence brilliantly exposed blustering prosecutor Reginald Manningham-Buller's crass incompetence in putting forward tainted evidence from nurses that contradicted their own log of prescriptions. To police disgust, the DPP refuses to proceed with other charges against the doctor.

1958

Glasgow Fiend Goes to the Gallows for Killing Eight

PETER MANUEL (31), charged in January with killing eight people and convicted of seven of those murders in May, was hanged at Barlinnie Prison in July. Thus ended a lifetime of theft, burglary, indecent assault and rape, and two years of wanton killing around Glasgow.

Manuel killed Ann Kneilands (17) in January 1956 when he dragged her to a wood and battered her around the head after assaulting her. This was the crime of which he was acquitted, the only hard evidence being his confession which he withdrew and reinstated from time to time after his arrest.

In September of the same year he broke into the Watt family house while Mr Watt, a master-baker, was on a fishing trip. There he murdered Mrs Watt and her sister and niece. Since it would have been just possible for Mr Watt to drive home in the night and commit the crimes, he was remanded for questioning in Barlinnie, where Manuel, too, found himself in custody for burglary. The good-looking murderer drew attention to himself by offering to produce evidence exonerating Mr Watt.

In 1957 Manuel was in Newcastle where police believe he murdered taxi driver Stanley Dunn. And last December he assaulted and murdered 17-year-old Isabelle Cooke, burying her body in a field near Uddington.

New Year's Eve found this brute in the Smart family home in Uddington, where he killed Mr and Mrs Peter Smart and their 10-year-old son. But at last a murder could be traced to him. Manuel subsequently tendered new £5 notes Mr Smart had drawn from his bank. Manuel confessed to the murders when he learned that his father was also in custody, being questioned about the presence in his house of property from the murder victims.

Manuel's victims: Left to right (top) Ann Kneilands, Marion and Vivienne Watt, Margaret Brown; (bottom) Isabelle Cook, Peter, Doris and Michael Smart

At his trial Manuel withdrew his confessions, arguing that Mr Watt was responsible for killing his own wife, sister-in-law and niece. He also dismissed his counsel and defended himself – with remarkable skill and aplomb, as the judge commented. But it didn't save him from the gallows!

Hung Jury in the Finch-Tregoff Trial

LOS ANGELES' sensational society murder case will go to a retrial because the jury cannot agree. Not in dispute, however, are the following points:

1. Dr Raymond Finch (42) was threatened with divorce proceedings by his wife, Barbara, who claimed he intended to kill her. She also claimed just about all his property by way of a fair settlement!

2. Dr Finch and his attractive secretary-mistress, ex-model Carol Tregoff (21), hired petty crook John Patrick Cody. Finch asked him to compromise Barbara. Carole asked him to kill her!

3. When neither compromise nor killing happened, Finch and Tregoff visited Barbara in July.

4. After the visit, Barbara was left with a fatal bullet wound in her back as a memento.

So did Barbara herself pull the gun on her unwelcome guests? Had they brought a knife and hypodermic syringes to kill her? Or was it all a tragic accident?

The jury couldn't decide. Let's hope the next one does better.

'Amnesiac' Blackmailer Hanged for Killing Policeman

GERMAN-BORN Gunther Fritz Podola (30) came to England from Canada this year. After stealing furs and jewellery from Mrs Verne Schiffman's South Kensington home, he telephoned her, pretending he had discovered compromising tapes and photographs in her mansion flat.

Fearing nothing on this score, Mrs Schiffman strung him along before informing the police. By the time Podola called her again, from South Kensington underground station, her phone was tapped, and detectives quickly surrounded the call-box.

Podola eluded them, however, and took temporary refuge in the foyer of an apartment build-ing. Here, he hid behind a pillar and shot dead Detective-Sergeant Raymond Purdy when the police-man approached him. Podola made good his escape and evaded capture for several days.

Police traced him to a small hotel where a group of officers broke down the locked door to the room in which he was hiding. Podola was hauled off into cus-tody. The black eye and bruises ev-ident on the accused's face were incurred, the police said, when the door flew open. Podola and his sympathizers said he was beaten punitively and as a result of this vi-olence could no longer recall any-thing about the circumstances of Sergeant Purdy's murder.

Gunther Podola (right) brought to court by detectives

At his trial in September it was suggested that Podola was unfit to plead because he could not re-member anything. The matter was put to the jury. They decided that a letter written by the accused while awaiting trial proved both his fitness to plead and that he was shamming. Podola was tried, con-victed and executed. Before his execution, his memory sponta-neously returned!

Düsseldorf Doubles Killer Gets Life Sentence

THE TRIAL IN GERMANY of 31-year-old Werner Boost for killing two courting couples and threat-ening a third has ended with his life imprisonment – for the oc-casion when he killed one of a pair of homosexuals embracing in a car.

Boost worked in collaboration with Franz Lorbach, who claims that Boost terrified and hypnotiz-ed him, forcing him to assist in the perverse murders. According to Lorbach, who has received a six-year prison sentence, Boost took pep pills and truth serum. He in-jected his victims with sedatives and then raped the women before killing them and their partners.

The two killed homosexual lawyer Dr Serve in January 1953, beating and robbing his male lover. In 1955 they killed Thea Kurmann and Friedhelme Behre, crushing their skulls before dumping the bodies in a water-filled gravel-pit. Early in 1956 they killed Peter Falkenberg and Hildegarde Was-sing, and immolated their bodies in a haystack.

In June of the same year a courting couple successfully scared them off. This gave the authorities the lead they needed: they now knew the "doubles killer" was two armed men. Shortly after this, Lorbach was arrested. While he was safely in custody, a forest ranger spotted Boost stalking an-other courting couple.

Lorbach's confession allowed charges to be brought, but the lack of strong corroborative evidence allowed three years to pass before Boost could be convicted. He has only now been found guilty of mur-dering Dr Serve.

CANADA'S YOUNGEST RAPIST MURDERS GIRL

LYNNE HARPER, a 12-year-old of Goderich, Ontario, went trust-ingly on the crossbar of 14-year-old Steven Truscott's bicycle when he offered her a ride. He will-ingly admitted this after Lynne's worried parents asked school-children if they had seen her. He added that he had dropped her off at a highway where he saw her accept a lift in a grey Chevrolet.

But Lynne's raped and strangled body was found in woodland near the Air Force base where her father worked. Young Steven was found to have a sore penis and scratches consistent with defensive wounds inflicted by the struggling girl. Found guilty of her murder, he is the youngest living Canadian to have heard the death sentence pro-nounced. His age, however, makes his reprieve inevitable.

IN BRIEF

BRIAN DONALD HUME, self-confessed murderer of Stanley Setty (*see* 1950), has killed again: this time a taxi-driver in Zurich, Switzerland, where he was robbing a bank. The Swiss courts have no intention of seeing him freed for a third murder, and he has been imprisoned for life.

1960

London Youths Kill Lad for 14 Shillings!

TWENTY-ONE-YEAR-OLD Alan Jee was one of the nicest young men you could wish to meet in South London. Polite, decent, hard-working, engaged to be married, and seemingly without an enemy in the world.

These attributes didn't stop four youths from attacking him as he walked through a dark alley in Hounslow after seeing his fiancée home. Francis "Flossie" Forsyth (18), Norman James Harris (23), Chris Darby (23) and Terence Lutt (17) jumped on him; threw him to the ground; robbed him of the mere 14 shillings they found in his pockets; and kicked him so savagely that he died in hospital two days later.

Chris Darby was found guilty of non-capital murder. The other three were found to be capital offenders, though Lutt's youth means he can only be detained at Her Majesty's Pleasure.

"Flossie" Forsyth's youth has led to some agitation against his hanging. But the brutal beating of Alan Jee to "shut him up", leaving blood all over Forsyth's shoes, invites truly humane people to feel more concern for innocent Alan, his family and fiancée.

The crowd at Wandsworth Prison for the hanging of vicious killer "Flossie" Forsyth

---

Headless Body Found in Midlands YWCA

TWENTY-ONE-YEAR-OLD Margaret Brown was working in the laundry-room of Birmingham YWCA hotel on December 23 when a heavy-set man burst in and attempted to molest her. Miss Brown screamed, scaring the man off. Staff then searched the building for him, and made a horrifying discovery behind the locked door of Room 4 in the annexe.

On the floor lay the body of 29-year-old shorthand typist Stephanie Baird. But not her head! That lay separately on a bloodstained bed! Post-mortem examination revealed that Miss Baird had been sexually abused after death. There was a note in her room, apparently left by the murderer, which read, "This was the Thing I Thought Would Never Come."

Not a fingerprint has been found to assist inquiries, but police are following up evidence that a "peeping tom" has lurked around the hostel for some weeks. A bus driver's report of a passenger dripping blood in his vehicle on the murder night may prove useful, too, as the blood group of the stains matches Miss Baird's.

Murdered YWCA resident Stephanie Baird

'Beast of the Black Forest' Got His Kicks from Porno Films

HEINRICH POMMERENKE, the "Beast of the Black Forest", has received prison sentences in Germany totalling 140 years after being charged at Freiburg with an astonishing catalogue of crimes:

**10 rape-murders
20 rapes
35 assaults and burglaries.**

This 23-year-old monster has been a sexual pervert ever since puberty, when he took to molesting girls outside a dance-hall in Mecklenberg. He began his career as a rapist in 1955, and in 1958 attacked two girls in Austria. His first murder victim was 18-year-old Hildegarde Knothe in 1959, whom he followed from a cinema to a park where he raped her before cutting her throat. In 1959 he discovered trains as a suitable site for sex murders. When he found student Dagmar Klimek sleeping on a transcontinental train bound for Italy, he assaulted her, pushed her out of the compartment on to the line, then pulled the communication cord and jumped out after her to rape and kill her where she lay. As his bestial assaults continued, his description began to circulate in the Black Forest area. He was picked up in Freiburg this year and made a full confession. He says that watching pornographic films made him "tense"! Well, he's got more than a century to cool off his lust, and it's safe again to take a walk in the Black Forest!

IN BRIEF

MICHAEL JOHN DAVIES paroled from his life sentence for the murder of John Beckley (see 1953). Davies still insists he was not the knife-wielder.

Woman Raped and Paralyzed by Gun Murderer

A MYSTERIOUS GUNMAN forced himself into the car occupied by Michael Gregsten and Valerie Storie as they sat in a field at Dorney Reach, near Slough, England. After forcing Gregsten to make a fantastic all-night drive around the edges of London, the gunman directed him up the A6 and into the layby on Deadman's Hill. There he killed Gregsten; raped Miss Storie; and fired several bullets at her, one of which entered her spine, paralyzing her.

She was found and taken to hospital the following morning. A police hunt for the brown-haired man with brown "staring" eyes she described turned up the peculiar near-fascist loner Peter Louis Alphon. He was reported by hoteliers as behaving suspiciously around the time of the murder, and identified by a Mrs Dalal of Richmond as the stranger who pulled up her skirt and threatened to rape her when she showed him a room to let, saying as he did so, "I am the A6 killer."

But Valerie Storie did not pick Alphon in an identity parade. Indeed, she picked out a seaman who was out of the country at the time of the murder.

The murder weapon was found abandoned on a London bus. Bullets fired from it were found in a hotel room next to the one where Alphon had stayed before the killing. Its occupant, incompetent burglar James Hanratty, was said to be wanted by the police, and the description of the A6 murderer now gave him staring saucer-like blue eyes, like Hanratty's.

Hanratty telephoned Superintedent Bob Acott to protest his innocence, but refused to give himself up, saying he would only be held for burglary. Police found him, nonetheless, in Blackpool. And Valerie Storie identified him positively after asking him to say, "Be quiet. I'm thinking." (Which he pronounced "finking", just as the murderer had done.)

Despite his insistence that he was in Liverpool at the time of the offences, Hanratty goes on trial in the New Year.

James Hanratty, charged with raping and maiming Valerie Storie and murdering Michael Gregsten

JAMES HANRATTY —the A6 killer First picture

A6 murder victim Michael Gregsten, with his wife

'Identikit' Picture Traps Antique Dealer's Killer

ALL OF ENGLAND'S national newspapers carried on their front pages the awkward-looking drawing of a fierce dark-haired young man. The image was not up to the usual standard of press portraiture. The picture was put together from jigsaw puzzle-like sections for the approval of witnesses, the idea being to obtain a reasonable likeness of a suspect by assembling the right sort of nose, eyes, lips, and so forth.

This new technique, called "Identikit", helped to track down the man who killed Mrs Elsie Batten in Louis Meier's antique shop at Cecil Court, Charing Cross Road, on March 3. Eurasian Edwin Bush (21) argued with Mrs Batten about the price of a dress sword, then killed her and made off with it. Subsequently, he tried to sell it.

At his trial, Bush attempted to win sympathy by claiming that Mrs Batten had provoked him with her racist remarks. True or not, this did not win him a reprieve, and the first victim of the "Identikit" became the latest victim of the hangman.

Rent Boy Kills Punter Who Didn't Give Him a Job

SEVENTEEN-YEAR-OLD Manuel Garces from the slums of Valparaiso, Chile, sold himself to wealthy homosexuals in the hope that one of them would help him escape from poverty and squalor.

One of them, Enrique Mercier, an elderly and respected lawyer, seemed to offer the hope of a better life, promising to find the lad satisfactory employment. Later, Mr Mercier was found dead in his office, wearing only a shirt and socks. He'd been beaten over the head and his wallet taken.

The office building staff confirmed to police that male prostitutes had visited the old gentleman after hours. Manuel was caught when he tried to pass a stolen cheque belonging to the dead man.

The lad told police that Mercier had not kept his promise to help him. He has been given 15 years' imprisonment, which doesn't seem too harsh a sentence for a crime born out of disappointment.

Did the Baron Really Say "Bodyguard, Please Kill Me"?

IN JANUARY THIS YEAR, Marthinus Rossouw of Cape Town met Baron Dieter Joachim Gunther von Schauroth, a playboy who inherited a farm in South West Africa, but was suspected of supplementing his income by deals in the illegal diamond trade.

Rossouw, a film buff who dressed in cowboy clothes and liked to be called "Killer", was promptly hired by the baron to be his bodyguard and general gofer. The baron also (according to Rossouw's later story) asked if he would be willing to kill someone for $14,000. Rossouw casually agreed that he would.

In March, the baron was found at a roadside a few miles from Cape Town with two bullets in the back of his head. Diamonds were scattered around the site, one of them an uncut beauty of four carats.

Rossouw denied knowing anything about his employer's fate. But when he could not give a satisfactory account of his whereabouts while von Schauroth was being murdered, he changed his story.

Now he claimed that the rich playboy had been in fear for his life because of his involvement with the illicit diamond trade, and in despair because his marriage was breaking up. He had insured his life for almost half-a-million dollars the previous year, and now pleaded with Rossouw to kill him so that the baroness could enjoy the insurance payout. When Rossouw hesitated, the baron gave him a loaded pistol and a cheque for Rand 2,300, which encouraged the bodyguard to live up to his nickname. He explained his initial delay in confessing with the story that the baron had made him promise to conceal the truth for a day or two.

In June Rossouw told this tall tale to an unimpressed court. Whether or not the baron had asked to be killed, this was murder, and he went to the gallows on June 29.

Pretty clearly the court felt that the whole story of "Murder by Request" was a lie. But the insurance companies saw definite value to themselves in it. They vigorously contested Baroness von Schauroth's claim, insisting that the baron's death was at best suicide, which was not covered by the policies. Faced with the possibility of extensive legal proceedings which would eat up the money, the widow was forced to come to a settlement out of court. She finally accepted payment of $28,000 – far from the $500,000 her husband had hoped would come to her.

Whether Rossouw's story was true, it seems that courts that accept common law precedent will take the opposite view from insurance companies. You may ask someone to kill you but be aware that the courts will accuse them of murder.

IN BRIEF

JAMES HANRATTY, tried for the A6 murder (*see* 1961), changed his defence in mid-trial when his Liverpool alibi collapsed. The sudden introduction of new witnesses claiming he was in Rhyl at the time of the rape and shootings did not impress the jury, and he has been hanged.

THIRD TIME seems still lucky for 21-year-old Sharon Kinne. Two years ago a jury cleared her of shooting the wife of a car salesman who tickled her fancy after the death of her own husband. Next the merry widow was charged with creating her own state of merry widowhood. Gun experts found incredible her claim that 2-year-old infant son Brian had pulled the heavy trigger and accidentally shot his dad. So did the jury. But Sharon appealed; was granted a mistrial; and in her third appearance in the dock for murder this year has been acquitted again.

Acquitted Husband Sent for Second Murder Trial

GOD FORGIVE YOU! He'll kill again!" cried Ted Garlick's mother-in-law when a jury decided Ted's suicide pact with her daughter did not amount to murder, even though Garlick had survived the gassing that claimed his wife.

The distraught lady was quite right. On October 12 this year, 16-year-old Carol Ann White disappeared after going out to ring her boyfriend from a call-box in West Drayton, England. Her purse was found under the telephone.

The following evening, Ted was walking his dog in the company of relatives when the animal raced away into a field. Ted followed, and found Carol's body. The girl had died from multiple stab wounds.

Police discovered that Ted had been seen walking past the telephone box the previous evening. He broke down under questioning and confessed to the crime. He had chatted to the girl as she stood by the callbox. When she teased the 25-year-old about his sexual incompetence he had lost his temper and stabbed her repeatedly.

He has handed the murder weapon to the police, and goes on trial in the New Year.

Killer Ted Garlick with his dog Curly

President John Kennedy Assassinated in Dallas

Lee Harvey Oswald

WHILE A SMALL CROWD watched the presidential motorcade pass along Elm Street, Dallas, on November 22, shots rang out, and President Kennedy's head was seen to jerk back. Before his startled driver could accelerate away, Mrs Jacqueline Kennedy had crawled across the trunk of the limousine to protect her husband.

In hospital doctors struggled to save JFK's life, enlarging a bullet wound in his throat to perform a tracheotomy. But massive injury to the side of the president's head meant their work was in vain. Texas Governor John Connally, riding in the seat in front of the President, was also injured, suffering a cracked rib and broken wrist.

Many bystanders thought the shots came from a picket fence in front of the President and to his right. Senator Ralph Yarborough, riding in a car behind the president, smelled cordite and spotted a former army veteran throw himself to the ground as a bullet passed him. Police found a sniper's nest and an abandoned Mannlicher-Carcoma rifle at a window on the fifth floor of a warehouse to the rear of the cavalcade's route.

Within an hour, Lee Harvey Oswald (23), who had been working in the room that morning, was arrested after acting suspiciously in another part of town. Oswald has given no coherent explanation of his actions.

This young man has a very peculiar history. He was discharged from the US Marines when he defected to the USSR, where he married a Russian girl. Since then he has redefected, bringing his wife Marina to the USA. During the summer he was active in New Orleans on behalf of a pro-Castro group. But there are no reports that he has ever expressed particular interest in Mr Kennedy.

President Kennedy's coffin is borne from St Matthew's Cathedral to Arlington Cemetery for burial

Oswald Shot by Strip Club Owner

AFTER 24 HOURS in the hands of Dallas Police Department, officers were transferring Lee Harvey Oswald, President Kennedy's alleged assassin, from their headquarters building when Jack Ruby, proprietor of the Carousel Club, barrelled forward from behind onlooking detectives and fired a pistol point-blank into Oswald's abdomen.

The whole nation witnessed the scene on television, as Oswald, simply dressed in a dark sweater, light shirt and slacks, doubled forward clutching himself with an agonized expression on his face.

Ruby says he acted out of sympathy for Mrs Kennedy on learning that she would have to return to Dallas for Oswald's trial. This concern sits uneasily on a man who came to Texas from Chicago with an influx of hoods, and whose sleazy occupation running strip clubs hardly suggests that his is a sensitive soul.

But whatever his intention, Jack Ruby (born Jacob Rubinstein) has stymied the inquiry into the President's assassination. Guilty or not, Lee Harvey Oswald had to be the starting point for a serious investigation into the killing, and now he has died without answering vital questions concerning the gun and the sniper's position found at his workplace.

1964

Prostitute's Tainted Evidence Reduces Millionaire's Sentence

STRIKING RED-HEADED call-girl Gloria Kendall testified in New York this October that millionaire punter Mark Fein sought her help when he killed his bookie. Gloria, who uses 30 different names as a call-girl, and whose criminal record classifies her as a "common prostitute", says that Fein showed her the body of Rubin Markowitz, which had wounds to the head and chest. Gloria arranged for a couple of guys to box up the grocery-store clerk and bookmaker and feed him to the fish in Harlem River, whence police dredged him up. The bookie's little black book was found to include both Gloria's phone number and Mark Fein's name, which had a debt of $7,200 recorded against it.

Thirty-two-year-old Fein's counsel hastened to point out that Miss Kendall "aint no Goody Two-Shoes. Can you pronounce Mark Fein guilty of first-degree murder on the testimony of Gloria?" he asked incredulously of the jury. The jurors saw his point

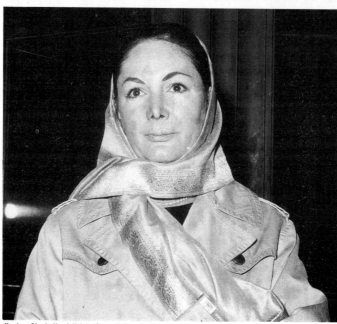
Hooker Gloria Kendall (aka Carmela Lazarus) arrives in court to testify against Mark Fein

and convicted Fein of second-degree murder, which sent him down for 30 years.

Nobody knows why he killed Markowitz over a gambling debt he could have paid ten times over.

Wife Goes on Murder Jaunt 'For the Ride'

ON APRIL 7, laundry van driver John West was battered and stabbed at his home in Workington, England. A neighbour saw a car speed away from the scene of the crime. In a pocket of a raincoat left behind by one of the attackers police found a medallion inscribed "G.O.Evans", and the name and address, in Preston, of one Norma O'Brien.

When questioned by police, 17-year-old Norma agreed that three years previously she had met a "Ginger" Evans who wore such a medallion. Traced to his Preston lodgings with Mr and Mrs Peter Allen, Gwynne Owen Evans (real name John Robson Welby) admitted the theft, but accused Allen of the killing. Allen returned the compliment. The jury decided both were murderers, and both have been hanged.

Oddest feature of the clumsy crime: Mrs Allen and her children accompanied the killers from Preston to Workington in the stolen car, simply for the ride!

Sharon Kinne Caught at Last – Arrested in Mexico

AFTER FOUR MURDER TRIALS, one terminating in her acquittal of the murder of Mrs Patricia Jones, the other three all mistrials when she was charged with killing her husband (*see* 1962), lethal 23-year-old Sharon Kinne has been caught with a smoking pistol in her hand. Literally!

In September this year Sharon went to Mexico City with a man. Four days later she was out on her own when she met radio announcer Francisco Ordonez and went to a motel room with him. When the proprietor heard shots and hurried to investigate, he found Ordonez dead on the bed, and Sharon about to vamoose with her hot .22 in her hand. She shot the proprietor in the back as he tried to withdraw, but he seized her and was still holding her when police arrived.

Sharon explained that she had not understood Mr Ordonez' intentions when she accompanied him to the motel, and shot him when he tried to rape her. The Mexican court did not believe this story and sentenced her to ten years' imprisonment.

Meanwhile, the Kansas City D.A.'s office asked for the murder weapon. Ballistic tests proved it had also been used to kill Patricia Jones, whose husband had taken Mrs Kinne's fancy. Sharon cannot be re-tried for that crime, but a fool-

ish appeal against the severity of her sentence has enabled the Mexican courts to prolong her imprisonment by three years!

Multiple murderess Sharon Kinne

London's Mysterious 'Nudes-in-the-Thames' Slayings Stop

The "Jack the Stripper" scare

THE WEST LONDON nude murders have suddenly stopped, after a massive police operation which entailed questioning all motorists discovered driving in Hammersmith and Kensington after midnight. The naked bodies of eight prostitutes have been found either in the Thames or on the foreshore near Chiswick, or dumped in garages and back alleys in this area of Britain's capital.

The scare began in February last year when a woman's body was washed up by Hammersmith Bridge. In April another appeared at Duke's Meadow. It was then recalled that two bodies had been found the previous November. As bodies continued to turn up, police observations prompted certain definite conclusions:

The killer was choking his victims when they practised fellatio on him. (Proved by missing teeth and semen traces in the throats.)

He was storing their bodies in or near a car-spraying works; proved by flecks of paint on them.

He was abusing the bodies again after death.

He drove a small van, seen a couple of times speeding away from the sites where bodies were found.

His occupation justified his driving around the West End at night.

The killer's secret lair, a sprayshop at Westpoint Trading Estate, West Acton, was stumbled upon with the discovery of Bridie O'Hara's body. The case was finally closed when a security guard for the estate – one of the three final suspects – committed suicide saying the pressure was too much.

Discovery of body in West London puts Police on trail of 'Nudes in the Thames' killer

THE NUDES IN THE THAMES

1963 JUNE – Elizabeth Figg, found in the river
NOVEMBER Gwynneth Rees, found in the river

1964 FEBRUARY – Hannah Tailford, found by Hammersmith Bridge
APRIL – Irene Lockwood, found in Duke's Meadow
APRIL – Helene Barthelemy, found in Swyncombe Avenue, Brentford

1965 JULY – Mary Fleming, found in Berymede Road, Acton Lane
NOVEMBER – Margaret McGowan, found in Hornton Street, Kensington
FEBRUARY – Bridie O'Hara, found at Westpoint Trading Estate, West Acton

Tucson 'Pied Piper' Leads Schoolkids to Murder

RUNTY LITTLE Charles Schmid (22) raised his 5ft 3in stature by wearing cowboy boots packed with cardboard and crushed Coca-Cola cans. He dyed his hair jet black, employed eyeshadow to give himself a heavy-lidded smouldering look, and painted a mole on his cheek.

This bizarre posturing impressed high school kids, the only ones who would pay "Smiddy" any attention.

He enjoyed being a charismatic personality among immature juveniles.

On May 31 last year Schmid told young John Saunders and Mary French that he felt like killing a girl. French decoyed 15-year-old Alleen Rowe to join them for a late-night drive in the desert. There Schmid raped her in front of Saunders, afterwards telling him to hit her over the head with a rock. Alleen ran off, but "Smiddy" chased her, caught her, killed her, and buried her with the help of French and Saunders.

In August this year, Schmid was consumed with jealousy when his 17-year-old girlfriend, Gretchen Fritz, boasted of having gone "all the way" with a boy in California. Gretchen and her 13-year-old sister Wendy disappeared. When Schmid boasted of killing them to Richard Bruns, the young man did not believe him. So "Smiddy" took him to the bodies in the desert.

Bruns, fearing his own girlfriend was next on Schmid's hit-list, went to the police in November. Schmid, French and Saunders are now awaiting trial.

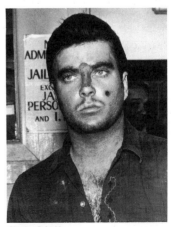

Charles Schmid

1966

Mayhem in London Outside Wormwood Scrubs

The scene of the slaying of police officers in Braybrook Street

THREE UNARMED London policemen have been gunned down in cold blood on Old Oak Common. The killings occurred when Detective Sergeant Christopher Head ordered his patrol car to stop so that he could investigate a blue Vanguard estate car parked suspiciously close to Wormwood Scrubs prison.

The occupants of the Vanguard, villains Harry Roberts, John Witney and John Duddy, were in fact contemplating burglary when approached by Head and Detective Constable David Wombwell. Roberts immediately opened fire, closely followed by his two accomplices.

The patrol car driver was shot dead before he could either help his comrades or escape the murderous villains. A passer-by took the number of the blue Vanguard, which was traced to a lock-up garage under Waterloo railway arches, rented to an individual called John Witney.

He confessed to having been in the company of Roberts and Duddy. The latter was easily tracked down in Glasgow, where he had family.

Ex-soldier Harry Roberts, experienced in jungle warfare, kitted himself out with camping gear and disappeared in the direction of Epping Forest. He was not caught until October, when a schoolboy found his camp in Hertfordshire woodland. Once surrounded, Roberts came quietly. The three murderers received life sentences at the Old Bailey in December.

Drifting Seaman Slays Eight Nurses: Rapes One, Misses One

ON JULY 14, passers-by were startled to see a young woman, precariously perched on the narrow window-ledge of a bedroom in the nurses' home at the South Chicago Community Hospital, screaming for help.

Inside the building, Pamela Lee Wilkeming, Nina Jo Schmale, Valentina Pasion, Patricia Ann Matusek, Mary Ann Jordan, Merlita Gargullo, Suzanne Bridget Farris and Gloria Jean Davie, student nurses in their early 20s, had been brutally murdered. All had been stabbed except Patricia Matusek, kicked in the stomach and strangled.

The girl on the window ledge, 23-year-old Corazan Amurao, was the sole survivor. She had hidden successfully under a bed as the killer took his victims one by one to their doom. She recounted what had happened that evening.

A lean-faced, pock-marked young man with a tattoo on his arm reading "Born to Raise Hell" rang the doorbell. When Miss Amurao answered it, she found herself facing a knife and a gun. The young man told her he only wanted money. Pushing his way in, he secured her and five other nurses with torn sheets. Around midnight, two other resident nurses returned, one accompanied by visitor Mary Ann Jordan.

When all the nurses were bound, the intruder became increasingly jumpy, until he took Pamela Wilkeming into an adjacent room. Her scream as he stabbed her was choked by the piece of sheet he drew round her neck. Twenty minutes later he returned for another victim; twenty minutes later for another. The remaining girls cowered under their beds, but only Miss Amurao escaped his search. The last victim, Gloria Jean Davie, was the only one he raped. He spent half an hour in normal and anal penetration, at one point politely asking her to put her legs around his back.

Miss Amurao's clear and accurate description led to the speedy arrest of the drug-abusing killer, who was picked up in hospital after trying to cut his wrists in a seedy

Richard Speck is led away after receiving the death sentence on eight counts of murder

flophouse. Ordinary Seaman Richard Speck (24) was easily identified by his tattoo, and his likeness to an "artist's impression".

The jury took just 50 minutes to reach a guilty verdict. Speck has been sentenced to death in the electric chair.

Sexy Welsh Blonde Manipulated Men to Murder for her

BUSTY BLONDE Kim Newell knows how to get what she wants from a man. Sex first. Lots of it. And then, whatever else she wants from him. An abortion, say. Money. All he can lay hands on. Assistance in murdering an inconvenient woman.

Back in Wales, in her teens, Kim worked as a confectioner's assistant. She enjoyed a passionate affair with Eric Jones, 20 years older than her and 20 years richer. When Kim became pregnant, she demanded an abortion. Once he'd done that, she had an even better blackmailing hook driven in to him, although she didn't use it at first. She went to Berkshire where she took a job at Borocourt Hospital. Here, she met big, slow Raymond Cook, a draughtsman training as a male nurse.

Ray was 10 years older than Kim and a great deal wealthier, thanks to a better-educated property-owning wife who was 11 years older than he.

Kim claimed to love Ray. And to need his (wife's!) money in ever-increasing amounts. She persuaded Ray to live with her. When that cut his allowance off, she sent him back: to insure Mrs June Cook's life.

Then Eric Jones was summoned from Denbighshire and told the police would learn all about the abortion he'd once given under-age Kim if he didn't come and give her another! He was also told to give Ray a hand in staging an accident to get rid of June.

On March 2, Cook took June drinking. On the way home in their red Mini, they were stopped by Jones, driving his blue Cortina, near Henley-on-Thames. June was dragged from the car, battered over the head with a jack, and pushed back into the driving seat. The car was driven cautiously into a tree at Rumerhedge Wood. Cook then got in the passenger seat to play injured. Astute village bobby PC Sherlock realized the "crash" had been far too gentle for the injuries June had sustained; he spotted, too, blood outside the car.

With Eric Jones's Cortina traced, and Kim Newell associated with him, the plot unravelled. The Lady Macbeth of Berkshire received the life sentence also awarded to her two dupes.

Kim Newell, charged with the Berkshire Mini murder, taken to court under police escort

Eric Jones, who was blackmailed into helping with the murder of Mrs June Cook

Rapist Schoolboy Left Toothmarks in Girl's Breast

FIFTEEN-YEAR-OLD Linda Peacock was found raped and strangled in the cemetery at Biggar, Scotland on August 17. Her right breast was so savagely bitten that clear impressions of unusual pitted canine teeth remained on her flesh, and the mark of a dropped filling.

When police checked a nearby school for delinquent boys, they soon figured that the young rogues were trying to cover for one of their number, Gordon Hay. The 17-year-old had been absent on the day of the murder, although he vigorously denied this. He was snared though by a match of the dental impressions which proved that his were the fangs that had buried themselves in poor Linda's bosom.

Since he is under 18, the vicious young man is detained at Her Majesty's pleasure. The appeal court has upheld this new form of forensic evidence – toothprints in erogenous zones.

1968

Dr Martin Luther King's Assassin Caught in England

JAMES EARL RAY, killer of Martin Luther King Jr, was arrested in London in June, and returned to the USA in July to go on trial next year.

Dr King was shot in Memphis, Tennessee, on April 4 as he stepped onto the balcony of the Lorraine Motel. Ray was in the hotel opposite, firing from a bathroom window. He fled immediately, dumping his weapon in the door of a shop. His subsequent peregrinations were so complicated, sophisticated and well-financed as to encourage suspicion that powerful paymasters guided the actions of this petty crook.

A small-time robber, Ray escaped from Missouri State Prison last year. After his escape he armed and placed himself perfectly to kill Dr King, coming to Memphis in May to support a demonstration. Though just what sort of organization feels it protects its own interests best by murdering the civil rights leader is unclear, especially as his was a voice of moderation, a bulwark against the militancy among some younger members of the movement.

After the murder, Ray reached Canada with forged documentation giving him identities of existing people, some of whom resembled him. After arriving in England, he made a trip to Lisbon and was about to go to Brussels when picked up at Heathrow. These side trips have never been explained.

Yet those best placed to know insist that Ray was a lone madman. It is unlikely that the FBI will make any effort to establish the truth. Director J. Edgar Hoover's loathing of Dr King is well-known. He has gone so far as to bug his bedrooms, and send prurient information to Mrs Coretta King in the hope of damaging King's role in the civil rights struggle.

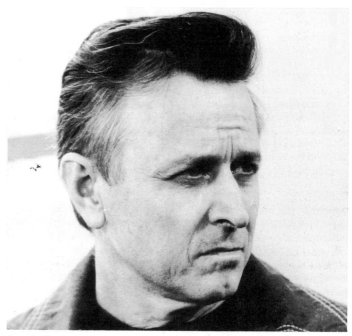

James Earl Ray, petty crook and jail-breaker who has been arrested for the murder of Dr King

English Schoolgirl Laughs at Victim's Funeral

PRETTY, PRECOCIOUS 11-year-old Mary Flora Bell is a self-assured liar, a playground bully, a schoolroom vandal – and a callous murderess!

On May 25, 4-year-old Martin George Brown's body was found in a derelict house in Scotswood, Newcastle, England. Next day, a nursery school which Mary and her friend Norma Bell (no relation) were later found vandalizing was broken into, and a childish note was left saying, "We did murder Martin Brown."

A few days later Mary called at the Brown's house and asked if she could see Martin. "No dear, Martin is dead," said the boy's mother. "I know. I wanted to see him in his coffin," was the little girl's chilling answer.

On July 31, 3-year-old Brian Howe went missing. Mary said she had seen him going to a vacant lot. Brian was found there, strangled, with cuts on his face and legs.

Mary told the police she had seen an 8-year-old with a pair of broken scissors beating Brian. This was interesting, as it had not been published that broken scissors were found by the body. Chief Inspector Brian Dobson was certain Mary was his killer when he saw her laughing and rubbing her hands as Brian's coffin was carried past her.

But it was 13-year-old Norma who cracked under questioning, and proved totally under Mary's influence, quite incapable of undertaking the murders herself.

Mary comported herself like a seasoned old lag, answering questions firmly yet evasively and demanding legal representation. This pretty little girl is evil incarnate and as such has shocked the great British public.

She has been found guilty of manslaughter and sentenced to life detention. No asylum will take her, and she has been sent to a special approved school.

> " I WANTED TO SEE HIM IN HIS COFFIN. "
>
> QUOTE **MARY BELL**

East End Gang Lords Jailed after Murders

> **TAKE NO NOTICE OF KRAY. HE'S JUST A BIG FAT POOF.**
>
> **GEORGE CORNELL**

TWINS RONNIE AND REGGIE KRAY (38) have been convicted of murdering fellow-villains George Cornell and "Jack the Hat" McVitie respectively. The Krays' life sentences carry no eligibility for parole for 30 years.

With that, the gangsters' terror-hold on London's East End collapses, despite their acquittal on the charge of murdering Frank Mitchell, "the Mad Axeman", whose escape from leisure in HM's prison the Kray brothers had engineered.

George Cornell was a leading lieutenant of the Richardson brothers (*see* 1966) who escaped conviction at the "torture" trial. Previously, in negotiations between the Krays and the Richardsons attended by important American gangsters, Cornell remarked, "Take no notice of [Ronnie] Kray. He's just a big fat poof."

Although Kray makes no secret of his homosexuality, and is certainly overweight, this insult could not go unavenged. Shortly after the "Mr Smith and the Witch Doctor" affray, Cornell was drinking at the Blind Beggar pub on Whitechapel Road when Ronnie Kray marched in with "Scotch Ian" Barrie and shot him dead at pointblank range. Then he walked out again, confident that no witness would dare to name him.

The following year, minor criminal Jack McVitie cheated the Krays out of a few hundred pounds over a couple of deals, and boasted about it. They invited him to a party in Stoke Newington, where Reggie

Reg (left) and Ron Kray, the twin lords of protection racketeering in London's East End

tried to shoot him with a pistol that jammed, and then stabbed him with a carving knife.

Scotland Yard chiefs destroyed the murderous protection racketeers by giving Superintendent Leonard "Nipper" Read a task force to operate out of Tintagel House.

After careful investigations, the force arrested the Krays and all their henchmen in a dawn raid, then assured terrorized witnesses that there was no one left to kneecap them. Result: the Kray twins are enjoying a deservedly long holiday at Her Majesty's expense.

Cannock Chase Child Murderer Caught

Flowers left in memory of Christine Darby

IT'S TAKEN TWO YEARS, but the evil pervert who raped and strangled Christine Darby (7) is behind bars. It was clear in 1967 that a dangerous child-molester was operating from a grey car along the A34 between Stone and Walsall, Staffordshire. Investigators were hampered by the fact that each time the monster struck it was in an area covered by a different police force; separate incident rooms and awkward liaison between the various forces guaranteed confusion.

The deaths of little Diane Tift, Margaret Reynolds and Christine Darby gave urgency to the detectives' work, however. When, last year, accumulating evidence pointed to Raymond Leslie Morris of Walsall, it seemed as though charges might not be possible, as Mrs Morris alibied her husband, saying he had been home with her on the evenings of the murders.

Morris, a motor engineer with a fetish about his own competence and excellence at anything to which he turned his hand, gave the police no assistance. He simply stonewalled all their questions.

But Mrs Morris changed her story when pornographic pictures of little girls were found in Raymond's drawer: pictures he had taken, and in one of which his hand with clearly identifiable watchstrap was visibly pushing the child to take up the position he wanted. The child was Mrs Morris's five-year-old niece! She has now given evidence against her husband, and is starting divorce proceedings.

Raymond Morris can look forward to a miserable life in jail: as a "nonce" or "beastie" (child-molester), he risks being maimed by outraged fellow-prisoners.

Charles Manson: Evil Master of Hippie Commune

Charles Manson in court

Shocking Sharon Tate Murder Solved

THE HORRIFIC DISCOVERY at 10050 Cielo Drive, Beverly Hills, appalled the world. The house was occupied by film director Roman Polanski and his beautiful young wife Sharon Tate and it changed instantaneously from a highly desirable residence to one of the world's most infamous murder sites.

When the cleaner came to work on the morning of August 20, 1969, she found:

In a car on the drive, the body of Steve Parent (18), delivery boy, pre-college student, hi-fi enthusiast, shot through the head.

On the lawn, Voytek Frykowski, 32, immigrant Pole, up-market gigolo, scrounger,

dope-dealer, stabbed to death. Abigail Folger, 25, coffee-heiress, current keeper of Frykowski, stabbed and clubbed to death.

In the sitting room, Jay Sebring, 35, fashionable hairdresser; Sharon Tate, 26, eight months' pregnant, film actress. They were roped loosely together around the necks, Sebring shot, Tate stabbed.

On the door, written in blood, was the word "PIG".

LaBianca Killings

The murder of grocery chain proprietor Leno LaBianca (45)

and his 38-year-old wife Rosemary at their home in the La Feliz district of Los Angeles the following night showed no obvious connection with the Sharon Tate killings.

Leno and Rosemary were stabbed. Leno's flesh was also incised with the word "WAR". A carving fork was protruding from his abdomen.

Violent housebreakers are common in urban America. The prosperous LaBiancas were typical bourgeois victims of such criminals, unlike the rather racketty "Beautiful People" living on Cielo Drive.

Written in Blood

What might have connected the two cases was the writing in blood. On the LaBiancas' wall: "Death To PiGS" and "RiSE". On their refrigerator door, "Healter Skealter".

A recent Malibu murder had also been accompanied by a blood graffito. Musician Gary Hinman, stabbed to death in his flat, had "POLITICAL PIGGY" written on his wall beside a Black Panther-style clenched palmprint "paw-mark".

But since an obvious perpetrator was under arrest for that murder – young actor Bobby Beausoleil, who had no good explanation for possessing Hinman's car – police were not inclined to look further.

Hinman and Beausoleil were young drug-using hippy types. The LaBiancas emphatically were not. The drug-using Tate-Folger entourage's social context was so superior to Hinman and Beausoleil that there seemed no likely connection.

Helter Skelter

In August and November, a commune of young hippies calling themselves "the Family" were raided, first at the Spahn Ranch near Hollywood, then at the Barker Ranch in Death Valley. The kids were (rightly) suspected of drug-dealing, auto-theft, sex with minors, shoplifting and cheque fraud. Many of the young girl hippies believed their charismatic leader, 43-year-old Charles Manson, to be an incarnation of Jesus Christ.

But police paid no attention to their painted graffito "HELTER SCELTER", which might have indicated that, like the visitors to the LaBianca house, someone could not spell "helter skelter" correctly.

Susan Atkins' Confession

In December, a "Family" member arrested for participating in murdering Gary Hinman, told her cellmate about the other murders. Twenty-one-year-old Susan Atkins shocked prostitute Ronnie Howard with her cold-blooded satisfaction over the slayings and clear hope of perpetrating more. For the first time in her life, Ronnie decided she must grass.

Susan quickly agreed to a plea-bargain with state prosecutors (which she subsequently abandoned) and told them how she and Leslie Van Houten (20), Patricia Krenwinkel (21), Linda Kasabian (22) and Charles "Tex" Watson (23) were sent by

> "I have done my best to get along in your world, and now you want to kill me....
> I don't care anything about any of you."
> "Truth is... I ain't never been anything but a half-assed thief
> who didn't know how to steal without being caught."
>
> Charles Manson

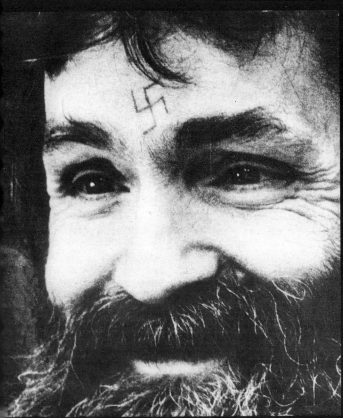

Charles Manson at the time of his sixth bid for parole, in 1986. It was turned down

TABLE OF MANSON FAMILY CRIMES

1969

AUGUST 4 – Murder of Gary Hinman by Bobby Beausoleil, accompanied by Susan Atkins and Mary Brunner.

AUGUST 8 – Arrest of Bobby Beausoleil.

AUGUST 9 – Murder of Steve Parent by Tex Watson. Murders of Jay Sebring, Abigail Folger, Voytek Frykowski and Sharon Tate by Tex Watson, Susan Atkins and Katie Krenwinkel; Linda Kasabian accompanying them.

AUGUST 10 – Murders of Leno and Rosemary LaBianca by Tex Watson, Katie Krenwinkel and Leslie van Houten. Manson headed break-in and tying-up of victims before leaving.

C.AUGUST 17 – Murder of "Shorty" Shea by Manson, Steve Grogan, Bruce Davis and probably others.

OCTOBER 12 – Manson and other family members arrested at Spahn Ranch on autotheft charges.

DECEMBER – Case breaks after Susan Atkins talks indiscreetly to fellow-prisoner.

Charles Manson to the Cielo Drive house (which they had formerly known when Beach Boy Terry Melcher lived there) with orders to kill all the occupants and write "something witchy" on the walls.

Watson killed Steve Parent, who was leaving the premises of 10050 after trying to buy hi-fi equipment from the houseboy, quartered in a separate building. Then the armed kids surprised the mildly stoned occupants of the house, Watson saying, "I am the devil and I have come to do the devil's work."

Sebring was shot when he protested; Frykowski and Folger chased onto the lawn and cut down when they tried to make a break for it.

Sharon Tate, the last of the victims to be killed, pleaded for the life of her unborn child. But Susan, nicknamed by the Family "Sadie Mae Glutz", was proud of her response, "Look, bitch, I don't care about you.... You're going to die and I don't feel anything about it."

Immediately after stabbing Sharon repeatedly, Susan licked blood off her hand, saying, "Wow, what a trip!"

Motive

According to Susan, the motive was to precipitate a black vs white war, following which Charles Manson would take command of the black victors and become king of the world. This Armageddon, called "Helter Skelter", was supposedly predicted in the song of that name recorded by the Beatles.

Prosecutor Vincent Bugliosi accepted Susan's story, and on this basis Manson, Atkins, Watson and four others were convicted of the Tate and LaBianca murders.

But Manson, a life-long unsuccessful petty criminal, says this story was all Susan's delusion. The true motive was cover for Bobby Beausoleil. Since Susan had left bloody graffiti at Gary Hinman's murder scene, it was hoped copycat killings might lead to Beausoleil's release from jail.

A still more plausible suggestion is that this might be true of the LaBianca killings, but Manson, who pimped his "Family" and dealt drugs in fairly sophisticated circles, may have accepted a contract to murder Frykowski and Folger, who were trying to monopolize marijuana dealing in South California.

This, too, would explain the group's subsequent murder of Spahn ranch-hand "Shorty" Shea, who knew too much.

BIZARRE TRIAL

As if the Tate murders weren't sensational enough, the goings-on at Manson's trial attracted more world headlines.

Led by Lynette "Squeaky" Fromme, pretty young hippy girls from "the Family" sat barefoot on the pavement outside the courthouse in vigil while the trial proceeded. They gave press interviews and displayed the fine embroidery-work worn by "the Family".

When Manson tried to disrupt proceedings and carved an X on his forehead, the girls, too, "X-ed themselves out of your world." When Manson altered his X to a swastika, so did the girls. When Manson shaved his head after his conviction, so did they.

1970

Incompetent Brothers Kidnap Newspaper Magnate's Wife

IN BRITAIN'S FIRST major kidnapping, brothers Arthur and Nizamodeen Hosein, from Trinidad, grabbed Mrs Muriel McKay, wife of the deputy chairman of the *News of the World*. The incompetent villains thought they were kidnapping millionaire Rupert Murdoch's wife, having trailed the company chairman's official car to Mr McKay's home in Wimbledon.

Mrs McKay was snatched from the house on December 29. Demands for £1 million ransom were then made by telephone and in notes and a letter to the newspaper's editor. Unfortunately the kidnappers were as hopeless at collecting the money as they were at identifying their victim, and attempts to follow their directions to telephone boxes on the London-Cambridge road were aborted. A suitcase of money was dropped, but the Hoseins failed to pick it up. Watching police did, however, identify Arthur Hosein's car reconnoitring the area, and fingerprints on the ransom demand notes tied the 34-year-old trouser manufacturer and his 22-year-old brother inexorably to the case.

Arthur Hosein was trying to live it up as the "squire" of Stocking Pelham, Hertfordshire, where he had bought Rooks Farm. Lacking the money to support his grandiose self-image, he succeeded only in

Police gather at Rooks Farm to search for Mrs McKay's body

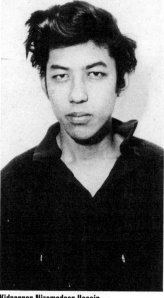
Kidnapper Nizamodeen Hosein

bringing on himself the derisive local nickname "King Hosein".

The brothers have made no confession, and no trace whatsoever of Mrs McKay has been found. There can be little doubt that she was murdered, and the Hoseins have been sentenced to life imprisonment for that offence, in addition to their convictions for kidnapping and blackmail.

But where is Mrs McKay? Local rumour has it she was fed to the pigs on Rook's Farm!

An evil-looking weapon left by the kidnappers at the McKay house

College Killer Hid Victims in Uncle's Laundry Room

NORMAN JOHN COLLINS of Michigan, the 22-year-old Ypsilanti co-ed murderer, was trapped by hair-clippings in his last victim's panties. Not his hair, not hers, but the hair of Norman's cousins, the Loucks kids.

While his uncle, policeman Dana Loucks, was vacationing with his family, young Collins had the use of his house. Before dumping the half-dressed body of 18-year-old freshman student Karen Sue Beckemann in a gully, the murderer kept it in the basement, little thinking that Mrs Loucks' habit of cutting the family hair down there would leave tell-tale evidence in the girl's panties.

Collins has murdered and mutilated seven girls since 1967 – all either college or high school students. He has shot, knifed, strangled and battered his victims, frequently even mutilating their sexual parts.

A good-looking motor-biker attending Eastern Michigan University, Collins regularly dated co-eds and led an active sex-life. Some, however, could tesify to savagery if a girl refused to sleep with him. Others knew that he had a peculiar phobia about menstruating women, and would curse a lover and throw her out if she were having her period. (The maniac "Bible John" who has been terrorizing Glasgow appears to have the same sick fear of nature.)

Now that the physical evidence links him definitely to the killings, Collins, a previous suspect, goes to trial in the New Year.

Mafia Boss Shot for Denying Mafia's Existence

IN 1964, Joe Columbo replaced Joe Magliocco as head of New York's "Profaci" Mafia family. Other crime bosses were grateful to "rat fink" Colombo, who revealed that Joseph C. Bonnano, also known as "Joe Bananas", had hired Colombo's boss, Magliocco, to "rub out" the current crime syndicate rulers.

The "Banana war" took place and ended in defeat for ambitious Bonnano. Joe Colombo then founded the "Italian-American Civil Rights League."

This extraordinary association claims that there is no Mafia, and that public attention to organized crime induces prejudice against Americans of Italian birth. Despite the absurdity of a leading Mafioso peddling this twaddle, it appealed to Italian immigrants, and the League won considerable support from politicians and church leaders. Last year 50,000 people attended its Unity Day rally at Columbus Circle, and New York State Governor Nelson Rockefeller accepted honorary membership.

Older and wiser Mafiosi were displeased. They know that, for them, all publicity is bad publicity.

Joe Colombo's denial of the Mafia's existence simply drew mocking press attention to it. Carlo Gambino, one of the bosses saved when Colombo betrayed Magliocco, had no hesitation in ordering a "hit" on the President of the Italian-American Civil Rights League. The contract was passed to Joe Gallo, who delegated it to Harlem mobsters.

So it was that on July 28 this year, Joseph Colombo's career ended as he stood in Columbus Circle, preparing once more to tell cheering throngs that it is racism to claim that crime is organized and Italians play a large part in it. Jerome A. Johnson, a black man wearing a press badge, came up to the platform and gunned down the gang leader before he could warm to his message of assuring the world that no such gunnings-down happen in Italian circles.

Johnson was himself instantly killed by Colombo's hoods. Colombo has survived, but has suffered such severe brain damage that his former level of stupidity has nose-dived to that of a vegetable. He continues to exist at this level thanks to a life-support machine.

Joe Colombo (centre) appears before a federal court in April

Colombo's funeral in Brooklyn, seven years after the attempt on his life which crippled him

'Murder-by-Negligence' Doctor Murdered in Texas

THE STRANGE CASE of Dr John Hill has ended with his murder by a professional hitman – himself shot by police before he could say who employed him.

In 1968 Hill's wife Joan died in Houston, Texas, after he had taken her for treatment to a hospital in which he had shares. It was suggested that this was unnecessarily far from their home; that Dr Hill had deliberately ignored his wife's sudden and serious indisposition; that he might have caused it, since she was buried with unseemly haste and her death certificate was signed without close examination.

There was no doubt that the doctor's obsession with classical music and Joan's equal passion for equitation left them little time together, and it was whispered that John Hill really married Joan Robinson for her father Ash's money. This last point was given validity when Hill remarried within three months of being widowed. Millionaire Ash Robinson promptly had his daughter's body exhumed, and after inconclusive autopsies suggested possible liver failure or possible meningitis as causes of death, Ash's influence secured the doctor's trial for murder this February.

The method alleged was negligent delay in treating Joan's illness. So when the second Mrs Hill (by now herself separated from the doctor) blurted out that he had tried to poison her, a mistrial was declared. Before the case could be heard again, John Hill was dead.

Suspicion obviously points in the direction of the vengeful Ash Robinson, but nobody believes that Houston can bring this particular "Big Daddy" to book.

1972

Bodies in Black Activist's Lettuce Bed

THROUGH THE 1960'S, ex-pimp and slumlord Peter Rachman's lead extortionist Michael de Freitas – later self-styled Michael X or Michael Abdul Malik – established himself as a radical black spokesman in England. His pressure group RAAS (actually a rude word in Trinidadian dialect, though Malik pretended it was an acronym for Racial Advancement and Action Society) and cultural commune "the Black House", were supported by naive celebrities like Beatle John Lennon and Yoko Ono.

But after a questionable conviction for encouraging racial violence, Malik fled the country when threatened with yet another prison sentence for extorting money using threats.

Back in his native Trinidad he set up as a spokesman for race consciousness, and started another commune in a suburban house in Arima. This year he was threatened with eviction when he was unable to exercise his option to buy his house, and it seems that in a fit of pique he may have told some followers to burn it down while he was on a speaking tour in Guyana.

The fire was a disaster for him. Police, looking at the garden of the gutted building, were puzzled by an unduly well-tended bed of lettuces. Suspecting that political activist Malik might have cached guns there, they dug it up and found

• Gale Ann Benson, pretty British daughter of former Conservative MP Captain Leonard Plugge.
• Joseph Skerritt, a young barber's assistant.

It seems Miss Benson was frightened by Malik's increasing Messianic delusions, and wanted out with her almost equally batty Messianic American boyfriend Hakin Jamal. Malik hired a hitman to kill her for this unforgivable betrayal of his divinity. Skerritt had to go when he asked too many questions about the missing white woman. Malik killed him personally with a machete.

Malik shaved off his beard and fled through the jungle for the Brazilian border when he heard the bodies had been found. But it takes skill to survive in those untrodden ways. The lethal agitator was quickly caught and sent back to Trinidad, where Prime Minister Dr Eric Williams, a scholar-statesman who has no need of jumped-up demagogues in his republic, will leave the case to the courts. Few Trinidadians will mourn if this troublesome charlatan ends in the death cell and learns why Trinidad and Tobago keeps a gallows to rid itself of embarrassments.

Chicago Deaf-Mute Charged with Killing Prostitute

IN 1965 illiterate Donald Lang (25) was the last person seen with streetwalker Ernestine Williams before her stabbed body was found in a Chicago alley.

It proved impossible to charge the black deaf-mute, who apparently could not follow the proceedings. He was confined for seven years in a hospital for the criminally insane.

Soon after his release this July, prostitute Earline Brown was found suffocated in Chicago's Viceroy Hotel. Lang was the last person seen with her. This time, bloodstains of the prostitute's group on his shirt provide compelling forensic evidence, and he will stand trial whether or not he can understand the proceedings!

Hertfordshire Poisoner Kills Workmates out of Curiosity

Poisoner Graham Young

WHEN HE WAS A CHILD, Graham Young poisoned his stepmother and made his father seriously ill in the hope of being returned to the care and control of his grandmother. He spent seven years in a secure institution for that crime.

Released, Young got a job with Hadlands, a photographic instruments firm in Bovingdon, Hertfordshire. Mysterious illnesses occurred soon after, and two popular workers, Bob Egle and Fred Biggs, died of disorders which doctors could not diagnose.

When police came to the factory to question staff over the case, 23-year-old Graham drew attention to himself by asking whether they had considered thallium poisoning as the cause of death.

They hadn't, but the young man's diagnosis was spot on! A search of his room turned up a library of books on poisons and further enquiries brought his past record to light. Graham found himself charged with murder.

His only motive seems to have been the interest of finding out whether and how the poisons would work. He also enjoyed a sense of power in being the only one to understand the mysterious "Bovingdon bug".

Killer Thought Human Sacrifices Prevent Earthquakes

IT'S BEEN A ROUGH 18 months for Santa Cruz, California, which has been terrorised by mass-murderers Ed Kemper (*see* below) and Herb Mullin.

Mullin, religiose son of a Marine colonel, may have blown his mind smoking dope and taking acid. Anyway, last year he heard voices telling him that human sacrifices would save southern California from the massive earthquakes that naturally occur along the Pacific coast. So he killed 13: a tramp; a lone girl; a priest; four campers; two potheads; a mother with two children; and an old man digging his garden.

Though Mullin has been in and out of mental hospitals, diagnosed paranoid schizophrenic, a jury that wants him locked up forever has refused to find him insane and declared him guilty of ten counts of murder. Once the schoolboy most likely to succeed, Herb Mullin now goes to prison for life.

Mass murderer Herb Mullin under escort. He was found guilty of murder, on ten counts

Ince Cleared — In Bed With Dolly

TWO MEN HAVE BEEN charged with last year's brutal Barn Restaurant, Braintree murder, in which restaurateur Bob Patience, his wife and daughter were all pointlessly shot by masked robbers. The thieves forced their way into the Patiences' residence, detached from the restaurant, following the popular and successful Guy Fawkes' night party and fireworks. Mrs Muriel Patience subsequently died of her injuries.

Petty crooks John Brook and Nicholas Johnson have been arrested after Brook foolishly showed an associate the gun he said had killed Mrs Patience. The pair go on trial next year.

Their arrest comes too late to be a real relief to the better known suspect George Ince. For George has already stood trial after three times being identified as the sinister stranger seen hanging round the Barn restaurant. George won immediate and easy clearance when pretty Mrs Dolly Kray told the jury George couldn't have been at the Barn on Guy Fawkes' night, because he was in bed with her.

Okay, that clears George of the murder. But it leaves him – (and Dolly!) – in some trouble with Dolly's husband, none other than Charlie Kray, brother of the notorious twins Ronnie and Reggie, whose pose as popular business-men-philanthropists was so rudely shattered by their imprisonment for murder (*see* 1969). Charlie's sharing their durance at present, though he protests that he only kept "the Firm's" books. However the underworld doesn't like wives and lovers frolicking while their hubbies are behind bars.

Playing with Kids, Texas-Style, Sets Murder Record

PASADENA POLICE were shocked when 17-year-old Wayne Elmer Henley telephoned to say he'd just shot 33-year-old electrician Dean Corll. For Corll was known locally as "a real good neighbour and a real good guy", who especially loved small children, giving them candy and rides in his van.

Turns out that what Corll really loved was big kids. He bribed Henley and his buddy David Brooks to lure drunk teenage boys to his Houston boatshed, where they would be handcuffed and tied up while loud music drowned their screams. A tarpaulin would catch their blood while Corll indulged his enjoyment of torture. He would spend up to a day in this before killing them.

The gruesome ongoing party stopped when Henley brought a girl by mistake. Corll threatened to kill the boy if he didn't rape and murder 15-year-old Rhonda Williams. Henley could not comply, and shot Corll instead!

Twenty-seven boys have been found in shallow graves around Corll's boathouse. Juan Corona's US mass murder record has been broken.

Gentle Californian Giant Decapitates Momma

AT 6FT 9INS, gentle Ed Kemper was too tall to be a policeman – he'd have scared the public. It didn't help either that he spent his adolescence in a secure mental hospital for shooting his grandparents!

Ed loved cops, and hung around the police station in his home town, Santa Cruz, California. Santa Cruz police just didn't believe it when Ed telephoned from Pueblo, Colorado, this April to confess to being the co-ed killer who ravished, decapitated and mutilated six college students in the previous year. But when Ed persuaded them to look in his house, they locked him up in a hurry.

Ed's mom was decapitated in her bed. Her battered head was on the mantelpiece, and it seemed Ed had thrown darts at it. The larynx, from which the termagant had screamed abuse at Ed and her suc-

Ed Kemper (left) seems pleased to be under arrest in Colorado, awaiting extradition to California

cessive husbands, had been cut out and thrown in the dustbin. In the sitting room, also decapitated, was her best friend, Sarah Hallett.

Now cops believed Ed's stories of picking up college girls as hitchhikers in his car, which had a passenger door that would not open from the inside; believed that he'd raped them, cut bits off them, kept heads in his wardrobe for days, eaten parts and masturbated into human carrion. Now they knew they had a gentle, charming, intelligent, likeable monster on their hands. Ed has been arraigned on eight counts of murder, and hopes to receive the death penalty.

1974

Lord Lucan Disappears After Slaying of Children's Nanny

Lord Lucan

PROFESSIONAL GAMBLER Lord Lucan has disappeared. Confusion surrounds the events of Thursday, November 7 at his former home in Belgravia, currently occupied by his estranged wife and their two children. Ascertained facts are as follows:

9.00 PM 29-year-old Sandra Rivett, the children's nanny, leaves the room where Lady Lucan and the elder child are watching television to make a cup of tea in the basement kitchen.

9.20 Lady Lucan goes to see why Sandra is taking so long and is struck over the head. She recovers to find a man struggling with her, and as she restrains him, by crushing his testicles, recognizes the assailant as her husband.

9.30 Lord and Lady Lucan retire upstairs to discuss the fact that Sandra Rivett is dead in the basement. While Lord Lucan goes to wash, Lady Lucan runs from the house and raises the alarm at a nearby pub, saying an intruder has attacked her.

9.45 Neighbours accompany her to find Lord Lucan has left. Miss Rivett's battered body is found stuffed in a US mail sack, a bent bloodstained bludgeon made of lead piping with an elastoplast grip lying beside it. Lady Lucan now says the intruder was her husband.

9.50 Lord Lucan telephones his mother to say that while passing the house he saw a stranger grappling with Lady Lucan and rushed in and drove him off, only to have Lady Lucan believe it was he who had attacked her.

11.30 Lord Lucan drives to friends in Sussex and tells them the same story. He also writes letters repeating it to other friends. He declares his intention of "lying doggo", and insists on driving away, at 1.15 am.

NOVEMBER 8 Lord Lucan's car found abandoned near Newhaven. In the boot, an empty US mail sack and a bludgeon made from the same lead piping as the one that killed Sandra Rivett. The obvious conclusion is that the earl hid in the house intending to kill his wife on the nanny's usual night off (Thursday). When Miss Rivett came downstairs, he mistook her for Lady Lucan and killed her.

Lord Lucan's friends deny this possibility, insisting that he will return and give a full account of himself. But they, like Lord Lucan himself, strike many people as a dislikeable bunch of aristocratic gamblers. Their snobbish contempt for the police and the fate of Miss Rivett is hindering the inquiry.

Their attitude is well illustrated by the outraged response of one of them to the suggestion that Lucan might have been attractive Miss Rivett's lover – "Sleeping with the *nanny*!". Their good opinion of the noble lord is not shared by the public.

Suggested change in Lucan's appearance

Unspeakable Brutality in Utah Robbery-Murders

AIRFORCEMAN DALE PIERRE and friend William Andrews robbed a hi-fi store in Ogden, Utah this April, and treated the proprietors and three of their friends with quite unspeakable cruelty.

The victims were herded into the basement, tied up and robbed. They were forced to drink Drano, a vitriolic compound of caustic acid used to clear blocked plumbing. A teenage shop assistant was raped, and all the victims were shot in the head. Finally, one who was only superficially injured was half strangled, and finished off by having a ball-point pen thrust into his ear.

Doctors saved the lives of two of them, who identified Pierre and Andrews when stolen property turned up at the USAF base. A half-empty bottle of Drano was found with stolen hi-fi equipment in Pierre's rented garage. Relatives and friends of the victims are furious that the US Supreme Court allowed the prohibition of capital punishment two years ago.

Black Muslim Youths Kill 15 'White Devils'

SINCE NOVEMBER last year, a group of eight Black Muslim youths calling themselves "Death Angels" have been killing white citizens in San Francisco. The climax of their efforts was "the Night of the Five", January 28, when J.C. Simon suggested that his comrade "Angels" join him for a really hectic night of shootings.

It was apparent to police that young black gunmen were deliberately shooting innocuous white passers-by; for which reason the killings were nicknamed the "Zebra Murders" – black on white.

The disapproving Black community supported the setting up of white vigilantes. The Black Muslims themselves espouse no such doctrine of destruction and violence. In April, Anthony Howard came forward in response to a reward offered, and informed on his fellow "Death Angels".

One hundred police officers raided an apartment block, making seven arrests. As a result, Larry Green, J.C.Simon, Jesse Cook and Manuel Moore will stand trial for the "Zebra Murders".

Adolescent Psychopath 'Franklin Bollvolt I' Freed to Kill

Patrick Mackay, aka Franklin Bollvolt I

PATRICK MACKAY (22) loved dressing up in spiked helmet and cardboard armour and parading before his mirror as "Franklin Bollvolt I, Dictator of the World". Seven years ago, psychiatrists called him "a cold psychopathic killer".

This April he proved it when the fully-clothed body of Fr Anthony Crean was found in the bath at his cottage in Gravesend, England, beaten to death with a hatchet.

Two years ago Fr Crean had sought the withdrawal of charges against Mackay for forging a cheque. Mackay recently visited the priest in a state of agitation after friends suggested the older man's interest in him was homosexual.

Fr Crean was confronted by an angry giant, who pursued him to the bathroom, cut him down, and gazed for an hour at his bloody handiwork as he ran water into the bath. Mackay confessed to this killing and much more.

In addition to many muggings, he confessed to the murder of Isabella Griffiths last year in Chelsea, and to that of Adele Price this February in Belgravia. Both old ladies were killed in their flats. To fellow convicts Mackay boasted of another eight killings, and detectives concluded:

Mackay certainly killed: Miss Mary Haynes (73), robbed and murdered in her Kentish Town flat; Frank Goodman (62), Finsbury Park tobacconist, robbed and murdered in his shop.

Mackay probably killed: Stephanie Britton (74) and her grandson Christopher Martin (4) in Hadley Green, Hertfordshire.

Mackay may have killed: Heidi Mnilk (17), stabbed and thrown off a train from London Bridge; Mrs Ivy Davies (54) in Southend; an unidentified tramp he claims to have thrown off Hungerford footbridge across the Thames.

Mackay did not kill: Sarah Rodwell (92), robbed of her pensioner's Christmas bonus on the doorstep of her Hackney home.

Pleading guilty to the manslaughter of Fr Crean, Mrs Griffiths and Mrs Price, and asking for 26 more robberies to be taken into account, Mackay has been sent to a secure unit for life.

A lethal weapon Mackay may have used for murder

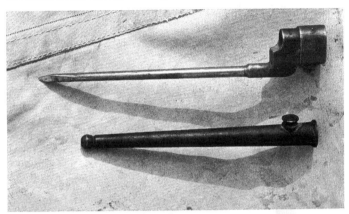

Nazi insignia found among Mackay's "Dictator of the World" costumes and props

Murder-Suspect Doctor Plucked off Plane at Take-Off

THE AIRLINER TAXIED out on to the Kennedy Airport runway; the flight to London was about to begin its long sprint before lifting away into the sky over New York when the pilot was ordered to return to the terminal and hand over passenger Charles Friedgood!

Sophie Friedgood, the middle-aged surgeon's wife of 28 years, died in June, and her husband certified the cause as stroke. The authorities then learned that the doctor had a young mistress with two children who was pressing him to divorce Sophie and marry her. When traces of the poison demerol were found in Sophie's body, police acted. The doctor also has to explain why he was trying to cross the Atlantic with $600,000 of his late wife's cash, bonds and jewellery in his hand-baggage, all secured on her forged signature!

Girl Promised Sex for Murder of Lover's Wife

LOVELY SOUTH AFRICAN model Marlene Lehnberg (19) made poor, one-legged Cape Coloured Marthinus Choegoe an offer he couldn't refuse: a car, a radio and sex with her, if he would kill Susanna van der Linde, whose husband Marlene wanted to marry.

Choegoe did the deed in November last year, stabbing Mrs van der Linde with a pair of scissors. He was soon arrested, because witnesses clearly recalled a man with a limp.

Marlene stood trial with him this March. Apart from her tantalizing incitement to murder, she may have helped in person, as crippled Choegoe could barely strike hard enough to kill.

Lehnberg and Choegoe were convicted and sentenced to death, but then won a reprieve.

1976

Southeastern States' Mafia Boss Murdered

FLORIDA MAFIA CHIEFTAIN John Roselli ended his days in the Atlantic, sealed up in a heavy oil-drum weighted with chains.

This should have been his final disappearance, but gases emitted by the decomposing body brought it to the surface and to the world's attention.

In his youth, Roselli was the mob's man in Hollywood. He shook down the studios for a million through a Mafia-controlled union. He also swindled Groucho Marx and Phil Silvers out of a lot of money in a bent card game.

After moving to the southeast, he worked closely with Sam Giancana in efforts to recover Mafia interests in Cuba. This led to the notorious conversations with the CIA which Roselli revealed to a senate committee last year. With government spies proposing *Boys' Own* paper stunts, such as poisoned cigars, against Castro, it's a safe bet that the Mafiosi took the government's money with a straight face and made no attempt to carry out these hits.

Talking to the senators proved to be a mistake, however. Sam Giancana was killed before he could give evidence before the same committee (*see* 1975). Roselli managed to testify but then made a serious professional error by rejecting advice to hire bodyguards. The man who knew all about sitting targets became one himself.

Crapulous Killer Turns Back the Clock in USA

GARY GILMORE IS A no-account, nickels-and-dimes petty crook. 18 of his 37 years have been spent behind bars. His most successful robberies have netted nothing more than old cars or a few bucks.

Yet this no-hoper is pulling the United States out of the Civilised 60's into the Sleazy 70's. Convicted of two pointless murders, he is insisting that the State of Utah be permitted to shoot him, thus overturning the Supreme Court decision of 1972 that judicial execution is cruel and unusual punishment. For ten years no one has been executed in America. Gilmore's gonna change all that, and drag his country down into equality with South Africa and the Soviet Union – the only developed nations that still practise the barbarism of capital punishment.

On parole to relatives in Provo, Utah, Gilmore proved a poor factory worker and ungrateful when given a car. Soon he left his family to shack up with thrice-married 19-year-old Nicole Baker and her three children. 37-year-old Gilmore was infatuated with Nicole's innocent beauty, but outraged by her predictably far-from-innocent association with other men. On July 13 the two had an explosive row and he kicked her out. On July 19 he took a gun and drove off to rob the Sinclair gas station in Orem, Utah. Student Max Jensen was on night duty there in the forecourt. Gilmore stuck him up, made him lie on his face, and put two bullets through his head, saying, "This one's for me and this one's for Nicole". He scooped $125 from the till and fled.

Next year he went into City Center Motel in Provo and shot the manager, Ben Bushnell, in the same way. Again his take was barely $120.

The clumsy creep betrayed himself however, in throwing his gun away. Trailing blood, he attracted police attention and was arrested.

Convicted, he is under sentence of death, and determined to go out that way, too.

Murderous Black Panther Caught

THE MYSTERIOUS "Black Panther", whose 17 sub-Post Office robberies across northern England and the Midlands has left three people dead, and whose spent bullets prove him to be the kidnapper and murderer of Lesley Ann Whittle, has been caught. Thirty-nine-year-old joiner Donald Neilson is a "survival" freak whose happiest times were spent in the army. So keen was he on army-style life that he forced his family to wear combat fatigues and join him in adventure games.

"Black Panther" Donald Neilson

Neilson, a short man who changed his name from Nappey because he considered it undignified, was arrested when two policemen in a patrol car saw him loitering suspiciously in Mansfield Woodhouse, Nottinghamshire. He pulled a gun on them and tried to force them to drive him away, but they stopped outside a fish-and-chip shop when his attention wavered. Two civilians waiting in the queue in the shop helped overpower the villain. Back at the police station, two black hoods found in Neilson's possession proved that this was the "Black Panther".

Neilson's uniform

He has been urgently sought since January last year, when he snatched 17-year-old Lesley Ann from her home in Shropshire, under the misapprehension that she was a rich heiress. He held her in the labyrinth of drains and culverts under Bathpool Park, near Kidsgrove. His elaborate attempts to collect ransom money, with dynotape messages left in telephone kiosks, failed, however, serving only to draw attention to the park. A security guard who tried to apprehend Neilson was murdered around this time.

When his lair was unearthed in March 1975, Lesley's body was found there, hanging by a wire noose. By her were a sleeping bag and survival equipment. But police discovered no evidence as to the identity of the "Black Panther" until Neilson's capture this December.

He goes on trial next year.

The wire noose with which Lesley was killed

New York 'Son of Sam', Couples Murderer Caught

THE MONSTER who has terrorized New York city for 13 months is in custody. The couples killer, whose bizarre letters declared that he killed on father "Sam's" orders, turns out to be 24-year-old Jewish mailman, David Berkowitz, and the demonic Son of Sam who controlled him is a dog!

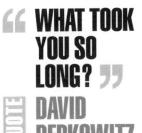

Berkowitz was caught because he left his car blocking a fire hydrant on August 10 while he killed 20-year-old Stacey Moskowitz and injured her boyfriend Robert Violante in their parked car in Brooklyn. Detectives investigated reports of a short suspect with scruffy blond hair behaving suspiciously in the vicinity, and connected a yellow Volkswagen with

David Berkowitz (centre, clean-shaven with dark hair) smirks as he is arrested for the "Son of Sam" killings

him. Husky Berkowitz, with short curly brown hair and Ford car, clearly did not fit the bill.

But routine checks on ticketed parking offenders near the murder sites put NYPD detectives in contact with the traffic bureau at Yonkers where Berkowitz lived. Police telephonist Wheat Carr, daughter of Sam Carr whose dog Berkowitz identifies as his evil genius, was shocked to learn that the neighbour whose bizarre misconduct had led her family to wonder

whether he might be connected with the murders was perfectly placed for the Stacey Moskowitz killing.

Soon Berkowitz was surrounded in his apartment. When police broke in they found weird satanic messages scrawled on the walls. Drafts of new "Son of Sam" letters were in his room and car.

At his arrest, a smirking Berkowitz asked, "What took you so long?" He has confessed to shooting 13 young men and women, killing six. He claims that the devil in the shape of Sam Carr's black labrador prompted the slayings. Brooklyn and Queens are relieved that the worst couples killer in living memory is off their streets.

The .44 pistol that gave the "Son of Sam's" killings the alternative name of the ".44 murders"

Black Landlord's Eviction by Manslaughter

FOR THREE YEARS Battersea landlord Berman Benjamin Bailey tried to clear tenants paying statutory controlled rents out of his house in Marjorie Grove. He bullied and hectored. He said to crippled Harry Cadwell, who has lived there since 1938, "This is a black man's house. I want you out."

County court orders served on Bailey enjoined him against harassment and interference. When his considerable contribution to bad race relations got him

nowhere, Mr Bailey took a final, murderous step against the tenants he wanted to be rid of.

One December night, he or his agents crept into the house, poured paraffin over furniture in the hall and set light to it. Ironically, the innocent victims of this inferno were Mrs Icylma Amos and her two little boys and Mr Gladstone Fuller, four of the black tenants he claimed to prefer to whites.

Bailey has been jailed for ten years for manslaughter.

Deadly Butler Takes Ex-MP for a Ride

WALTER SCOTT-ELLIOT was once a Labour junior minister. He was also rich, with an equally rich wife, and could well afford a stylish butler like Archibald Hall for his London home.

On December 9 last year Hall gave Mr Scott-Elliot a heavy dose of sleeping pills and tranquillizers. But even so, it was odd that the old man accepted his butler's telling him they were suddenly going for a drive to Scotland. Odder still that he should accept a bewigged woman he'd never seen before as his wife!

What Hall didn't tell his employer was that Mrs Scott-Elliott lay dead in the car boot. Burglar and con-man Hall had introduced his confederate Michael Kitto into the Scott-Elliot's flat to examine the premises during the night, under the impression that Mrs Scott-Elliott was in hospital. When she turned out to have been discharged unexpectedly, the two suffocated her.

The plan was to bury her in a Scottish burn where Hall had successfully hidden an earlier victim: a villain whose violence threatened his security in a comfortable job.

Mr Scott-Elliot proved too much of a handful, so he was killed in Cumbria, and left there with his wife. Then Mary Coggle, the confederate who had masqueraded as Mrs Scott-Elliott, turned awkward and demanded the lady's fur coat. So she too was killed. Finally Hall's half-brother, whom he had never liked, joined him and Kitto. The half-brother's body was in the car boot when North Berwick police discovered that its number-plates were false. Hall ran, but was quickly picked up. He is now serving a life sentence for his crimes.

Red Brigades Terrorists Murder Italy's Ex-Premier

ALDO MORO, five times Prime Minister of Italy, was kidnapped on March 16 when his car was ambushed as he drove to a special session of Parliament.

The left-wing "Red Brigades" terrorists claiming to be holding him sent messages to the government, accompanied by photographs of Moro holding the day's newspaper, to prove that he was alive. They demanded the release of 14 of their leaders, on trial in Turin. When the government refus-ed to accede to this blackmail, Sr Moro was shot. His body was left in a car parked near the Communist Party headquarters and the offices of the Christian Democrats. The "unholy alliance" between these two parties has aroused the ire of the extremist of the left, whose crimes are taken more seriously than the actrocitie perpetrated by neo-Fascists and Mafiosi over the years.

IN BRIEF

MURDERER CHARLES FRIEDGOOD (*see* 1975) has provoked a new law in New York state. Henceforth, it is illegal for a doctor to certify the death of his own next of kin.

Killer Clown Stuffed Boys Under his House

FOR SIX YEARS building contractor John Wayne Gacy has gone to gay zones around Chicago, picking up young men and driving them back to his home on Norwood Park. There he would tie them up, torture them, and finally kill them. He pushed the bodies in the crawl space under his floor until that got full. Then he started burying them in his garden.

At the same time, Gacy presented a popular and acceptable public profile. A Democratic Party ward worker, he was photographed shaking hands with First Lady Rosalynn Carter. As Pogo the Clown he put on whiteface and costume to delight kids in hospital or at parties he threw in his mausoleum. But Gacy the secret slaying sodomite got careless.

Last year a young man complained that Gacy pulled a gun on him when he came to apply for a job. Gacy wriggled out of that say-

First Lady Rosalynn Carter unwittingly shakes hands with America's worst mass murderer, John Wayne Gacy

ing the man was blackmailing him. This March he let 27-year-old Jeffrey Rignall go after chloroforming and torturing him for a day, figuring that a man who didn't know his name or address when he came round in Lincoln Park wouldn't be able to identify him. Rignall watched out for weeks until he saw Gacy's car and turned the number over to Chicago police – who did precisely nothing.

Des Plaines police were more determined when missing 15-year-old Robert Piest was shown to have been in Gacy's company. They watched Gacy, questioned him, followed him; and finally two policemen received his hesitant confession. With 27 bodies under his house, three buried in his garden, and four more thrown in Des Plaines River, Gacy is under arrest as America's worst mass murderer.

Secret Weapon Assassination of Cold Warrior

Magnified photograph of the poison pellet

Murdered Bulgarian refugee Georgi Markov

GEORGI MARKOV was a refugee from Bulgaria. When he annoyed the Communist authorities he fled to Italy. Ten years ago he was granted political asylum in Great Britain.

Since then he has been broadcasting to his native land on the BBC World Service – too effectively for the regime, it seems.

On September 7 he was walking along the Strand in London, on his way to read the evening news bulletin from Bush House, when he felt a stinging sensation in the right thigh. It appeared he had been prodded sharply by the umbrella of a man in a bus queue, who apologized profusely for the injury in a strong foreign accent before hailing a taxi and disappearing in the traffic.

Mr Markov's leg grew stiff. By 11.00 pm he felt feverish and went home. The following day he was in hospital, where the puncture in his thigh puzzled doctors. Also giving concern was Mr Markov's white blood corpuscle count which rose alarmingly. Two days later Markov was dead.

During the post-mortem examination the pathologist extracted a miniscule pellet measuring 1.52 mm across from the dead man's leg. The pellet was found to be hollow with two microscopic holes bored in the sides. Forensic tests determined that Mr Markov had been poisoned with ricin, a rare derivative of castor oil seeds. Research on this substance has mainly been carried out in Hungary and Czechoslovakia.

The metal from which the pellet was made is an alloy of platinum and iridium; the workmanship that went into making the pellet is far beyond the engineering skills possessed by an ordinary jeweller. A similar metal was found in the back of Vladimir Kostov, another Bulgarian defector, who was shot with an umbrella-gun in Paris last year. Mr Kostov survived, so the poison dosage must have been increased for Mr Markov.

No prizes for guessing who is behind these James Bond-type killings of dissident Bulgarians.

IN BRIEF

IRA HIGH PROFILE murders this year include Airey Neave MP, killed as a car-bomb was detonated by a tilt device when he mounted the ramp to leave the House of Commons underground car park; and Earl Mountbatten of Burma, killed in his booby-trapped motorboat while on holiday in Northern Ireland.

Airey Neave, MP, IRA victim

Killer Confesses, the Speaking Ghost was Right

MEDICAL ORDERLY Allan Showery would never in a million years have been convicted of murdering 48-year-old Teresita Basa on the original evidence turned up by police. A Filippino doctor's wife told police that, five months after Manila-born Teresita was found stabbed, burned and wrapped in sheets in her apartment, the dead woman's ghost came to her in a vision and named Showery as her killer!

Teresita, like Showery, was an employee at Edgewater Hospital. Embarrassed detectives paid him a visit to ask him what he had to say to the supernatural accusation. They were very surprised to find some of Miss Basa's jewellery hidden in his apartment.

Still, Basa's lawyers said murder on ghost testimony was easy to defend. They were disgruntled when Showery confessed, accepting 14 years' imprisonment for the murder!

John Lennon Assassinated in New York

FORMER BEATLE John Lennon was shot down outside his home in the Dakota Apartment Building, New York, on December 8. His killer, freaky 25-year-old Mark David Chapman, called out "Mr Lennon" as the singer walked past him. Then Chapman fired five times, four bullets striking Lennon at pointblank range.

Chapman's life has veered between rebellion and drug abuse in his early adolescence, and born-again Christian work for the YMCA. After failing at college in Arkansas, he went to Hawaii and attempted suicide. A period in a mental hos-

pital appeared to effect complete recovery, and he worked successfully with geriatric patients for a while afterwards.

He came to New York with the deliberate intention of killing Lennon, believing this would fulfil something of J.D. Salinger's fictional "Catcher in the Rye's" crusade against "phoneys".

Mark David Chapman has the paranoid's crazy conviction that he is far more important than the facts warrant. This hopeless man believes he has won some kind of immortality by killing one of our time's most creative minds.

Lovely Dorothy Stratten, raped, sodomized and murdered by her estranged husband

'Playmate of the Year' Slain by Pimp Husband

BEAUTIFUL DOROTHY STRATTEN appeared as "Playmate of the Month" in August *Playboy* last year and was heading for stardom as "Playmate of the Year 1980".

But she couldn't take her hus-

band with her. Paul Snider was a pimp when he met Dorothy Hoogstraten in Vancouver and persuaded her to let him send photo spreads to *Playboy*. The magazine employed her, and Snider came along as her manager. When he obviously wasn't wanted there, he married her to tie her to him. Dorothy fell in love with film producer Peter Bogdanovich, then... well, then I guess Paul just couldn't take it any more.

When Dorothy called to talk about divorce, he tied her up, ravished her, shot her, ravished her corpse all over again, and shot himself. It's a sad old world if you get out of your depth in the glamour spin.

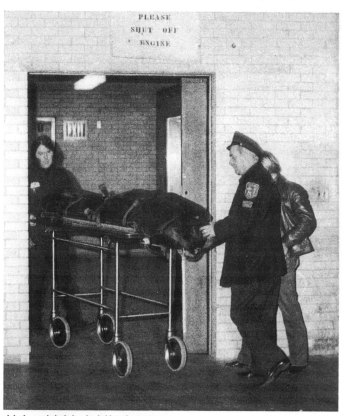
John Lennon's body is wheeled into the mortuary

Rape-Killer Demands Death

AT THE AGE OF 12, Steve Judy broke into a neighbour's house, and raped, stabbed and beat her. Last April, aged 22, he noticed Terri Chasteen driving along the highway near Indianapolis. He drew alongside her, flashing his lights and pointing at her tyres. She stopped to see if she had a flat and he disabled her car, offering her and her children, a lift to a gas station. Instead he drove to lonely White Lick Creek with the words, "I guess you know what's going to happen now." She reluctantly sent the kids into the woods. Then, Judy raped her and, as she screamed, he strangled her. When the kids came running back Judy drowned them in the creek. His truck was soon indentified and he was arrested. At his trial he sneered at the jurors, "You'd better put me to death, because next time it might be one of your daughters." He was sent to Death Row.

Jeremy Thorpe Cleared of Murder Conspiracy

Jeremy Thorpe arrives at the Old Bailey with his wife, Marion

LEADER OF BRITAIN'S LIBERAL PARTY Jeremy Thorpe, exposed last year as a one-time latent homosexual, offered no defence to the charge that he and three others plotted to assassinate his accuser, male model Norman Scott. Instead, his counsel argued that the main prosecution witnesses – Scott himself, former Liberal MP Peter Bessell, and amateur hitman Andrew Newton – were so unreliable that the prosecution had not made its case. The jury concurred.

In 1960, young Scott stayed with Mr Thorpe at his mother's house and other places, receiving presents and affectionate letters from him. According to Scott, frequent homosexual acts – at that time illegal – took place. According to Thorpe this is untrue, although he confesses to homosexual leanings toward Scott.

Over the next 14 years whenever Scott's fortunes fluctuated he returned to Thorpe with appeals for money or help, always with the implicit threat that he might (through weakness rather than malice) expose their alleged relationship. The jury was asked what they made of the camp ending to a letter in which Thorpe (who nicknamed Scott "Bunny") promised help in the words, "Bunnies can and will go to France."

In the end, according to Peter Bessell, Thorpe urged him and Liberal party activist David Holmes to eliminate Scott. Through the agency of Cardiff club owner George Deakin, Andrew Newton was contacted, and in return for a promise of £10,000 agreed to make the "hit". He bungled it, however, shooting Scott's Great Dane dog, Rinka, on Exmoor in southwest England, but then failing to kill Scott because his gun jammed.

Despite this, part of his fee was delivered by carpet merchant John le Mesurier, an acquaintance of Holmes and Deakin. These last three men stood in the dock as Thorpe's co-conspirators.

In the event, Mr Bessell's off-colour business past made him an unreliable witness, and the flakiness of Scott and Newton made their uncorroborated testimony suspect. Conclusion: there was no case to answer.

Yet Mr Holmes, according to his counsel, would have pleaded guilty to a charge of conspiracy to frighten Scott. And Newton certainly drove Scott and Rinka to lonely Exmoor, where he killed the dog before driving away.

So, in the first murder charge ever brought against a major British political leader, we are still left asking – what happened?

Virginian Headmistress Harris Guilty of Homicide

DR HERMAN TARNOWER, author of *The Scarsdale Diet*, liked classy women, but he liked to treat 'em like broads, not like class. Sure, they could come on expensive holidays. Sure, he bought 'em expensive presents. But they always knew he was doing the same for other women.

Mrs Jean Harris, headmistress of classy Madeira School for Girls in Virginia, was Hy's main girlfriend for ten years.

But over the last three she became increasingly angered by his relationship with 12-years younger Lynne Tryforos; Mrs Harris was 44 in 1977.

On March 10 this year, she drove from Virginia to Scarsdale to have it out with Hy. She took a gun – to shoot herself, she says. When she found Lynne's clothes all over Hy's bathroom, Mrs Harris flew into a rage and pulled the gun. It went off, injuring Hy's hand, but classy Hy just said calmly, "Jesus, Jean! Look what you've done!" There was a short struggle, and the gun went off again. Twice.

Mrs Harris says she meant to kill herself. The jury, learning of a bullet in Hy's back, doubted it. She has been convicted of second-degree homicide.

Jean Harris about to be whisked away from court after hearing a "guilty" verdict from the jury

"Teddy Bear" Murder Gang Sent Down

HENRY MACKENNY, JOHN CHILDS and Terence Pinfold are hopeless robbers. Their 1978 attempt to rob a Security Express van ended when they ran away leaving both car and weapons behind. Their next attempt, in 1979, might have been a success, had an accomplice not left the keys of the getaway car in overalls at the scene of the crime, leading police straight to them.

However, as contract killers they were a success, with an extraordinary way of disposing of bodies. They took them to Childs' flat, covered the floors with polythene sheets, cut up the cadavers, and burnt the pieces in the tiny eighteen-inch grate.

They hit upon this idea in 1974 when they eliminated Pinfold's partner in the Teddy-Bear business, Terence Eve, earning themselves their nickname. They then made themselves available for contract killings, usually charging between £2000 and £4000. Between 1975 and 1980 they killed:

• George Brett, brother of a silver bullion robber

• Brett's ten-year-old son Terry, who impetuously jumped in the car for a ride with the strangers

• Robert Brown, a runaway convict who learned about Eve's murder

• Robert Sherwood, proprietor of a Herne Bay nursing home

• Ronald Andrews, whose wife was having an affair with MacKenny.

The gang have been given life sentences.

Peter Sutcliffe: The Yorkshire Ripper

Hard-Worked Police Unfairly Criticized in Yorkshire Ripper Case

Peter Sutcliffe, the Yorkshire Ripper

CLUES AND SUSPECTS

Sutcliffe emerged as a suspect under the following leads, only to be lost among thousands of others:

- Owner of a car with wheel and axle dimensions matching tyre-tracks left by the Ripper
  (First investigation –1 of 10,000 possible suspects. After linkage with NVR computer –1 of 2 million possible suspects!)
- Recipient in wage packet of new £5 note given to one victim
  First investigation –1 of 8,000 possible suspects (all interviewed within a few months). After sophisticated re-run of notes' issue techniques had been carried out –1 of 30 possible suspects; arrested before this re-investigation was complete.

GOOD OLD-FASHIONED police work ended the five-year terror of the Yorkshire Ripper. The cunning sex maniac avoided his favourite red light districts throughout 1979 and 1980, striking down five women in respectable residential areas.

However, in January 1981, when he returned to pick up a prostitute in Sheffield, the dogged Yorkshire police surveillance of working girls and, more importantly, their clients, paid off.

Sergeant Robert Ring recognized 24-year-old Olive Reivers as soon as he saw her with a man in a car down a dark lane. Olive had been cautioned for soliciting and had a forthcoming court appearance for a second offence, so the man's tale that he was "Peter Williams" out with his girlfriend cut little ice with the vigilant Sergeant Ring.

When the number plates on "Mr William's" car proved to be stolen, he confessed that he'd not wanted to be recognized kerb-crawling. His claim, "I'm bursting for a pee," won him a couple of minutes in the bushes, then it was back to the cells for an interrogation which soon had the local force calling in the Ripper Murder Squad.

The next morning, when Sergeant Ring reported for duty and found this petty thief still being questioned, he remembered that quick pee, and raced back to search among the bushes in Melbourne Lane. There he found a ball-pin hammer and sharp knife: the deadly trademark weapons with which, for five years, lorry-driver Peter Sutcliffe struck down women in Yorkshire and Lancashire, and mutilated their bodies.

The Yorkshire Ripper case was over.

Start of the Scare

Public anxiety began early in 1976, when prostitutes Wilma McCann, Barbara Booth and Emily Jackson were savagely murdered in Leeds. Detective Chief Superintendent Denis Hoban speculated that this was a man obsessed with wicked women: "Other women could be in danger," he advised the public - "not ordinary women in the street, but probably women who follow this way of life. Any street girls, models on the seamier side of Leeds, and the prostitutes who may know or suspect a client that may be this way inclined and violently opposed to their way of life, should come forward and see us."

In fact, just such an obsessive was Barbara Booth's murderer, a student with a bizarre mission to suppress girls who smoked and chewed gum in public! As is normal with such delusional killers, he was picked up quickly and made no denial of his crimes.

Meanwhile, the more sinister sadistic maniac Sutcliffe had already attacked and injured two perfectly respectable women, and in June 1977 would provoke the most extreme rage and panic by his murder of pretty 16-year-old shop assistant Jayne MacDonald on her way home after a night at a "bierkeller" disco.

Thirteen thousand people were interviewed in the aftermath of this murder. Nearly 4,000 written statements were taken, and 400 people seen near the playground where Jayne was killed were traced and interviewed within weeks.

But the sheer weight of evidence (*see* Box) handicapped police, and a cruel hoaxer misdirected the investigation for over a year .

The Hoax Tape

In June 1979, Assistant Chief Constable George Oldfield received an anonymous tape recording through the mail. "I'm Jack," a man's voice began. "I see you're having no luck catching me. I have the greatest respect for you, George, but Lord, you're no nearer catching me now than four years ago when I started."

Oldfield and the police have been criticized for letting this taunt dominate their investigation, but there were powerful forensic reasons for doing so. The tape was mailed from Sunderland by a man who also sent letters signed "Jack the Ripper". Initially dismissed as a hoax, these came to seem central clues in 1979 because:

An envelope from the hoaxer had been sealed with saliva from a blood group B secretor. This matched semen found in the orifices of Preston prostitute Joan Harrison, whose murder the hoaxer also claimed.

Light machine-oil traces on one of the envelopes exactly matched light machine-oil traces left by the Ripper on victim Jo Whittaker's body.

Highly original detective work was called into play. The tape was sent to brilliant dialectologist Stan Ellis at Leeds University. He reported that the speaker's accent came from Castleton, a small village near Sunderland.

Every man who lived in the village or who had grown up there was questioned. Yet each and every one of them had cast-iron alibis eliminating them from one or more of the murders. Alas, the misleading tape itself apparently exonerated Sutcliffe, who spoke with a Bradford accent.

The Ripper

When caught, the Ripper proved to be a good-looking, young lorry-driver, highly esteemed as a reliable workman by his employers. His Czech wife, Sonia, was unaware that he loved visiting sleazy red-light districts.

Formerly employed as a grave-digger, Sutcliffe claimed that God's voice, emanating from a grave, ordered him to kill prostitutes. This silly story, contradicted by the obviously sexual nature of his activities, did little to help his case. Compulsive he may be, rather than deluded, but nutty as a fruitcake given the nature of his compulsions.

Never fear, the Yorkshire Ripper, is locked up securely for life.

Victims: Left to right (top) Helen Rytka, Tina Atkinson, Jo Whittaker; (centre) Emily Jackson, Wilma McCann, Jean Jordan; (bottom) Irene Richardson, Yvonne Pearson, Jayne MacDonald

VICTIMS

1975
JULY • Annie Rogulskyj, waitress, Keighley. Severely injured.
AUGUST • Olive Smelt, office cleaner, Halifax. Severely injured.
OCTOBER • Wilma McCann, prostitute, Leeds. Murdered, mutilated.

1976
JANUARY • Emily Jackson, housewife/prostitute, Leeds. Murdered, mutilated.
MAY• Marcella Claxton, prostitute, Leeds. Severely injured.

1977
FEBRUARY• Irene Richardson, prostitute, Leeds. Murdered, mutilated.
APRIL• Tina Atkinson t/n Pat Mitra, prostitute, Bradford. Murdered and mutilated.
JUNE • Jayne MacDonald, shop assistant, Leeds. Murdered, mutilated.
JULY • Maureen Long, prostitute, Bradford. Mutilated, survived.
OCTOBER • Jean Jordan, prostitute, Manchester. Murdered October 1. Corpse mutilated October 9.
DECEMBER • Marilyn Moore, prostitute, Leeds. Battered, survived.

1978
JANUARY • Yvonne Pearson, prostitute, Bradford. Murdered and mutilated.
Helen Rytka, prostitute, Huddersfield. Raped, murdered and mutilated.
MAY • Vera Millward, prostitute, Manchester. Murdered, mutilated.

1979
APRIL • Jo Whittaker, office worker, Halifax. Murdered and mutilated.
SEPTEMBER • Barbara Leach, student, Bradford. Murdered and mutilated.

1980
AUGUST • Marguerite Walls, civil servant, Leeds. Strangled.
SEPTEMBER • Dr Uphaya Bandara, mature student, Leeds. Survived battery and strangling.
NOVEMBER • Jacqueline Hill, student, Leeds. Murdered, mutilated.

1981
JANUARY• Olive Reivers, prostitute, Sheffield. Saved by arrest, unassaulted.

1981

Australian Dingo Baby Mother Charged with Murder

LAST AUGUST the world was stunned to learn of the dingo that entered the Ayers Rock campsite in Australia and stole 1-year-old Azaria Chamberlain. Trackers recovered nothing save Azaria's bloodstained clothing. Hearts went out to her parents, Pastor Michael Chamberlain and his wife Lindy.

But soon evil rumours began to circulate: that Azaria was spastic, and her parents destroyed her rather than cope with her handicap; that the Chamberlains' Seventh Day Adventist Church demanded Azaria (a name meaning "Gift of God") as a human sacrifice.

(In fact, the Adventists' extraordinarily high standard of personal integrity is enviable. All who met Michael and Lindy Chamberlain were impressed by the strength and courage the couple drew from their religion.)

The local coroner did his best to quash this vile gossip, expressing the hope that anyone reopening the case might "rot in hell". Despite this, people who fear the extermination of dingoes in consequence of the baby's death, and others with a prejudice against minority religions, have forced the authorities to hold a second inquest.

Every single person who heard Lindy Chamberlain cry "The dingo has got my baby!" totally believes her story of seeing the wild dog backing out of the tent shaking its head to control something in its mouth. Not a camper from Ayers Rock doubts that the dingo stole the child.

But pathologist Professor James Cameron of the London Hospital flew out with two British colleagues to testify that Azaria's clothes show no traces of dingo saliva, and speculative experiments suggest that they were removed from the baby by human hand and not canine teeth. This evidence must be inconclusive, as Azaria's outermost garment, a matinée jacket, has not been recovered.

Even so, Lindy has been charged with murder and Michael as accessory, and these unfortunate parents go on trial next year.

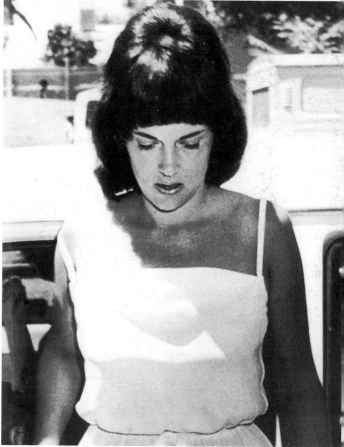

Mrs Lindy Chamberlain, charged with murdering her baby daughter

---

Castrated Child Killer Shot in Court by Mother

GERMAN CHILD-MOLESTER Klaus Grabowski submitted to castration in 1975 after he nearly strangled one of his victims, but then had himself treated with hormones and recovered his virility.

In May last year he lured 7-year-old Anna Bachmeier into his flat to play with his cat. There he strangled her with her tights. When police learnt that the convicted paedophile lived so near the missing child, they questioned Grabowski, who soon confessed and led them to the buried body.

But his trial this March was going his way, with prosecutors barred from asking why he had removed Anna's tights, and his story of little Anna's threatening to blackmail him receiving a sympathetic hearing. The judge was evidently taking a liberal and lenient line, viewing Grabowski as a penitent pervert, and the jury was not hearing enough about the accused's deliberate restoration of his sex drive.

As he looked likely to receive a light sentence for manslaughter, Frau Marie Anne Bachmeier, the little girl's mother, took matters into her own hands. In open court she shot the murderer dead, and calmly awaited her own arrest.

New York has its own 'Jack the Ripper'

HIGHLY INTELLIGENT, amoral and sadistic, that's how Blue Cross computer-operator Richard Cottingham struck the court, when he stood charged with the murder and assault of 19 New York women this May. Yet the arrogant amoralist remarked to one of his victims, "Prostitutes need to be punished," echoing Victorian Britain's infamous "Jack the Ripper" letter, whose author declared himself "down on whores".

Cottingham was traced through fingerprints found on the handcuffs he used to secure two of his teenage prostitute victims. Unsolved prostitute murders going back to 1979 were then traced to him. He has been sentenced to 197 years' imprisonment for 15 murders. Most shocking of all is that such a maniac should rampage through America's largest city without anyone even noticing his presence. Just how heartless can New Yorkers be about the precarious lives of its prostitutes?

> " **PROSTITUTES NEED TO BE PUNISHED.** "
>
>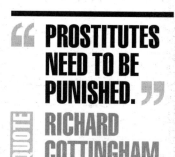
> QUOTE **RICHARD COTTINGHAM**

Atlanta Child Murders Stop after Suspect's Arrest

Wayne Williams

ATLANTA, GEORGIA has been terrorized by a serial murderer who has killed a black juvenile almost every month since 1979. All but two of this beast's victims were boys; the one victim to have been sexually assaulted was a little girl.

The black community nationwide has been stirred to fury, maintaining that:

1. The killer must be a white supremacist.

2. Atlanta police are not really concerned about murdered black children.

The first point is challenged by police, who note that the victims were abducted from black communities, where any suspicious white man would have been observed. The deduction is supported by the FBI Academy's Behavioural Sciences Unit, whose studies of habitual violent criminals show that sex maniacs almost invariably strike within their own racial group. These killings suggest the work of a black teenager commanding some respect from his victims.

The protestors' second point might well have been true originally, but with mounting nationwide campaigning and fear of riots was certainly invalid by this year. Senior detectives from all over the country have been pulled in to help, and President Reagan – hardly the black community's most sensitive friend – pledged $1.5 million of federal funding for the inquiry.

In July, two policemen patrolling a bridge over the Chattahoochee river at night heard a splash, and saw a man drive away in a station wagon. Another patrol stopped the vehicle before it could leave the bridge. The driver turned out to be 23-year-old Wayne Williams, an ambitious would-be photographer. When Williams denied stopping on the bridge, the officers advised him that he would be brought in for questioning if anything suspicious was found in the river; the body of 21-year-old murder victim Jimmy Payne had been found at the spot previously.

Two days later 27-year-old Nathaniel Cater's body was recovered from the Chattahoochee, and Williams was arrested. Dog hairs and carpet fibres found on ten of the child victims are identical to those in Williams' flat. The murders have stopped since his arrest. Although Williams has been charged with killing two adults, he is really on trial as the Atlanta child killer.

Dr Jay Smith (left), suspected of Satanism, bondage orgies and murder

'Prince of Darkness' was Satanic Head of Murder High School

ENGLISH TEACHER Bill Bradfield of Upper Merion High School, Pennsylvania, has been convicted of theft and deception, following the discovery that he was the beneficiary of $730,000 worth of insurance and the recipient of $25,000 of investments taken out by his deceased colleague Susan Reinert.

Everyone knows, however, that the authorities are preparing a murder case against Bradfield. Susan's body was found in her car in 1979, dead by asphyxiation. She had apparently been kept in chains before her death.

Deeply implicated in some way is school principal, Dr Jay Smith, who is believed to have conducted Satanic orgies. Chains matching abrasions on Susan's body were found in his cellar. His comb was found in Susan's car, and a brooch of Susan's was found in his car. Dr Smith is being held in custody for firearms, drugs and theft offences, but sooner or later it is expected he will be shown to have played a major part in killing Miss Reinert.

IN BRIEF

ARNFINN NESSET, manager of Orkdal Valley Nursing Home, Norway, arrested this March and charged with murdering 22 elderly patients between 1972 and last year by injecting curacit. His motive is unclear, though he has embezzled a small amount of patients' money (about £1200) which he passed on for Salvation Army and missionary work.

Enquiries at homes where Nesset worked in previous years suggest he may have killed 62 people!

Police load the body of one of the Atlanta child victims into a hearse

Irish Attorney-General Resigns after Pal is Arrested

Attorney-General Patrick Connolly (left) returns to Dublin to tender his resignation

AN UNEXPECTED crisis hit Taoiseach Charles Haughey's Fianna Fail government in Ireland when police arrested 36-year-old murderer Malcolm MacArthur – in the Attorney-General's private flat! To make matters worse, Attorney-General Patrick Connolly blandly flew off on a long- planned holiday in America!

Playboy MacArthur, who has dissipated an inheritance of £80,000, ran out of funds while junketing in Tenerife this July, and came back to Dublin determined to fill his pockets by armed robbery. The University of California graduate stayed with his old family friend Connolly, and went to historic Phoenix Park to steal a getaway car.

Bridie Gargan, a 25-year-old nurse, was sunning herself beside her Renault when the ham-fisted would-be crook forced her into the car with a dummy handgun and hit her over the head with a hammer. As he raced along in the Dublin traffic, an ambulance driver spotted the hospital sticker in his rear window, and assumed he was a doctor taking a sick patient to hospital. With its siren blaring and lights flashing the ambulance cleared a path for him through the crowded streets to St James's Hospital. On arrival MacArthur whizzed in at the vehicle entrance and whizzed straight out again at the exit! Two miles away he abandoned the car and Miss Gargan, who died in hospital four days later.

Despite Mr Haughey's instant despatch of a private jet to fetch the errant Attorney-General back from America, and his immediate acceptance of the impolitic Mr Connolly's resignation, the indiscretion contributed to Fianna Fail's loss of the autumn election.

Wife Picked Paraquat for Poison Pie

IT GIVES A WOMAN a nasty turn if her husband comes home unexpectedly to find her curled up in the arms of his best friend. It's still more startling if your lover races down your garden path, vaults the gate and pelts off along the street stark naked. And it puts your marriage at risk if your husband then gives you a beating. So thought Essex girl Susan Barber (28) when husband Michael surprised her in bed with Richard Collins in May last year. But Susan was not to be put off her stroke! With Michael at work the next afternoon, she called in Richard for another love session.

Afterwards they went down to the garden shed and collected some Gramoxone, a weedkiller

containing the deadly poisonous paraquat. Now paraquat tastes disgusting, but Susan still managed to make a really tasty meat pie with just enough paraquat to kill Michael slowly.

After an illness which seemed much like pneumonia, Michael died in hospital. Nobody suspected a thing: the cause of death was said to be Goodpasture's Syndrome, a condition much rarer than the common cold but perfectly natural. One pathologist dissented: he reckoned the body showed traces of paraquat. He sent samples from Michael's digestive tract to the National Poisons Unit for analysis. Back came the reply – nothing untoward to report. Dr David Evans was mystified. It looked as though

Poisoner Susan Barber partying with one of her lovers after the death of her husband

the widow had got away with murder.

Richard didn't last long in Susan's bed, though. Soon she was broadcasting for lovers on CB radio. Her call sign was "Nympho' – and she wasn't exaggerating!

Her casual lovers on one-night stands were taken aback to find that Susan's idea of a good time included calling up a stranger on CB

to listen to their love-making.

The fun stopped this year. Dr Evans followed up the case and discovered that someone at the poisons lab had just lost the first set of the victim's samples and sent back the negative report! Now it's been proved that Michael ate paraquat pie. Susan's got a lifetime in prison, and Richard's earned a couple of years in jail for helping her.

Doping Tourists in India

FRENCH VIETNAMESE supercrook Hotchand Bhawanni Gurmukh Sobrajh – but just call him Charles – preys off tourists and drug buyers in the Far East. He dopes tourists and steals their money and papers. He buys, sells and steals drugs. He's not averse to jewel theft either. And if people get in his way, they're liable to end up dead!

This noxious 38-year-old representative of the "me generation" carried his "good old-fashioned greed" too far in Delhi this year when he met a party of French tourists in the Bikram Hotel. The suave Paris-educated con-man warned them of the horrors of dysentery, and generously distributed medicine among them.

Only Charles's medicine was a sedative, aimed to k.o. the lot of them while he rifled through their luggage. Unhappily for him, he got the dosage wrong. They fell ill, and with 20 French tourists collapsing all over the hotel lounge, Sobrajh found himself under arrest.

For two of his past murders in India he's received seven years' hard labour and life. Now eight other countries want a shot at putting this lethal smoothy on trial!

Digging up one of Sobrajh's victims in Thailand

Charles Sobrajh under arrest in Delhi

Ginger, You're Barmy! We Say to Murderer

HORRIBLE JOHN "Ginger" Bowden, a 26-year-old drunk from Camberwell, London, has a record as long as your arm for robbery, assault, blackmail and wounding. At liberty, for a change, over the last couple of years, he and his mates Michael Ward and David Begley took to preying on lonely old people and down-and-outs.

This January they struck up acquaintance with former amateur boxing champion Donald Ryan. They took him back to Mrs Shirley Brindle's council flat in Camberwell and there felled him with a machete, dropped him in a scalding bath, and cut him into pieces with an electric carving knife.

After the loathsome Bowden had a good giggle at the murdered man's head, they scattered parts of him around waste ground and then put the head in a dustbin before going back to sleep among the blood and residual gore.

On receiving a minimum 25-year sentence, Bowden yelled at the judge, "You old bastard! I hope you die screaming of cancer!" His lordship was too polite to return the compliment, so we'll do it for him: "Same to you, Ginger."

> " YOU OLD BASTARD! I HOPE YOU DIE SCREAMING OF CANCER! "
> QUOTE JOHN BOWDEN

Berserk Police Killer Shoots Himself in a Hide

FOR 17 DAYS in June and July 38-year-old Barry Prudom ran amok in northern England. In Doncaster, he shot PC David Haigh who stopped him for a traffic check. Haigh's notebook recorded his car number, so police knew who they were looking for.

In Girton, Lincolnshire, he shot George Luckett dead and severely injured his wife, making off in their car to north Yorkshire where he injured PC Kenneth Oliver.

In Old Malton he shot Sgt David Winter three times at point-blank range, after thinking, "I'll have this bugger".

In Malton he held elderly Mr and Mrs Maurice Johnson and their son Brian hostage for a couple of days. He established amicable relations with them, and even described his previous murders.

On July 4 he retreated to a hide outside the Johnson's house. There he shot himself after police had surrounded it and opened up with stun grenades, rifle and shotgun fire. And nobody knows why he did it all.

IN BRIEF

WAYNE WILLIAMS convicted of two murders. The complete cessation of Atlanta child killings since his arrest convinces police he was also responsible for them.

1983

West Coast Hillside Strangler Convicted — by an Eyelash

I'S TAKEN FIVE YEARS, but at last both the "hillside stranglers", who tortured, raped and murdered nine Californian women and girls in 1977, and a tenth the following year, have been convicted.

Judge Ronald George, who refused to allow prosecutors to drop charges against Angelo Buono (47) two years ago, was accused of conducting a "judical extravaganza". But the mothers of 15-year-old Judith Miller, 14-year-old Sonja Johnson and 12-year-old Dolores Cepeda – all bound, raped, sodomized, strangled, and left naked in lewd postures on parkland – will not feel the millions of dollars, nor the time of 400 witnesses in the USA's longest criminal trial has been wasted. Buono goes to life imprisonment without the possibility of parole.

The trial of Buono's cousin and accomplice, Kenneth Bianchi (31), was equally odd. Bianchi spent 1975-78 with upholsterer Buono, a beer-swilling slob who entertained prostitutes in his grungy Los Angeles home. When, in 1977, they started their killing spree with a prostitute, Bianchi's fastidiousness came into play, and the naked body was carefully washed before being obscenely exposed on a hillside.

Eight killings later, Bianchi moved to Bellingham, Washington. When he killed two young women in Bellingham, he was quickly identified as the last person seen with one, and LA police suspicions of him in the Hillside stranglings were revealed.

But Bianchi claimed to suffer form split personality, asserting that his alter ego "Steve" committed crimes, which central personality Ken deplored. Several psychologists supported this claim, and only later was its fraudulence exposed.

Bianchi feared Washington state's death penalty by hanging, and wished to serve his imprisonment in California's more comfortable jails. So when guaranteed

Confessed "hillside strangler" Kenneth Bianchi testifies in a Los Angeles hearing against his accomplice, cousin Angelo Buono

immunity from a capital conviction, he pleaded guilty to the Bellingham killings; then proceeded south to testify against Buono.

Buono's conviction proved difficult because, reversing character, he scoured his filthy house before forensic teams examined it. Not a trace remained of the blood and semen that had once stained the premises. Or the dead girls' belongings. Except... a single eyelash! Just one eyelash, identifiably belonging to one victim remained in the house. And that sent Buono to prison for life.

While Bianchi, to his disgust, (and the public's satisfaction) has been returned from warm California to cold Washington.

Woman Shampooed to Death and then Walled Up

LONG-DISTANCE lorry-driver Luigi Longhi has the weirdest sexual fetish. He becomes aroused shampooing women's hair! In May 1981, Longhi picked up hitch-hiker Heike Freiheit in Germany, and persuaded her to come to his Padborg apartment for a jolly good shampoo. It proved so satisfying that both fell asleep after the foamy climax. But Heike awoke to find herself tied up and gagged, with Longhi lustfully lathering her again.

When he ran out of shampoo, he rubbed her scalp with cottage cheese, honey and salad dressing. When she drummed her feet on the floor to summon help, he strangled her and stuffed her in a space behind the wall, where a workman repairing the roof found her this year.

Longhi has been sent to indefinite psychiatric confinement.

Blocked Drains at London Flat Give Away Killer

The kitchen of the top floor flat, 23 Cranley Gardens

THE DRAIN-CLEARER called to 23 Cranley gardens, Muswell Hill, London, this February didn't care for the job. The outside underground pipe was clogged with meat. And somehow... it seemed... almost human. Still, knocking-off time was approaching, and he went home shelving his worries for the night.

Next day, almost all the meat was gone! But a little bit remaining seemed to be a definite finger. Police learned from other tenants that the occupant of the top-floor flat, 37-year-old Job Centre clerk

Dennis Nilsen, had been up and down all night, flushing loos and prodding around in the drain.

When Nilsen got home from work he didn't beat about the bush. He showed detectives human remains bagged in polythene in his flat. He showed them the big saucepan in which he cooked himself curries – when it wasn't in use for boiling down his victims' heads!

He confessed to 15 murders, both in Muswell Hill and at his previous flat in Willesden.

Nilsen, a homosexual, drew his victims from the grey netherworld of runaways and drifters. He picked them up in pubs; invited them home for more drinks; and strangled them with ties, often preserving the bodies for a few days and even sketching them.

One-Eyed Matricide Hillbilly Confesses to Texas Murders

Henry Lee Lucas: multiple murderer

SQUALID, SMELLY little Henry Lee Lucas (46) has only been arrested for two murders in Stoneburg, Texas. But, with his grubby confederate, Floridian Ottis Toole, he just may be the biggest multiple murderer ever!

Early this year, 83-year-old Mrs Kate Rich of Stoneburg disappeared. The friendly widow had no enemies and little worth stealing. Her only shady acquaintance was Henry Lee Lucas who once worked a couple of days for her, with his young common-law wife Becky.

Lucas amiably insisted he knew nothing about Mrs Rich's disappearance. Nor, it seemed, about Becky's! Snake-handling Pastor Moore swore to Henry's good character, and supported his story that Becky had left him. But when police checked Lucas on the national crime computer, they found a record as long as your arm, including autotheft, sexual assault and – wait for it – matricide! This man spent seven years in prison for killing his prostitute mother!

Under pressure, Henry at last confessed to killing Becky (and ravishing her body) when she wanted to leave him; killing Mrs Rich (and ravishing her body) because he felt like it. He proved this by taking police to the crime-sites. But now he is confessing to more and more rapes and murders, often in association with Becky's uncle, Ottis Toole. And police all over the country are sending in reports of unsolved crimes which they hope this horrible little man may clear up.

Alaskan Baker Hunted Down Live Women

ROBERT HANSEN IS AN acne-pitted runt, and no great lover. The Alaskan baker is, however, a distinguished hunter, holding records for shooting wild sheep with bow and arrow. But it seems he's shot rarer game with his trusty rifle – women!

For the last ten years, Anchorage police have noticed a high disappearance rate among the hookers of their sleazy strip. But it wasn't till hunters started turning up bodies in graves along the Knik River that Police started to suspect a serial killer. One with a plane to transport his victims into the outback.

Early this year a hooker came forward with a story that pinpointed Hansen. He'd picked her up with the offer of $300 for oral sex; took her to his home where he tied her up, raped, tortured, and threatened to kill her. Then he drove her to the airfield where she escaped as he tried to board her on his plane. Her story backed up the complaint of a stripper who had run naked through the streets to escape Hansen who, she was sure, intended to murder her.

After breaking Hansen's alibi, supplied by a businessman who believes that whores are dispensable, police now hold him responsible for 17 slayings over the last 10 years.

IN BRIEF

THIRTY-TWO Red Brigades terrorists convicted in Italy for croimes including the murder of Aldo Moro (see 1978). Prosper Gallinari (33) is named as Sr Moro's executioner.

BILL BRADFIELD convicted of murdering Susan (see 1981), and also her two children, who disappeared at the same time and have never been traced.

Gay slave boy batters top people's S-M gal pal

THE MURDER OF beautiful model Vicki Morgan by her homosexual lodger Marvin Pancoast has unleashed a flood of gossip and innuendo around the White House. It appears that Ms Morgan was the sado-masochistic playmate of President Reagan's friend and kitchen cabinet member, the late department store millionaire Alfred Bloomingdale.

"Trustworthy and distinguished citizen" Bloomingdale joined the presidential Foreign Policy Advisory Committee. Ms Morgan's $10 million "palimony" claim in 1982 shows that she thought Bloomingdale's "trustworthiness" lay in giving her a monthly allowance of $18,000, in return for which she serviced his "distinguished" appetite for "flog-and-snog" orgies.

The courts cut Vicki's claim down to size, and never questioned the lots of naughtiness that she and Bloomingdale got up to before his death.

Pancoast was being evicted from Vicki's house for failing to pay his rent, though his statement, "I was tired of being her slave boy," might suggest that he too was dragged into kinky games – and didn't like them. Anyway, he beat her to death with a baseball bat as she slept.

Most people couldn't care less about this homosexual drifter's wayward crimes. They're more interested in the videotape his attorney, Robert Steinberg, says Pancoast owned. This supposedly shows Vicki and Bloomingdale playing very naughty games with very distinguished people.

But Steinburg says the tape is lost, and his client goes down for 26 years to life.

> **" I WAS TIRED OF BEING HER SLAVE BOY. "**
>
> QUOTE **MARVIN PANCOAST**

Vicki Morgan, pervert's partner and murder victim

Marvin Pancoast, murderer

Alfred Bloomingdale, millionaire pervert

Sexy Surrogate Mum Shoots her own Kids

POSTWOMAN, 29-year-old Diane Downs made headlines as one of America's first "surrogate mothers", letting a childless husband impregnate her and carrying his child with the approval of his wife.

Fellow workers in Arizona knew her as an insatiable lady, who slept with any good-looking man she could. When Lew Lewiston decided that an affair with Diane was too demanding, and concentrated on putting his marriage straight, Diane moved to Oregon, hoping absence would make the heart grow fonder.

When it didn't, she decided that her children, Dannie (3) Cheryl (7) and Christie (8), were the real obstacle to her commanding Lew's love. So she shot them, shot herself in the arm, and then drove to hospital with a story of a "shaggy-haired gunman" who had attacked the whole family.

Christie and Danny survived Diane's best efforts to kill them, and under patient and supportive questioning by sympathetic officials revealed that there had been no gunman, just their own dear mom who had done the shooting. The judge who sentenced Diane hopes she will never be released.

MP Links Rose-Grower's Murder to *Belgrano* Scandal

LABOUR MP Tam Dalyell wants Mrs Thatcher's government to come clean about the sinking of the Argentinian battleship *Belgrano* when it steamed away from the "exclusion zone" around the Falklands during the conflict in the South Atlantic. He believes a puzzling murder in Shropshire holds a vital clue.

Seventy-eight-year-old Miss Hilda Murrell was one of the country's leading rose-growers. On March 21, when she returned to her country cottage after shopping in nearby Shrewsbury, an intruder seized her, forced her into her own car, and drove her seven miles to a copse, where she was stabbed and left to die.

No valuables were stolen from Miss Murrell's house. Police assume that she disturbed a burglar before he found anything worth taking. But Mr Dalyell says her papers had been rifled, and a manuscript she was composing had disappeared.

He notes that Miss Murrell's nephew was a naval intelligence officer at the time the *Belgrano* was sunk, and believes that he may have given his aunt information which would expose the government's lies to Parliament and the public.

Mr Dalyell and the police are in agreement on one thing. Both believe Miss Murrell interrupted a break-in, and was overpowered and driven out to the country where the panic-stricken intruder stabbed her. Only the police think the burglary was just "Bill Sikes" looking for swag, and Mr Dalyell thinks the burglars were government agents.

He's not alone in suspecting this. Anti-nuclear campaigners believe that her missing article, ex-

Hilda Murrell, murder victim

posing the inefficiency and danger of the proposed Sizewell B nuclear reactor, proves that Secret Servicemen acted to silence a critic of the nuclear energy policy by which the government sets such store.

Police are anxious to interview a man wearing a dark suit and trainers who was seen jogging away from the place where Mrs Murrell's body was found.

While sensible observers agree that the police conclusions are far more persuasive than conspiracy theories, they concede that the hectoring and priggish stridency and inflexibility of Thatcherism on almost any issue invites paranoid

RC Hippie Found Dead: Black Lover Suspected

SLEEPY GULFPORT, NEAR St Petersburg, Florida, was awakened in the middle of a hot autumn night by a terrified woman's scream. Only one, though, so most people went back to sleep.

Young married neighbourhood watch leader George Lewis, however, happened to be out in his garage working on his car. He looked out, up and down the street, seeing nothing suspicious except a long-haired bearded man hurrying away from the house diagonally across from Lewis's.

That house belonged to black postgraduate student David McKay.

But with David away at a conference in New England, and nothing seeming untoward about his darkened house, Lewis paid no more attention.

Which is a pity. For a day later, McKay's attractive, slightly older white girlfriend Karen Gregory was found assaulted and stabbed inside the house. Seen by her conventional Roman Catholic family as "the last of the hippies", Karen at nearly 30 was just settling her life down and starting a serious job under David's stabilizing influence. Indeed, she had been moving her things into his apartment, where she was about to take up residence,

when her murderer found her.

Despite his obvious good influence on her, David became prime suspect when the body was discovered. Gulfport police laboriously worked out just-possible air connections that might have raced him from New England and back to commit the crime.

But David passed a lie-detector test with flying colours, and is in the clear. Gulfport police have egg on their faces, as promising fingerprints in the house were all left by investigating officers. Only a smudgy footprint in blood holds hope of solving this crime.

Racist Neo-Nazi Fascists Shoot Talk-Show Host

DENVER TALK-SHOW HOST Alan Berg's station promoted him as "the man you love to hate", but they never imagined that uttering controversial opinions on the airwaves merited death: Berg was cut down by a hail of gunfire as he stepped from his car this June.

Berg's possible enemies, it was suggested, ranged from Libya's Colonel Gaddaffi to the KKK. But in October, FBI agents raiding a cache of arms in Idaho came across a machine-pistol which had fired the bullets into Berg.

The group hiding the arsenal was a neo-Nazi organization styling itself the Bruders Schweigen (Silent Brotherhood).

In a December shoot-out with police, their leader, Robert Jay Matthews, was killed. Their "assassination squads" targeted liberals, Jews and homosexuals. Eleven of the fascists face indictment next year for a range of offences, including Berg's murder.

IN BRIEF

WEARING PINK PYJAMAS for her execution, Mrs Velma Barfield received a lethal injection at Central Prison, Raleigh, North Carolina on November 2. Six years of appeals ended when the courts agreed she had poisoned tobacco farmer Stuart Taylor after diverting to herself his inheritance from former employers, whom she also poisoned.

1985

White House Farm Murderer not Mad Model 'Bambi' After All

IN AUGUST, English papers reported that ex-model Sheila "Bambi" Caffell went berserk and slaughtered her adoptive parents and twin boys at the White House Farm, Tolleshunt d'Arcy in Essex. Police were called before dawn by Sheila's distraught brother Jeremy with the news that his father, Nevill Bamber (61), had telephoned saying something was very wrong.

When the police broke in, they found Nevill's body in the kitchen, shot in the face and neck amid signs of a terrific struggle. Upstairs the 6-year-old twins had been shot in bed, as had Mrs June Bamber. Beside her on the floor lay "Bambi", clutched in her hand the .22 semi-automatic rifle which had wrought all this carnage and finally shot her twice in the throat.

Jeremy told of his sister's persistent mental disorders. He was sick on the spot when officers said what they had found. His evident grief spoke for itself, so it came as a shock when two months later he was arrested for the murders.

Nevill's nephew David Boutflour never thought "Bambi" could have done it. She was too small to have battered her father down before shooting him. Two discoveries convinced David that the police had missed vital evidence.

> A forced lavatory window disproved the theory that the mayhem was the work of someone living in the house.
>
> The rifle's silencer was found, wiped and put away in the cupboard downstairs where it belonged.

They reopened the investigation when Jeremy's girlfriend, Julie Mugford, went to the police with her story after a quarrel with him. She claimed that Jeremy, though given a small farm of his own by his father, yearned to inherit the large White House Farm and live extravagantly; that he had made various plans to destroy his family

– which she took to be jocular fantasies – until the murders actually took place; and that he envied "Bambi" the flat in London Nevill had given her. Forensic scientists have now established that "Bambi" was shot twice, first with the silencer on the rifle then with it off. Since she could not have shot herself, taken the silencer downstairs, returned to the bedroom and shot herself again, Jeremy finds himself arrested and awaiting trial for appalling murders he still denies.

Jeremy Bamber and girlfriend Julie Mugford at the funeral of the family he murdered

The murder weapon with tell-tale silencer

Satanic 'Acid King' Killer Hangs Himself

RICKY KASSO, 17-year-old "Acid King" of Northport, New York, got his kicks from drug abuse and satanism. The two mixed badly when young Gary Lauwers fell into his hands on June 16 last year. Kasso had long suspected Lauwers of stealing "angel dust" from his pocket, and beaten him up for this on several occasions. But on June 16, the two boys seemed friendly again as they left a party to go into the woods and take some mescaline.

Somehow the quarrel revived, and in a drugged frenzy Kasso stabbed Lauwers repeatedly, screaming, "Say you love Satan!" and explaining to horrified companions "He's gotta say he loves Satan."

Gary's body was found on July 4. It took a year to assemble enough evidence to arrest Kasso, who declared he would kill himself if ever he were incarcerated – and he did. On July 6 this year, the "Acid King" was found hanging in his cell.

 **SAY YOU LOVE SATAN!**
RICKY KASSO

104

Policeman Stabbed to Death, but Killer Walks Free

BRITISH JURIES do not take kindly to policemen dressed as terrorists invading private property without a warrant, as the officers investigating the missing Brinks-Matt bullion discovered this January.

Deeply suspected of receiving stolen ingots was businessman Kenneth Noye, whose house in Kent was used by special forces during the war and is believed to contain underground bunkers.

Mr Noye does not welcome visitors. His locked gates open only to people who identify themselves before closed-circuit television cameras. Rotweiller dogs roam the grounds. Keen to inspect this suspect territory, Detective-Constable John Fordham and Detective-Sergeant Neil Murphy spearheaded a covert police operation. Dressed in camouflage jackets with balaclava helmets covering their faces save for sinister eye-holes, the pair went in over the wall.

The operation went wrong at once as the dogs noisily discovered them. Murphy signalled on his radio that the break-in was compromised, and made his way out. Fordham stood still to prevent the dogs attacking him, and was on the premises when Mr Noye came to investigate the brouhaha, carrying an electric torch and a kitchen knife. With him were his wife and a friend, both armed. As a result of the encounter, DC Fordham was stabbed to death.

The police assumed they had a straightforward case of murder by a suspect evading arrest. The jury, noting that the policemen were illicitly on private property, were impressed by a photograph of a man standing in shrubbery dressed in the gear worn by Fordham and illuminated by a torch. Such a sinister figure, they felt, might unnerve the toughest householder. Any unguarded move by such an intruder would certainly justify a quick and violent response. If the responding householder was carrying a weapon – well, the intruding policeman just asked for all he received! The killing of DC Fordham goes down in the records as an accident.

Victim of his own daring: Detective-Constable John Fordham

Murdering Canadian Minister's Appeal Refused

COLIN THATCHER, Minister of Energy and Mines in Saskatchewan, was a blustering bully. In 1981 his wife Jo Ann divorced him, winning the largest settlement ever awarded by a Canadian court.

Just over a year after these proceedings, a mysterious attempt to murder Mrs Thatcher occurred. Somebody fired a shot through her window in Regina, hitting her in the shoulder.

In January 1983, somebody finished the job off, bludgeoning Jo Ann down in her garage and then shooting her through the head. This same somebody dropped a credit-card slip signed Colin Thatcher.

Incredibly, such was the former minister's political power that it was not until last October that he stood trial. His bluster did little to impress the court, though, and he was convicted. His blustering appeal failed this May, and so he will remain in prison for life.

IN BRIEF

Entrepreneur Eliminates Family to Escape Disinheritance

STEVE BENSON'S Florida businesses always failed. Not that it mattered: his adoring mother, Margaret, poured out money from the family's tobacco fortune to keep him going. But when she learned that Steve (34) had transferred $325,000 from the businesses to buy himself a house, she told him she was cutting him out of her will.

On July 9, the police in Naple, Florida, were called to investigate a massive explosion outside the Benson mansion. They found Steve sitting in a state of shock beside the smoking remains of Margaret's car, and the remains of Margaret, Steven's sister Carol Lynn Kendall, and her son Scott. Inside the car experts found remains of two pipe bombs, with Steven's palm-prints on one of them. He goes on trial for murder next year.

An emotional Steve Benson in court

1986

London's Railway Rapist Caught after Terrorizing 26

AFTER A PUBLIC APPEAL in May and June for information about missing TV company secretary Anne Lock, a man has been arrested and charged with her murder, and the rape-murders of Alison Day and Maartje Tamboezer, and some 26 rapes committed around London since 1982.

Short, spotty John Duffy was a railway carpenter. One of the first clues to uncovering this persistent rapist was the fact that he always struck close to railway stations. Deduction? For some reason – probably connected with his work – he knew their layouts and the secluded lanes behind them where he trapped his victims.

He nearly always tied his victims' hands behind their backs – fingers straight, thumbs aligned, in a "praying" position. He also used a type of brown string manufactured from paper which was almost exclusively used by British Rail.

The rapist also combed the pubic hair of his victims after assaulting them, and used tissues to wipe his semen from their vulvas. This was clearly a cunning man, who was trying to destroy tell-tale biological evidence that could lead to his conviction. In his murders he similarly tried to destroy vital clues: for example, by throwing Alison Day's body in the River Lee, and stuffing tissues into Maartje Tamboezer and Ann Lock's vaginas which he then ignited.

Despite these extreme measures, his semen has been identified on Maartje Tamboezer, and fibres from his clothing have been found on Alison Day's waterlogged sheepskin jacket.

Suzy Lamplugh, the missing estate agent's negotiator

DON'T START THE HUNT TOO SOON!

Police started a "missing persons" investigation unusually early on Suzie Lamplugh. Their reasons for caution when young women go missing were well illustrated over the first weekend of the hunt.

Another young lady was reported missing, and the press linked this story with Suzie's disappearance. Her name was headlined all over the country – to her extreme embarrassment when she surfaced from a naughty weekend on Monday morning, and had to confess that she and her lover had not emerged from the bedcovers to look at newspapers or television news for the whole time she was desperately being sought!

London Police Fear Missing Estate Agent is Dead

THERE NOW SEEMS LITTLE HOPE that 25-year-old Susannah Lamplugh, the estate agent's negotiator who disappeared from her work on July 28, is alive.

Pretty yuppie Suzie left Sturgis Estate Agents in Fulham Road at lunchtime, taking the keys of 37 Shorrolds Road with her; she apparently intended to show a client, named on her jotter as "Mr Kipper", round this property.

When she had not returned from the address late in the afternoon, police were informed. They quickly recognized that Suzie was not the type to run away and disappear for private reasons; and her handbag, left on her desk, seemed mute evidence that she intended to return. A massive search was immediately launched.

Ms Lamplugh's car was discovered parked in Stevenage Road – a mile away from Shorrolds Road and in the wrong direction from her office. Witnesses declared they had seen her in her car or with a man – possibly carrying a bottle of champagne.

All leads were followed, but even a police visit to Belgium to investigate a Mr Kuyper whose abandoned car was found in London proved fruitless. There can, alas, be little doubt that the unfortunate Susannah Lamplugh has been kidnapped and killed.

Man Goes on Trial for Murdering Nicola and Karen

FOR ONE OCTOBER night and a day, police and citizens of Brighton, England, searched Wild Park for missing children Karen Hadaway (10) and Nicola Fellows (9). When they were found, in a "hide" among thick undergrowth, both had been strangled and partially undressed; Nicola had also been raped.

An important clue proved to be a man's sweatshirt abandoned close to the murder site. Its owner, 20-year-old Russell Bishop, joined searchers with his dog on October

10, and was the second person on the scene when Matthew Marchant found the bodies.

Thereafter, Bishop described accurately the positions in which Karen and Nicola lay, although both Mr Marchant and Police Sergeant "Smudger" Smith who had urged Bishop to hurry across and see what Marchant had found, confirmed that he never went close enough to the overgrown hide to be able to see more than a flash of bright clothing. Bishop goes on trial next year.

Jet Set Rent Boy was Rough Trade Killer

MICHELE DE MARCO LUPO is London's leading sadistic rent boy. You wanna be flogged by a man in a mask? He's your guy. He'll flog men, women – anyone, for high prices. Wealthy international masochist swingers pay his expenses and more to have him fly the Atlantic and lash their eager little bottoms.

But simple binding and beating does not fully satisfy him – sexy gay Michele wants to go further than

commerce or the law allows.

He did so with railwayman James Burns, strangled in a derelict house in Warwick Road on March 16. He did so with James Connolly, strangled in a Kennington railway shed on April 3. He did so with IRA suspect Damien McClusky, strangled in an empty basement in Cromwell Road. He did so with an unknown tramp, encountered on Hungerford footbridge and strangled. But David Cole, picked up at Nine Elms, and destined to be Lupo's next victim, got away. He led police officers investigating the Burns and Connolly cases around gay bars till he spotted Lupo.

Lupo confessed at once, and told a great deal more into the bargain. How he loves sinking his teeth into the bottoms of his corpses. This particular little habit will undoubtedly lead to his conviction when he goes on trial next year.

IN BRIEF

Police comb the site of the murders

Wild Park, with footpaths running to the murder hideout

Miss Whiplash Found, Bound and Drowned in Bath

MRS CHRISTINE OFFORD was a specialist prostitute. Calling herself "Miss Whiplash", the 35-year-old ran a "torture dungeon" in Queens Gate, London. There punters could be tied up and gagged and flogged and have clips put on their nipples, and endure all the other extraordinary procedures that masochists enjoy undergoing at the hands of booted and corseted young ladies.

For her private and personal pleasure at her £100,000 home in Hounslow, however, Miss Whiplash much preferred caressing and making love to other women. Fellow prostitute Margaret Dunbar (29) was Mrs Offord's main lover and she was not pleased when Christine ended their lesbian liaison of several years last year.

Margaret decided to hire Robert Casaubon-Vincent and Barry Parson

of West Sussex to "rough up" her lover, and so bring her back into line

These two toughs went way over the top. They tied up Miss Whiplash, then threw her in the bath at her Queens Gate home before crushing her throat with one of the iron bars in her dungeon.

It was all most unfortunate, according to the women's friend, Mrs Pamela Shaw – at least as far as Margaret was concerned. "It happened when she was high on drink and drugs and she only intended slight harm," she assured the court.

Nevertheless Miss Dunbar has been sent down for seven years along with her hired thugs.

Berserk Gunman Rampages Through Quiet English Town

THE SLEEPY BERKSHIRE TOWN of Hungerford will never forget August 19. On that warm summer afternoon, 27-year-old Michael Ryan charged along its streets shooting at all and sundry with a Beretta pistol, a carbine, and a Kalashnikov automatic rifle.

Ryan, a bachelor loner who lived with his mother and was obsessed with guns, started his carnage with an attack on pretty housewife Susan Godfrey, who had taken her children for a picnic in Savernake Wood. Dressed in combat fatigues and armed to the teeth, Ryan strapped her children in her car before making her walk into the woods with a groundsheet. Why he then killed her, only he knew. The probability is that he tried to rape her and lost his temper when she resisted.

On his way back to Hungerford he shot up a service station. Then, on the streets of his home town, he shot dead 13 people, critically injured two more; and wounded a further 11. His mother and several close neighbours were among the dead. Another neighbour, 77-year-old Mrs Dorothy Smith, survived. Ryan fired at her and missed after she shouted at him, "Is that you making all that noise? You're frightening everybody to death. Stop it!" The resolute old lady spat back at his retaliatory fire with, "You stupid bugger!"

A policeman in a patrol car

Police marksmen join the hunt in Hungerford for rampaging gunman Michael Ryan

managed to radio for help before being killed. Ryan ultimately shot himself after holing up for an hour in John O'Gaunt School and negotiating with encircling police.

Home Secretary Douglas Hurd was as shocked as the public to learn that Ryan's gun licence covered his entire armoury – including the military Kalashnikov. New laws are promised to keep such instruments of death out of irresponsible private hands.

Smoke pouring from the house Ryan shared with his mother. He set fire to it after murdering her

Diane Downs Escapes for a Naughty Weekend

MURDERING MOTHER Diane Downs escaped from Oregon Women's Correctional Center this July after her appeal was turned down.

Good-looking Diane's impenitent ruthlessness, and total inability to accept responsibility for her actions, make her an extremely dangerous woman. Authorities feared that she might have engineered her escape in order to seek out and injure crime historian Ann Rule, whose excellent book *Small Sacrifices*, published this year, exposes Diane's wickedness.

There was also the danger that she might seek out her surviving children, Christie and Danny, now happily adopted by the lawyer who prosecuted her.

All were given police protection in safe places until, 11 days later, the escaped murderess was traced to a nearby house where she had set up with temporary boyfriend Wayne Sheifer and three of his men friends.

Diane issued statements about the reason for her escape, giving as her main motive the wish to look for her daughter Cheryl's "real" killer. She undoubtedly acted from a normal desire for freedom; a normal need for a male lover; and an abnormal love of notoriety.

Baroness's Blind Ex Battered

RETIRED ARCHITECT SIMON DALE WAS found brutally battered to death this September in the kitchen of his mansion in the heart of Shropshire, Heath House. Dale, who was nearly blind and becoming increasingly eccentric, had lived alone there for 14 years, ever since he and his wife Susan were divorced in 1973. In recent years he came to believe that Heath House was the true seat of the legendary King Arthur, and excavations in the house and grounds would unearth the Round Table.

His murderer failed to turn off the oven before leaving the house, so, when Dale's body was discovered two days later, his intended supper of toad-in-the-hole cooked to a cinder.

Police suspicions have turned to his ex-wife Susan, a great- grand-daughter of slave-liberator William Wilberforce, and now the ex-wife of Baron Michael de Stempel, a German with an obscure Baltic title, whom she married in 1984. He, however, refused to consummate the marriage and, after an attempt to have it annulled, the pair divorced in 1986. Baron de Stempel alleged that his wife had forced him to live in a tent in the garden of their home.

With all her capital tied up in Heath House, which she bought and refurbished personally during her marriage to Dale, the baroness found herself short of cash. Police think that she conspired with her children to recover the house and her money and get rid of the old man by battering him to death in cold blood with a jemmy bar.

Marie Hilley Dies – for Real, this Time!

CONVICTED ALABAMA murderess Marie Hilley absconded from prison while out on a weekend's furlough in February, and was subsequently found dead of exposure. Marie had "died" before and resurrected herself as her own imaginary twin, but this time her death was for real.

Marie's career in crime began in 1975, when she poisoned her 45-year-old husband Frank. She then proceeded to live it up on his insurance. In 1978 her daughter nearly died of arsenic poisoning, after Marie had heavily insured the girl's life. Investigation of this misadventure led to further delvings into Frank's death, revealing arsenical poisoning as the cause.

When it looked as though she was cornered, Marie jumped bail and fled to Florida where she married a boat-builder in 1980. Then she went away and announced her own death, returning to Florida to console her husband as her "twin" sister Teri! It was as "Teri Martin" that she was arrested in 1983, and subsequently convicted.

Is Gloucester Killer Suzy Lamplugh's Murderer?

RAPIST JOHN CANNAN had only been out of one of Her Majesty's residences for her less savoury subjects for three days last year when estate agent Suzy Lamplugh disappeared (see 1986).

Now that Cannan has been charged with the murder of Bristol newlywed Shirley Banks, the question of whether he was also responsible for the abduction of the missing Ms Lamplugh arises.

Mrs Banks disappeared after going shopping in October. Weeks later her naked body was found decomposing by a stream in the Quantock Hills, 45 miles away.

Cannan was questioned because of his long record of sex offences. The tax disc of Mrs Banks's car was found in his possession, and her car was traced to his garage where he was crudely repainting it.

Good-looking ladies' man Banks has a string of legitimate girl-friends, some of whom tell of the sudden violence that can replace his smooth charm.

In prison he was nicknamed "Kipper", because of his love for Seventies-style clothing and kipper ties. Suzy Lamplugh's last appointment, according to her jotter, was with a mysterious "Mr Kipper".

John Cannan, charged with killing Shirley Banks and suspected of being "Mr Kipper"

IN BRIEF

CONVICTED OF homosexual murders and sentenced to life imprisonment (in solitary confinement as an AIDS sufferer): Michele Lupo (see 1986). So much for Lupo's priggish and uptight health freak's anti-smoking stance!

ACQUITTED OF the murders of schoolgirls Karen Hadaway and Nicola Fellows: Russell Bishop (see 1986). Witnesses to Bishop's movements cast reasonable doubt on his access to Wild Park at the time of the murders, despite suspicion engendered by his own constantly changing story and some circumstantial evidence against him.

EXECUTED FOR horrifying Utah audioshop murders (see 1974): Dale Pierre.

DISAPPEARED FROM their home in Jersey: wealthy Lloyd's underwriter Nicholas Newall and his wife Elizabeth. Cleaned-up bloodstaining in their house suggests foul play some time after the couple's last known meeting with their sons Mark and Roderick.

1988

London's Stockwell Strangler Convicted, Given 40 Years

Kenneth Erskine, the Stockwell Strangler

THE TERRIFYING STRANGLER who invaded old people's bedrooms in Stockwell, south London, for three months in 1986 has been given the longest minimum sentence ever imposed in Britain. Half-Antiguan Kenneth Erskine will not be released for 40 years, when he will be 66.

This horrible creature sodomized and strangled four elderly men and three elderly women. Another potential victim, Fred Prentice of Mortlake, 73, managed to escape his clutches. He struggled and activated an alarm, causing the intruder to flee.

Mr Prentice's description was not essential to the police invetigation. Apart from the statistical knowledge that the strangler was probably black (*see* below on psy-

chological profiling), a negroid hair had been found in the room of murdered Mrs Eileen Emms. Subsequently, a fingerprint left in Mrs Jane Cockett's room identified Erskine, who had a previous conviction for burglary.

But the real difficulty was in tracing him. Police trailed him to more than 300 squats and bedsits in London, and still never found his main place of abode. Erskine was caught because, although he had at least £3,000 from break-ins, he went on collecting unemployment benefit. He was arrested at the Social Security office. Erskine proved stupid to the point of halfwittedness, and so uncontrolled that at times his arms had to be restrained to stop him masturbating in open court.

THE VICTIMS

APRIL 1986
Mrs Eileen Emms (78) West Hill Road, Wandsworth

JUNE
Mrs Jane Cockett (67) Warwick House, Overton Rd, Stockwell
Valentine Gleim (84) and Zbigniew Strabawa (94) both of Somervelle Hastings House, Stockwell Park Road

JULY
William Carmen (82) Sybil Thorndyke House, Marquess Estate, Islington
William Downes (74) Holles House, Overton Rd, Stockwell
Mrs Florence Tisdall (80) Ranelagh Gardens, Fulham

Psychological Profiling and Computers Transform Detection of Serial Murder

JUST EIGHT YEARS AGO all England reeled before the seemingly unstoppable Yorkshire Ripper (*see* p. 94). Two juries this year convicted men whose crimes presented similar difficulties. Both Railway Rapist John Duffy and Stockwell Strangler Kenneth Erskine attacked victims unknown to them, and did not steal identifiable property for marketing. Two factors make it unlikely that a serial killer will ever again be at large for long in Britain.

It is well-known that police questioned Sutcliffe nine times before his arrest during a routine check of prostitutes working the car trade. But the truly massive collection of card-index files made simultaneous recovery of the various entries identifying him impossible.

These days, computerization would instantly identify him as a prime suspect. Sutcliffe would turn up again and again in the investigation: as one of scores of car-owners frequently spotted in red-light districts; one of hundreds of possible recipients of the new £5 note passed to one victim; one of thousands of car-owners whose tyre and axle sizes fitted tracks left beside another victim.

Psychological profiling, developed by the FBI Academy at Quantico, has also proved amazingly fruitful. Instead of accepting the introspectively derived psychoanalytic categories of human personality, the Quantico Behavioural Sciences Unit works from statistically quantified interviews with convicted violent crim-

inals and the practical experience of evidence left at scenes of crimes.

Following this technique, Professor David Canter of the University of Surrey correctly advised police that the Railway Rapist would prove to be a small, physically unattractive, unhappily married man from Kilburn or Cricklewood, doing semi-skilled work for British Rail, and interested in the martial arts. The planning of his crimes showed an "organized" personality, compared with Erskine's opportunistic "disorganized" violence.

FBI statistics also show that sexual offences against old people number among the very, very few types of sex crime more commonly perpetrated by black than white offenders.

110

New Scientific Technique Catches the Right Man

IT'S NOT JUST your fingerprints that give you away now: your blood, sweat and tears can all be identified precisely, not just categorized into groups. Laboratory "blooding" or "genetic fingerprinting" can take cells from your body, or drops from its fluids, and show a pattern of darks and shades, similar to a supermarket bar code, which identifies you and you alone. It's the end of the road for the anonymous rapist – unless he uses a condom!

Twenty-eight-year-old Colin Pitchfork has just had to surrender to the irrefutable evidence of science. Back in 1983, 15-year-old Lynda Mann was raped and strangled on Black Pad footpath near Narborough, Leicestershire, England. Blood tests on eight suspects proved inconclusive.

In 1986, 15-year-old Dawn Ashworth suffered a similar fate in Narborough's Ten Pound Lane. A simple-minded mental hospital kitchen worker confessed under questioning. His semen, sent with that found in Dawn's body to Dr Alec Jeffreys' laboratory, produced the genetically fingerprinted report that he was innocent, and that Dawn's killer had also killed Lynda.

Blood and saliva samples were taken from all males in the area. At first the operation seemed a failure, because tests did not throw up the murderer. But this was only because crafty killer Colin Pitchfork persuaded a friend to go in his place. When the deception was exposed, Pitchfork was well and truly caught. He confessed.

His trial this January lasted a mere half a day. He has been sentenced for two murders, two rapes and the conspiracy to avoid giving specimens.

Mormon Murderer Gives Up: Tries To Kill Himself in Jail

Police inspect the wreckage of Mark Hofmann's car

BRILLIANT DOCUMENT DEALER and forger Mark Hofmann (33) has reached the end of the road. After practising massive frauds on the Mormon church, killing one associate who could have blown the whistle on him, and the wife of another who opened the parcel intended for her husband, Hofmann knows he will never again dazzle the book world. And he's tried to kill himself in prison.

By his own account, this is his second attempt at suicide. Police are more cynical, and believe the bomb blast which destroyed his car and crippled him three years ago was the accidental explosion of materials intended to blow up yet another person who might have exposed him.

Hofmann, an eighth generation Mormon, became interested in his church's history while of college age. He collected rare documents relating to the history of the cult, and delighted Mormon elders by apparently discovering papers which supported favourable claims for Mormonism.

When Hofmann started producing papers which undermined founder-prophet Joe Smith, Mormon officials were even more anxious to acquire and suppress these dangerous documents. Hofmann ultimately made about $2 million from gullible collectors and queasy Mormon leaders.

Hofmann was a brilliant technical forger. He bamboozled documents examiner Kenneth Rendell, who almost to the last minute tried to verify his most suspicious document: a letter claiming that a salamander rather than "the angel Moroni" had inspired Smith's "Book of Mormon". And when he produced a version of a famous lost early American settler's document, the Library of Congress verified it and seriously contemplated paying $1 million for it.

In 1985, however, Hofmann's frauds were endangered. A former associate, Steven Christensen, had been hired for a consultancy which would certainly lead to his exposure. Business partner James Gary Sheets was owed money which just wasn't going to be available. Hofmann delivered parcel bombs which killed Christensen and Sheets' wife Kathleen.

One day later Hofmann's car blew up, severely injuring him. For a moment it took the heat off. Hofmann seemed to be another intended victim of a mysterious anti-Mormon bomber. But determined self-educated policemen succeeded where trained experts had failed. They uncovered Hofmann's skilful scientific techniques. They forced him into a corner. And last year he pleaded guilty to two counts of second-degree murder.

IN BRIEF

JOHN DUFFY, the Railway Rapist (*see* 1986), convicted of two murders and five rapes.

Acquitted of Ann Lock's murder because the decomposed state of her body prevented such scientific evidence as would preclude "reasonable doubt".

Other rape charges remain open on file against him.

1989

Murder Causes Race Uproar in Massachusetts

EIGHT-MONTH PREGNANT Carol Stuart's murder in Boston last October provoked white fury against black street violence. The handsome, rising young Stuarts – Charles a furriers' manager, Carol a lawyer – were good Catholics expecting their first baby.

According to Charles, the couple were waiting at a set of traffic lights in the black neighbourhood beside the hospital where Carol took pre-natal classes when a robber hit them. Twenty-nine-year-old Charles, severely injured with a gunshot wound in the abdomen, managed to croak a call for help into his car-phone. The mugger, in black jogging-suit with a red stripe, had also shot Carol in the head and taken her jewellery.

Carol and her baby died in hospital. Charles was lucky to survive. Politicians, churchmen and opinion formers denounced urban black criminality. A petty black crook was implicated by his juvenile nephew (who loved boasting of Uncle Willie's crimes). Black spokesmen were embarrassed and tongue-tied, though Uncle Willie denied complicity and the nephew later retracted his story.

This year, Charles's brother Matthew revealed that, when the Stuarts were supposedly being attacked, he actually met Charles's car by prearrangement to collect Carol's rings and a pistol. He had retained her engagement ring and thrown the pistol in the river, from where police retrieved it.

Charles's main error actually made his story plausible: the shot supposed to give credence to his yarn injured him more seriously than he had intended. Charles left home in a hurry as Matthew's story was about to break and threw himself into the river before he could be arrested.

The black community is understandably furious that a white yuppie combining wife-murder with a cheap insurance scam should be instantly believed when he randomly accuses a black man of his own vicious crimes.

The body of murderer Charles Stuart recovered after his suicide

TV Sculpture Tracks Family-Slayer After 20 Years

JOHN HARDY was a decent middle class accountant, with wire-rimmed spectacles and receding hair; so was John List. John Hardy was a faithful married Lutheran, quietly introverted, rarely talking much above a whisper; so was John List. John Hardy had no children; nor had John List – well, not after the autumn of 1971. Prior to that he had two girls and a boy. He lost them, and his wife, and his mother, in one fell swoop. And the world lost John List for 17 years!

The entire List family had to leave their Rutgers, New Jersey, home suddenly to nurse a sick relative in North Carolina, so letters from List informed the children's schools, the bank, the public utilities, the church, and anybody else who needed to know.

The Lists' mansion on the edge of town stood silent and deserted, with random electric lights burning as a precaution against burglary.

The occasional failure of those light bulbs led neighbours to reflect that the Lists had been away from home an inordinate length of time. After a month passed, police broke into the List mansion.

There, in the freezing ballroom, neatly laid out, were the three children and Mrs List, all shot. Upstairs in a cupboard, List's mother Alma, also shot.

Investigations revealed that List was almost broke as a result of bad investments, and that he had "borrowed" from his mother to compensate. It was inferred that, unable to control his womenfolk without the aid of purse-strings, he shot his wife and mother, killed his children as they came home from school, and fled. Very successfully: his car was in the airport carpark. Mr List had disappeared.

Crime-reconstruction television company Cosgrove-Muerer broadcast a sculptor's impression of how List must look today, with further receded hair and flaccid muscles. And behold, many people recognized retiring Mr Hardy of Richmond, Virginia., who denied it, of course. But his fingerprints match List's old army records, and he's now under arrest for murder as John List.

Jack the Ripper Identified at Last

CRIME-SOLVING TV company Cosgrove-Muerer (*see* John List story on these pages) has proposed a solution to the 100-year-old mystery of Jack the Ripper that satisfies experts from Scotland Yard and the FBI. The company hired FBI psychological profilers Roy Hazelwood and John Douglas (*see* 1988) to examine the evidence and produce a profile, as they would in a modern case.

The agents agreed that of all the suspects ever suggested, the only one who can be the true Ripper is the Polish Jewish immigrant identified by CID chief Sir Robert Anderson at the time of the murders, as author Martin Fido proposed a year ago. A panel of experts, including representatives from Scotland Yard and the Milton Helpern Forensic Science Institute, unanimously concur.

IN BRIEF

Baroness Moves from Frying Pan to Fire

Baroness Susan von Stempel is driven away after her court appearance

SHROPSHIRE BARONESS Susan von Stempel and her children have been acquitted of conspiring to murder her ex-husband, Simon Dale (*see* 1987). So the slaying of the virtually blind architect in the kitchen of the house from which Susan was trying evict him remains unsolved.

Many other interesting facts came to light during the case, though. Detectives noticed that the Baroness's cottage was stuffed with valuable antiques and furniture. These proved to be the property of her late aunt, Lady Illingworth, and were left to Susan, or so she claims, at the old lady's death in 1986. The signature on Lady Illingworth's will appears to be a forgery, perpetrated by the Baroness de Stempel.

Susan's hugely rich "Aunt Puss", as Lady Illingworth was known, left Claridge's to live with the de Stempels in 1984. Within a year she was no longer rich, her funds transferred to the Baroness. "Aunt Puss" was herself transferred to a hostel, with the misinformation that she was a sex-obsessed alcoholic, liable to wander off. When "Aunt Puss" died, she wasn't given the Catholic funeral she had wanted. Susan had her cremated – and then declined to pay the bill or collect the ashes.

Baron de Stempel was around when Lady Illingworth was defrauded, so he too stands in the dock with Susan and her brood.

Madman 'Yosser' Kills Copper, then Himself

The scene of the shootings of Inspector Codling and Sergeant Bowden

ANTHONY HUGHES (42) of Baguley near Manchester, England, seemed so dangerously barmy that neighbours nicknamed him "Yosser", after the tragic victim of unemployment and bad social services in Alan Bleasdale's TV series *Boys from the Blackstuff*.

However, Hughes can seem far from tragic. He has served long prison stretches for armed robbery and a particularly nasty incident when he posed as a policeman to rape a 19-year-old girl and told her he was the Yorkshire Ripper.

At 2.00 am on September 14 he was in Birch Service Station on the M62 when Inspector Raymond Codling and Sergeant James Bowden, performing routine vehicle checks at the place, asked him a pertinent question about his motor bike. Hughes responded by shooting both men, killing Inspector Codling instantly. Then he rode furiously to Manchester in search of a Catholic priest. Finding Fr Maurice Keenan away from home, Hughes shot himself dead

Despite mild agitation for the restoration of capital punishment in the light of this bloody and senseless crime, it is obvious that no deterrent of any kind would have been the slightest use with someone as deranged as Hughes, and no retribution could be inflicted on a suicide.

Bishop Convicted of Assaulting Child

RUSSELL BISHOP, acquitted of the murder of two little girls in England in 1986, has now been given life imprisonment for the attempted murder of a third.

On February 4, Mr and Mrs David Clifton were enjoying the exhilarating view from Devil's Dyke, Sussex, when a naked little girl with tears streaming down her face appeared, bleeding from gorse scratches, and announced, "I've been kidnapped."

The 7-year-old child (whose name may not be published) was roller-skating near her home in Brighton when Bishop grabbed her and bundled her into the boot of his red Cortina. As he drove to the lonely beauty spot, the girl had the presence of mind to remove her roller skates in the hope of making a better escape. She also banged on the boot lid with a hammer she found.

On reaching Devil's Dyke, Bishop squeezed her throat till she passed out. Eventually she came round in the gorse where Bishop had thrown her, presumably leaving her for dead. Doctors say that the child was extremely lucky to survive Bishop's strangulation.

At Bishop's trial the child gave very clear and courageous video evidence against her attacker. Forensic scientists found hammer marks where she testified to striking Bishop's car boot lid, and a thread matching the fabric of her jumper in the boot. Most damning of all, DNA "fingerprinting" confirmed that her saliva and Bishop's semen were both on a pair of men's track suit trousers discarded at the scene of the crime.

Bishop's sullen claim that they were not his, and that the police had framed him by stealing a used contraceptive from his house to contaminate them, cut no ice with the court. He goes to jail to join the "nonces" so despised by hardened criminals.

Haysom-Soering Case Concluded after Extradition Battle

AT LONG LAST Virginia prison gates clang shut on arrogant Jens Soering, son a German diplomat. His co-criminal, American student Elizabeth Haysom, started her two 45-year stretches in 1988.

In 1986 the pair were picked up in London for passing dud cheques to retailers Marks and Spencer before returning their goods for cash at different branches. They were very well equipped with false identification and cheque books for this simple scam.

A search of their lodgings produced an astonishing cache of letters. These two, it seemed, had fled America after murdering Elizabeth's parents. Jens had carved them up with a butterfly knife while Elizabeth went to the theatre to establish an alibi for herself and her lover. Virginia police confirmed this and Elizabeth was sent back to America to stand trial.

But Jens fought extradition through the House of Lords and the European courts. His aim? Ideally, to be tried in his native West Germany, where he would be lightly sentenced as a juvenile and soon regain his freedom. In any case, he did not want to risk going to the electric chair, an unpleasant prospect which Virginia held out. Now, after a judicial compromise with the German authorities, who will not extradite for capital punishment, he's got life.

But why did they kill the elderly Heysoms in the first place? Astonishingly, it seems, because Mrs Nancy Heysom enjoyed a covert lesbian relationship with her bisexual daughter and hoarded mildly pornographic pictures of Elizabeth naked!

The young couple's supercilious arrogance has forfeited their hope of public sympathy.

Ozzie Vampires Lure and Kill Man

AUSTRALIAN TRACEY WIGGINTON is a lesbian vampire. Her girlfriends, Lisa Ptaschinski, Kim Jervis and Tracey Ann Waugh, have little scabs on their wrists showing where they open their veins to let Tracey suck their blood.

Tracey has been drinking animal blood since her teens. As an adult she clumped around Brisbane in hob-nailed boots and T-shirt and jeans. Until she wanted something special, that is, when she could make herself as attractive to men as her friend, pretty little Tracey Ann Waugh.

After a champagne supper the four went hunting, Tracey and Kim Jervis bringing along ninja butterfly knives. When they saw waiter Edward Baldock making his drunken way home, they stopped the car and came on to him like vamps. Wigginton, Jervis and Waugh were all over him, and invited him to have sex on the river bank.

Down at the river, Kim and Tracey Ann got cold feet and stayed behind. Tracey Wigginton and Lisa Ptaschinski made their way down to the bank, where Ted stripped and cautiously put his wallet in his shoe. They undressed to disarm his suspicions, and as he approached them, Ted spotted a credit card he'd overlooked, and slipped it, too, in his shoe. Then he prepared for prolonged ecstasy

Accused: Tracey Ann Waugh. Accused: Kim Aileen Jervis. Accused: Lisa Marie Ptaschinski.

Guilty: Tracey Avril Wigginton.

The Australian lesbian killers, with Wigginton shown at bottom left, and victim Edward Baldock

with the slender, naked girls.

Tracey alone enjoyed it. With the two knives she flailed at Ted Baldock, stabbing him over 50 times, and almost cutting his head off. Then she buried her mouth in his throat and sucked his blood. After she'd washed off Ted's gore in the river, the girls went home.

The police caught up with them when it was realized that the credit card Ted put in his shoe belonged to Tracey. She confessed and pleaded guilty to his murder in October. The other three go on trial next year.

Boxer Terry Marsh Acquitted of Attempted Murder

FRANK WARREN may have enemies, but which of them wanted him dead on November 30 last year? An Old Bailey jury decided that it wasn't former light-welterweight world champion Terry Marsh.

Warren, who has grown rich as an unlicensed boxing promoter, offending the British Board of Boxing Control, was Marsh's manager. He steered him to the world title, but then everything fell apart.

Frank had just arranged another big fight for his new champion when Terry gave the *Sun* newspaper an interview. In this he revealed that he suffered from epilepsy. The implication that Warren knew of his condition and was still willing to let him fight was damaging and caused quite a stir.

Not surprisingly, relations between the two men soured irrevocably.

But why should Terry want a professional "hitman" to pump bullets into Warren as he approached the Broadway theatre, Barking, last year? According to Terry's estranged wife, Jacqui, because he believed Warren had used him; made himself rich and then thrown him away once he had no further use for him. She made a statement to the police to this effect, then retracted it. So Terry walks free.

Warren's underworld connection through his uncle Bob –once a thug in the pay of Billy Hill – has been aired, as have his troubles with other promoters, but none of it explains who was out to get him on that autumn evening.

Former world champion boxer Terry Marsh, found not guilty of assaulting his former manager

Vain murderer Michael Shorey, who killed his girlfriend and her room-mate

God's Gift to Women Kills Lover and Friend

HANDSOME 35-year-old Michael Shorey pulled girls as and when he felt like it. The streetwise West Indian accounts clerk was a sharp dresser with a neat line in chat. He picked up *East Enders*' TV star Sandy Ratcliff in a bar for a £10 bet, and became her lover when she was at a low ebb.

But he was already engaged to 31-year-old Elaine Forsyth, and he couldn't take it when Elaine had enough of his lies and swaggering and broke it off. He strangled her with a sash cord. And when Elaine's flatmate, Patricia Morrison, came in, he strangled her, too. Then he left both bodies in a car.

He was caught when he asked a friend to help him get bloodstains off a carpet. Despite Sandy's tentative attempt to give him an alibi, he's received a life sentence for failing to swallow his pride.

IN BRIEF

JONATHAN MOYLE, 28-year-old Briton, found hanging in his hotel wardrobe in Santiago, Chile, was treated as a suicide by local police, but a judicial investigation has agreed that he was murdered. Political or arms-dealing connections are suspected.

1991

Missing Oxford Student Slain by New Zealand Lover

Student Rachel Maclean

WHILE ENGLAND FEARED that Rachel Maclean's disappearance at the start of her Oxford term meant another Suzie Lamplugh-style disappearance (*see* 1986), police decided that her New Zealand boyfriend, John Tanner, knew more than he was telling.

John was the last person to see Rachel alive – at the buffet on Oxford station where he said good-bye before returning home to Nottingham. He claimed that Rachel went to drink coffee with a man he didn't know, who offered her a lift back to her digs in his car.

With no subsequent sighting of the missing student, and a letter at her digs showing Tanner had written to her as soon as he got home, police couldn't act. There were no signs of grave-digging in the garden and no smell of rotting flesh in the lodging-house. Then Inspector Parker found a loose board in the basement.

When that was opened up, there was Rachel's body in the crawl-space. Giveaway putrefaction had been prevented by a cool, damp through-draught.

With the body exposed, a penitent Tanner cracked and confessed. He killed Rachel in fury when she said they must break off their relationship.

Drug Wars in London

THERE ARE MORE GUNS on the streets of London than ever before. All caused by foreseeable gang warfare, since the timid Dangerous Drugs Act prohibited doctors from prescribing narcotics to addicts, so that the villains can make money out of the junkies.

Biggest battles seem to centre on territory south of the Thames, where Turkish Ahmet "Abbi" Abdullah's family-based mob battles it out with the Brindles, connections of that old stalwart of the Richardson Bros' torture mob, "Mad" Frankie Fraser.

In March, Turkish Abbi was taken out quickly and cleanly by a masked gunman who walked up to him in a betting shop, put a gun to his head, and despatched him. Leadership of his mob then passed to his relatives, the Arifs. Abbi's cousin Dogan Arif is said to be the biggest drug dealer in London today, though a shoot-out and arrest has put him behind bars, where it is hoped he may stay for a long time.

Meanwhile in September, two masked men who were certainly not Turkish, judging from their accents, strode blatantly into The Bell pub in Walworth and shot fairly indiscriminately across the room, successfully gunning down their main target, Frankie Fraser's young nephew David Brindle, as he tried desperately to pull himself over the bar. "That's for Turkish Abbi," was one gunman's cynical comment. Neither apparently cared that they had accidentally killed innocent bystander Stanley Silk in their incompetent operation.

In fact, so casual and careless have the boys become about bystanders and old-fashioned villainous proprieties, that some of the hardest "faces" from good old London gangland are going quietly into retirement in the country.

Russian Cannibal "Metal Fang" at Large

THE SOVIET UNION LIKES to suggest that serial murder is an outcome of capitalist degeneracy. So Mr Brezhnev's publicists did not give great international fame to the horrible cannibal Nikolai Dzhumagaliev when he was arrested in Kazhakstan in 1980.

The soft-spoken, well-dressed monster stood out among fellow-workers on a building site near Alma-Ata, and his gentlemanly manners made it easy for him to enjoy his favourite recreation of walking along the riverside with attractive women. Despite terror in the republic as women seemed to be disappearing, nobody noticed anything suspicious in the fact that Dzumagaliev usually invited friends round for generous suppers of roast meat after he had enjoyed such promenades.

But when the gentleman whose complete set of white-metal false teeth gave him a horribly appropriate nickname invited a couple of casually-met hard-drinkers to come home and share another bottle, they made a discovery his intimates had never dreamed of. In his fridge lay a woman's head and intestines.

Metal Fang was put on trial and charged with 17 murders.

The court found him clearly insane, and he was committed to a mental institution.

Last year he escaped. Glasnost or no Glasnost, Mr Gorbachev's administration did not want the panic that would be created by the thought of this frightening figure on the loose. Nothing was reported until he was recaptured in Uzbekistan this August, after apparently trying to pick up women in Moscow. Now he is safely back under lock and key, and Russia can breathe again with this nightmare figure, who might have come from one of the country's more frightening folk tales, secure.

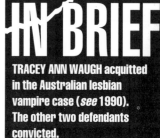

TRACEY ANN WAUGH acquitted in the Australian lesbian vampire case (*see* 1990). The other two defendants convicted.

'Pussy, Pussy! Eat up Your Nice Mrs Perry!'

JOHN PERRY'S first two marriages ended in divorce. When the 52-year-old aircraft fitter from the Welsh border married pretty Filippino Arminda, she knew nothing of his reputation for marital violence. But John soon reverted to type, and Arminda, too, had divorce papers served on him. The two quarrelled over Arminda's affair with Barry Burns – then she disappeared.

Four days later, when Inspector Ross Duffield called to ask where Mrs Perry was, John replied at once, "I've done a good turn. I've fed her to the animals." He showed the astonished policeman the bags of cooked flesh in the garage. In an armchair sat Katie, the tabby cat, replete after her meal of Arminda

Katie, the tabby cat who ate Mrs Perry

Rich Cannes Widow Murdered

ON JUNE 24, POLICE WERE called from Nice to investigate a villa on the edge of Cannes, whose occupant, the wealthy widowed heiress to a motor-car spark plugs fortune, had not been seen for a couple of days.

In the locked cellar, the gendarmes found 65-year-old Mme Ghislaine Marchal. Her throat and body had been stabbed repeatedly; her head battered with a piece of bloody wood that still lay beside her. Curiously, the door had been barricaded from the inside with furniture.

There was one important clue. The French words for "Omar has killed me", scrawled in blood on the inside of the cellar door. It seems that Mme Marchal used her last energy to denounce her killer.

Omar's identity is known. He is a Moroccan immigrant odd-job man who did Mme Marchal's gardening. Quiet-spoken and polite, with very little French at his command, he has never been suspected of any previous crime. But his wife has just had a baby; several thousand francs that were in Mme Marchal's bag have disappeared; and no-one can suggest any other theory.

Some problems remain. Omar seems to have a good alibi for one of the days on which Mme Marchal might have been killed, and an excellent one for the other. There is not a trace of blood on any of his clothes and possessions. And the accusatory words on the door are written with a blatant and elementary grammatical error that one cannot easily imagine Mme Marchal perpetrating, even in extremis. But few people doubt his guilt, despite his denials.

DIY Builder Fights Planning Decision with Bullets

A PLANNING OFFICER'S intransigence led Albert Dryden to commit murder in front of television and news cameras – the first such killing in Britain.

Albert wanted to use his £15,000 redundancy payment, from the closure of Consett steelworks, to build a bungalow in the country for his mother, but Derwentside planning officer Harry Collinson told him this was out of the question. The official jokingly remarked that anything built on the plot of unspoilt agricultural land Albert had bought couldn't be more than three feet high. Bearded eccentric Albert took this as permission. He dug a deep pit, and built his bungalow in it!

When Collinson ordered him to destroy the monstrosity, Albert tried every legal stratagem to save his handiwork. Inevitably, he lost. Just as he was on the point of giving up the struggle, a badly worded official letter gave him the impression that he had won five weeks' grace. So when Harry Collinson turned up with demolition workers, Albert was waiting for him.

As the dispute had reached the local papers, pressmen, police and a television crew were present at the encounter. They watched in horror, then fled, when Albert shot the bureaucrat with an antiquated pistol before giving himself up.

Bearded weirdie Albert Dryden shoots planning officer Harry Collinson in front of press cameras

Schoolmarm Seduces Pupil, Makes him Kill Husband

SWINGING PAMELA SMART, rocking "Maid of Metal" on local radio when she was at college in sunny Florida, found herself a 22-year-old housewife, married to an insurance salesman in freezing New Hampshire by 1989. She was also media advisor to the local school board, and a counsellor at Winnacunnet High School.

Husband Greg, once a passionate punk rocker like Pamela, was settling down to provincial yuppiedom and commonplace infidelity, with a little fling on an out-of-town trip just before Christmas 1989 – barely six months into the marriage. He made the mistake of telling Pamela all about it during a quarrel. In no time the slender siren lured 15-year-old schoolkid Billy Flynn into her office and showed him naughty pictures of her in her undies. Then she took him home when Greg was away, and showed him naughtier videos. Then she took him to the bedroom, so starting Billy on a sex-drenched life that came up to every teenage lad's dreams. When he was well hooked on her body, Pamela told him there'd be no more "fun" for Billy-boy – unless he killed Greg!

Driven by desire, Billy persuaded two friends to help him. They stole a gun and shot Greg dead in a faked burglary on May 1 last year. But they talked, and first they, then the steamy seductress, went on trial. A year later, pretty Pamela has been locked up for life without the possibiity of parole.

Steamy Pamela Smart

Jeffrey Dahmer: 'Milwaukee' Cannibal Monster

Jeffrey Dahmer, the chocolate-factory worker who ate parts of his 17 victims

Gay Cannibal Monster Caught in Milwaukee: Parts of his 17 Victims Stored in his Flat

> *Ma'am, Ma'am. Like I explained to you, it is all taken care of. It's as positive as I can be. I can't do anything about anybody's sexual preferences in life.*

QUOTE Desk sergeant, refusing to act on information which might have prevented five murders.

ON JUNE 4, 1978, Jeffrey Dahmer graduated from high school. Two weeks later he committed his first murder.

Stephen Hicks was hitching home from a rock concert at Chippewa Park, Ohio, when Dahmer picked him up and invited him in for a few beers. When Hicks said he had to leave, Dahmer, who had been left on his own in an empty house by his divorcing parents, snapped. He hit Hicks over the head with a barbell and strangled him with its handle.

He hid the body in the crawlspace under the house for a few days, then stripped off the skin and flesh with chemicals, smashed the skeleton to smithereens with a sledgehammer, and spread the bone fragments and viscous matter on open soil, leaving nothing like a newly-turned grave to attract attention.

Life with Grandma

Following failure at college and a dishonourable discharge from the army, Dahmer, a young alcoholic homosexual, went to live with his grandmother in Milwaukee's upmarket suburb of West Allis.

She encouraged his interest in tropical fish, unaware of his passion for haunting sleazy gay bars and bath-houses after his low-grade work in a chocolate factory finished.

He was barred from one bath-house for drugging his sexual partners in cubicles. By this time Dahmer had discovered he preferred an unconscious partner. When, in November 1987, he killed Stephen Tuomi in a room in the Ambassador Hotel, he discovered he liked it even better if his partner was dead.

He took Tuomi back to Grandma Dahmer's basement for disposal. He also fried and ate one of Tuomi's biceps.

Early in 1988 he killed two more rent boys picked up in gay clubs. But the increasingly smelly garbage he was depositing, the remains of his victims, made even his grandmother wish he would move out.

In September he moved to a cheap apartment of his own on Milwaukee's downmarket West Side.

The Sinthasomphone Scandals

The day he moved, Dahmer offered 13-year-old Laotian refugee Somsack Sinthasomphone $50 to pose for photographs. Somsack was given drugged coffee, indecently fondled and photographed in lewd postures.

But the child wandered woozily out of the deathtrap apartment, and Jeffrey found himself arrested and charged with enticing a minor for immoral purposes.

Between his conviction in January 1989 for assaulting Somsack and sentencing two months later, Dahmer killed another young man. He painted the skull of this victim, retaining it as a potential ornament for a necrophiliac "shrine" he proposed erecting in the living-room of his home.

His prison sentence was suspended, on condition that he lived for a year in a correctional institution from which he could still work at the chocolate factory and support himself.

With that punishment completed, Dahmer took a flat in Oxford Apartments, a flat that would become infamous. As virtually the only white man around, he began to make his rooms the smelliest on the block, with decaying flesh stashed away. He killed four more young men in 1990, paused for six months, and

DAHMER

"Intoxicated Asian, naked male (*laughter*), was returned to his sober boyfriend (*more laughter*)." Policeman reporting the incident which was in fact kidnapping and sexual assault with actual bodily harm, and escalated to murder following his decision to return the young man to Dahmer.

Police carry away bagged human remains from Jeffrey Dahmer's flat

killed another three in the spring of 1991.

Then, on May 26, quite by chance, he picked up 14-year-old Konerak Sinthasomphone, the younger brother of his former victim, Somsack. Like his brother, Konerak was not entirely overcome by Dahmer's drugs, but after suffering brutal abuse wandered unsteadily onto the street when Dahmer slipped out to buy beer. Since he was naked and bleeding from the buttocks, he attracted instant attention. Nicole Childress and Sandra Smith ran to help him and call the police.

When three cops turned up, Dahmer reappeared. He handled the police with aplomb, taking them to his room and showing them Konerak's clothes and suggestive polaroid photographs he had snapped of him. He claimed that Konerak was his steady boyfriend, and a lot older than he looked – 19, in fact. He said the two were into S-M. The cops believed him.

Nicole Childress and Sandra Smith didn't. They protested (rightly) that Konerak was obviously a child and that his bleeding anus indicated something worse than mutual spanking games. The cops brushed them off and threatened to arrest them if they went on protesting. Their precinct colleagues

brushed off Sandra's mother, too, when she telephoned her continuing anxiety. They assured her it was just two adult faggots who enjoyed beating each other – and all quite legal, however distasteful. Milwaukee police would live to regret their recorded calls and responses. As soon as they left, Dahmer made up for lost time and murdered Sinthasomphone.

Sandra and Nicole, like almost all Dahmer's victims, were black; Dahmer and the cops were white. After Dahmer's arrest, mass protests would draw attention to the tendency of police to disregard information given to them by black citizens.

The End

Despite the failure of Milwaukee's finest, Dahmer had only two months and four more victims to go.

On July 23 he picked up 32-year-old Tracy Edwards – a heterosexual who was not willing to join in sex-play or drink drugged coffee. But Dahmer got a handcuff on one of Edwards' wrists, and used that and a knife to hold him prisoner for four terrifying hours.

Edwards escaped when Dahmer's attention flagged. He stopped two policemen in a patrol car and asked them to release him from the handcuff. After hearing his story they went back to Oxford Apartments to investigate this strange homosexual kidnapper.

Dahmer offered the sullen explanation, "I just lost my job and I wanted to drink some f-ing beer." He resisted their attempts to come into his flat. An attempt to arrest him resulted in a struggle which ended with Dahmer screaming on the floor. A thorough inspection of the flat uncovered:

A human head in the fridge
3 heads in the floor-freezer
a human heart in the fridge-freezer compartment

a blue barrel jammed with body parts and bones
two skulls in a computer packaging box
three skulls and some bones in a filing cabinet
two skulls in a kettle
a penis and some hands in another kettle

The Milwaukee cannibal's career was over, and Dahmer was dragged away in custody, howling like a mad dog.

DAHMER AND RACE

While Milwaukee policemen's regrettable failure to take the complaints of black witnesses seriously may justify the race protest demonstrations led by the Reverend Jesse Jackson in the wake of the murders, the secondary suggestion that Dahmer himself was racially motivated seems ill-founded. Dahmer's victims break down into the following categories:

1 American Indian
1 Half-Jewish Puerto Rican
1 Hispanic
1 Asian
2 White
11 Black

This mix is very close to the demographic population of the poor districts of Milwaukee and Chicago where Dahmer made his pick-ups. So it seems certain that he took his victims opportunistically at random. With all his faults Jeff Dahmer is no racist, although he found the worst possible way of demonstrating his freedom from prejudice!

Sensation in Milwaukee with the discovery of a homosexual cannibal serial murderer

Prostitute Robbed and Murdered her Punters

AILEEN "LEE" WUORNOS (38) lived in run-down trailers in Florida with her girlfriend, Tyria Moore, socialized at run-down bars, and made her money by soliciting worn-out men. Guess it all got a bit too dismal, and Lee just had to hit back. She went from being a no-hoper to America's first sexual serial murderess!

When the half-clothed bodies of men with condoms beside them continued turning up along highway I-52, Florida police concluded that some prostitute must be killing her punters. The victims included: social services investigator Dick Humphreys; truck driver Buddy Burress; repair shop owner Richard Mallory; rodeo rider Chuck Carskadoon; concrete loader David Spears; and Bible-toting preacherman Peter Siems. Some of the families of these guys are angrier about the fact that Aileen has exposed their loved ones' appetite for paid-for sex than that she killed them!

Picked up at a bar, Aileen confessed to six slayings, though she gave details of seven, and there may have been more! Her victims were big middle-aged men. Aileen says they tried to rape her, but defence psychiatrists say they represented her father in her mind.

Aileen's childhood was a disaster: brutally thrashed and sexually abused, she learned before puberty that boys would give her money if she let them "put their things" into her. She spent the money she got from schoolgirl prostitution on endless cigarettes. Unhappy little Aileen was despised by the kids who used her. She fell into the hardened prostitute's icy self-contempt and defensiveness toward the world before she had full-grown pubic hair.

The fact that Aileen robbed every man she killed went against her. Last year, juries in her trials for four of her murders rejected her pleas of insanity and gave her a date with Ol' Sparky.

This year another county's court found her insane and unfit to plead! Now what's Florida going to do with its madwoman under sentence of death?

Killer-hooker Aileen Wuornos

Victim David Spears

Wuornos' first victim, Richard Mallory

South London Drug Wars, Brindle Brothers Acquitted

THE ACQUITTAL OF BROTHERS Patrick and Anthony Brindle this May, charged with murdering prominent drug dealer Ahmed "Turkish Abbi" Abdullah in March 1991, closes a bloody act in south London's raging gang war.

Its worst episode was the murder of the Brindles' brother David at a pub in Walworth in August last year. Two gunmen's incompetent scatterfire killed one innocent customer and wounded others. One killer is supposed to have yelled, "That's for Abbi!" as they shot Brindle in the back.

The Brindles have a sister married to Abbi's cousin, Dogan Arif, said to be South London's drug czar, even though he is residing in a high-security cell.

"Mad Frankie" Fraser, the Richardson brothers' old henchman, is the Brindles' uncle. "Mad Frankie" caught a bullet himself last year, as he passed the Turnmill Disco in Clerkenwell. True to form, he told police he was Tutankhamen, and refused to talk about his injury!

FEMINISM AND MURDER

American feminists have got themselves in a state about murderous women. Pamela Smart (*see* 1991) — well, she's easily excused for murdering an unfaithful husband. But the politicized gals ain't quite sure whether to praise or blame her for educating young Billy Flynn in bed. Is she catchin' up on beastly men by playin' their game of sex with kiddies, or is she lettin' the side down?

Betty Broderick (*see* these pages). Okay, Dan was a heel and deserved all he got, but what had his second wife, Linda, done? And can the great mystique of mother-love survive evidence that Betty put her own hurt pride and greed before the kids she mightily distressed?

Neither Betty nor Pamela rates high with the Red Lesbians, who think women must substitute lesbian Marxism for marriage and the "American Dream". Aileen Wuornos is their heroine: lesbian in her personal tastes; financially exploiting men's nauseating wish to have sex with women; killing some.

As for her robberies — well, to a Marxist "property is theft", and lesbian feminists believe every prostitute is unhappy and exploited and wants out. So Aileen was just cute to liberate those guys' wallets.

Andrei Chikatilo, whose 53 known killings give him No. 1 spot in the world serial killer league

Freak Blood Grouping Saved Russia's Record Mass Killer

BACK IN 1984, when 48-year-old Andrei Chikatilo was arrested in Rostov, police believed they'd got the serial killer terrorizing the city. However, tests showed his blood belonged to group A; the sperm found on bodies recovered over the past few years was AB.

Yet as early as 1978 he was a murder suspect. A small girl's body was found in the river Don, and blood-spattering in a squalid shack where Chikatilo used to entertain prostitutes proved she had been killed there. Another resident of the street, who had once been convicted of sex-murder as a juvenile, con-

fessed under interrogation, and was executed for Chikatilo's crime.

It was red faces all round for Red officialdom when it was revealed that Chikatilo is that one-in-a-million individual, one whose semen registers a different group from his blood.

In Brezhnev's USSR the scandals would have been covered up. (Sexual serial murder was purely a product of decadent capitalism!) But Chikatilo was arrested in 1991, under Gorbachev. He has committed at least 53 murders, a world record for modern times.

Chikatilo was convicted in Yeltsin's Russia, and sentenced to death.

America Divided over Ex-Wife's Revenge on Husband

THROUGHOUT NOVEMBER and December last year, America watched Betty Broderick's second trial in San Diego for the murder of her ex and his wife.

Dan Broderick III was a brilliant lawyer earning $1 million a year. In 1983, aged 38, he started a secret affair with receptionist Linda Kolkena, and told Betty, his wife of 14 years, she was "old, fat, ugly, boring and stupid." Two years later he finally admitted to extra-marital sex. He was unrepentant and aggressive into the bargain, depriving Betty of custody of their four children and kicking her out of the marital home. His legal skills enabled him to get the better of her in every way. Betty retaliated by making his life a misery, leaving profane tirades on his answerphone. Finally, in 1988, she went at dawn to shoot Dan and Linda as they slept.

Half the women of America feel Dan got what he deserved. Others are less sure, given Betty's insistence that money matters more than parenthood. Anyway, she was convicted of second-degree homicide in January, and her case looks like becoming a recurrent controversy on Oprah Winfrey's show.

Love & Death with the Fox Cubs

SANDRA WIGNALL and her husband Robert had one charming habit. Of a summer or autumn evening they would go out to the woods and feed the fox cubs. This they were doing on September 9, when Sandra added a new pleasure. Kneeling before her husband, she unzipped his fly and started to satisfy him orally.

But hardly had pleasure been achieved and decorum restored, when three men approached them from the bushes and asked Robert if he had seen their dog. As he replied that he had not, they suddenly attacked him, battering him over the head. He shouted to Sandra to run and hide, which she did. When she returned, her husband was dead.

Running for help, she encountered three youths out walking, and to their immense surprise, asked them if they had just killed her husband. All this was told to the police – and the nation, on television. At

the scene of the crime, one of the killers had dropped a gold bracelet engraved with the letter H.

And then for police and public came a complete surprise. The focus of the enquiry changed, and sympathy drifted away from the bereaved widow Wignall when it transpired that she had a lover with a need for just such money as might come from Robert's life insurance. And the lover had a friend with a criminal record who had owned a gold H-engraved bracelet. And Robert Wignall was starting to suspect that his wife was seeing someone else.

Sandra Wignall, Terence Bewley and Harry Mount will now have to explain to the courts why all their actions seem consistent with the theory that they plotted together to kill Robert, using Sandra's gratuitous act of love to disarm his suspicions, and make any embarrassment she evinced in telling her tale seem plausible.

Nurse Murders Four Children: Damages Nine

Beverley Allitt (centre), the nurse who killed children in her care

STATE ENROLLED NURSE Beverley Allitt attacked her first victim within a week of starting contract work in Ward Four at Grantham Hospital, Lincolnshire, England. Baby Liam Taylor died on February 23, 1991, of an inexplicable heart attack.

Two weeks later, on March 5, 11-year-old Tim Hardwick died; epilepsy was diagnosed.

On April 4, 9-week-old Becky Phillips died at her parents' home after a short stay in hospital; cot-death, the doctors decided. Becky's parents were so grateful to Beverley for her caring support of the child that they made her godmother to Becky's twin, Katie. When Katie was hospitalized, her godparent struck again, failing to kill her, but causing permanent brain damage.

One week later, blood from 5-month-old Paul Crampton, who suffered three near-fatal attacks in March, was analysed. It was found

to contain a massive overdose of insulin. Grantham Hospital was alerted, and a close watch was kept on Ward Four.

Despite this, Beverley killed again before the month was out, injecting 15-month-old Claire Peck with potassium. Finally, in May, Nurse Allitt was arrested and the killings stopped.

After her arrest Allitt developed anorexia and lost five stones in weight. She spent the entirety of her trial this year in Rampton Secure Mental Hospital.

Her real problem, however, is the extreme attention-seeking disorder Münchhausen's Syndrome. Bev graduated from florid lying through self-injury and hypochondriac illnesses to inflicting illness and death on those in her care.

Now she stands as England's greatest 20-century female mass murderer.

Frightful Cruelty to Young Girl

IN MID-DECEMBER LAST YEAR, three workmen came across a terribly burned naked girl screaming for help at a roadside near Stockport. They helped her to a nearby house from where the emergency services took her to hospital. The girl, 16-year-old Suzanne Capper, went into a coma and died three days later.

Fortunately, before she lost consciousness she was able to say exactly who had imprisoned, tortured, and finally murdered her. The police went straight to the Manchester address where she had been held, and arrested Jean Powell (23), Bernadette McNeilly (24), Anthony Dudson (17), Glynn Powell (29), Clifford Pook (18) and Jeffrey Leigh.

These young people lived the lives of squalid drop-outs. They dealt in drugs, stole cars, and shoplifted. They were fascinated by the occult and the horrific. The house in Moston to which Suzanne had directed the police was filthy, with old car seats lining the walls, and dreadful traces of the ways in which the gang had held and tortured Suzanne in an upstairs room.

Suzanne was not a very bright girl. Her only serious ambition was to become a hairdresser. But she was easily lured away from that by the superficial appeal of free and easy living as represented by Jean Powell's gang. She took to leaving her stepfather's house and staying there, even though on at least one occasion she was beaten, made to do housework, and made to take Powell's three children to school.

What led this horde of drop-out hooligans to so detest Suzanne Capper that they behaved so unspeakably to her? Possibly in the first instance, the fact that she was a little simple-minded. Cruelty to those of low intelligence is common enough.

But the obnoxious young people had their own set of inadequate explanations for "punishing" Suzanne. She had brought pubic lice into their casually promiscuous beds. She had made unwelcome sexual advances to Jean Powell and given her the impression that she wanted her to go to bed with an allegedly rich Arab of her acquaintance. She was suspected of stealing a missing pink duffle coat.

And so the dreadful six shaved the hair off her head and body. They

beat her with a belt, a heavy spoon and a fork. They locked her in a cupboard overnight. They tied her to a bed and left her to foul herself with her own excrement. When they decided to bath her, they scrubbed her flesh raw with disinfectant. They burned her with a cigarette; over-injected her with amphetamines, and played loud music at full volume through headphones. They wrenched out her incisors with pliers, breaking one. And finally they took her out to the fields, threw petrol over her, and left her to burn.

For this appalling wickedness, the elders are serving life sentences, and the youngers have drawn long custodial sentences.

Video Nasty for Murder

Two of this year's most distressing cases have drawn attention to the possibility that horror videos are stimulating children and young people to horrible activities.

In both the James Bulger murder and the Suzanne Capper torture and murder, the video *Child's Play III* has been held in some quarters to have played some part in the appalling events. Some one in the house where Suzanne Capper was imprisoned and tortured had recorded the sinister words from the horror picture, "I'm Chucky – wanna play?" over and over again on an audiotape. And given that Chucky is finally destroyed by burning, people have wondered whether the video nasty was responsible for some nasty ideas.

And the father of one of the boys responsible for James Bulger's abduction and murder had borrowed the same video shortly before the crime. While it seemed improbable that the lad had watched it, the possibility has alarmed the public and led to renewed calls for some form of censorship.

Children's Crime Provokes Near Riot in Liverpool

ALARMING SCENES of mob fury took place in Liverpool this February when police took boys in for questioning in connection with the murder of 2-year-old James Bulger.

The infant was abducted from a shopping centre. Security cameras showed that two boys, aged about 10 or 12, led him away when his parents had taken their eyes off him. Witnesses believe they saw James in some distress, being led by other children in the direction of the railway bank where his body was found, savagely mutilated.

Although violent crimes are sporadically committed by children (the horrific rape and murder of 4-year-old Tracey Wair by a 12-year-old boy in 1977 is a good example), they do not often attract massive public attention. Mary Bell (*see*

Police hold back an angry crowd as two boys are charged with the murder of James Bulger

1968) was the last major case in Britain. Her sensational trial aroused vehement feelings that she was a thoroughly abnormal child. The James Bulger murder has unleashed a torrent of guilt and anger about deteriorating moral standards in society being responsible for such crimes.

Outrage at James's fate is understandable, but it seems irresponsible to assume the suspects to be guilty and also to attribute to them motives that have not yet been fully explained or explored in a court of law. The circumstances of James's death will remain a mystery until that case is conducted.

Convicted Rape-Simulator's Case Re-Opened

IN 1991 YVONNE SLEIGHTHOLME of England, who went blind while awaiting trial, was convicted of killing her ex-lover's wife. In December 1988 Mrs Jane Smith was found dead by her farmer-husband outside their house. Her body was half-dressed and had injuries consistent with a sexual assault.

At her trial Miss Sleightholme claimed that Smith had hired three killers to carry out the murder, fearing expensive divorce proceedings, although he had only been married seven months. Smith tearfully denounced her story as "wicked, wicked lies," and the jury agreed.

This January Yvonne's appeal against conviction was dismissed, the appeal court finding there was no error in the judicial summing-up at her trial. But, with new solicitors, Yvonne is determined to try again, claiming new evidence uncovered must be heard.

Extradition Proceedings After RN High Seas Arrest

EXTRADITION PROCEEDINGS in Gibraltar and Paris have been started to bring brothers Roderick and Mark Newall back to the Channel Islands to face charges in connection with the death of their parents (*see* 1987).

Lloyd's underwriter Nicholas Newall and his wife Elizabeth disappeared from their Jersey home after their sons had visited them for a champagne dinner to celebrate Mrs Newall's 48th birthday. The brothers allegedly left their parents alive and well after midnight.

There were no signs of forced entry, nor of theft; but equally, no signs that the Newalls had left of their own volition: their passports were in the bungalow and their breakfast table was laid.

Roderick Newall (centre) is taken to face extradition proceedings in Gibraltar

From minute blood stains found in the house, police deduced that the Newalls had been killed there, after which the place had been scrupulously cleaned up and the central heating turned up high to dry out all traces of mopping-up. It looked like an inside job, done by somebody who knew their way around the house.

Mark and Roderick inherited their parents' wealth when it was assumed the couple were dead. Within a few months, Roderick resigned his army commission and put to sea in the family's 66-foot

yacht, *Austral Soma*. In August last year the Royal Navy frigate *Argonaut* apprehended 26-year-old Roderick at sea and took him to Gibraltar. Here, "new evidence" was presented to the courts in a move to extradite him. Roderick fought the proceedings, desperately trying to have a tape-recording excluded which apparently implicated another person as well as himself. Since his arrest he has made three suicide attempts.

This year, extradition proceedings were started against Mark, too, now resident in Paris.

Murder in Broad Daylight by Contract Killer

SELF-MADE MILLIONAIRE 55-year-old Donald Urquhart was gunned down as he walked along Marylebone High Street in London in broad daylight with his Thai girlfriend, Pat Iamspithone. After the attack the killer made off on a Yamaha motorbike.

Forensic science laboratories link the killing with last year's murder of south London off-licence owner Roger Wilson. However, this might mean only that the same professional killer was hired for the two murders.

Underworld gossip hints that the killer's name is known, and that he received £20,000 for the murder. The police suspect that Urquhart courted danger by going into the illegal gaming machines business currently controlled by south London gangsters.

House of Horror in Gloucester

Rosemary before she married Fred West

AN ADDRESS WHICH WILL forever reverberate with all the horror associated with 10 Rillington Place or 49 Hilldrop Crescent is 25 Cromwell Street, Gloucester. For here, at the end of February, police started investigations and excavations that would go on into the summer, and result in the discovery of 9 bodies buried under the house and patio; another body in another house formerly owned by builder Frederick West, and two bodies in a field near his boyhood home at Much Marcle.

West, a builder, had done a great deal of work, extending and renovating his house. At one time in the 1970's, the upper floors had been divided into small single bedsits which could be let to students and casual travellers. By the time national interest focussed on the house, the first floor had been converted into a bar and entertainment area, with adjacent bedroom. A more strictly locked bedroom on the upstairs floor had a four-poster with spotlights and a concealed microphone. Some friends and neighbours were aware of Fred West and his wife Rosemary as an uninhibited couple who gave each other leave to sleep with whomsoever they pleased, enjoyed saucy orgiastic parties with their friends, and played pornographic videos for family entertainment.

Others, the public was astonished to learn, knew Rosemary West to be an active home-based prostitute, advertising as "Mandy Mouse" in the contact magazines, and entertaining a steady and lucrative stream of male visitors.

Police interest in the "House of Horror" had been provoked by information that it might yield something of interest to do with the fate of Fred and Rosemary's

A police officer carries a box of human remains from 25 Cromwell Street

daughter Heather, who had last been seen in 1987 when she was 16. Her parents claimed she had left home with a lesbian in a blue mini. But the first body dug up under the patio was declared to be Heather's, and Fred West was taken away to be questioned and charged, shouting, "I didn't kill her!"

The other bodies found in Cromwell Street all turned out to belong to young women, many of whom had disappeared as early as the 1970's, and most of whom had last been seen alive at bus stops somewhere in the neighbourhood of Cromwell Street.

In the field near Much Marcle the police found, as they had expected, the remains of West's first wife Catherine "Rena" Costello. She and her daughter Charmaine had disappeared in 1968 and 1971 respectively. Charmaine's body would be discovered in West's

other Gloucester house, 25 Midland Road.

West was charged with murder almost as soon as the investigation began, and each new body was added to his charge-sheet as it was identified.

Rosemary spent longer at liberty. But when charges against her started to be brought, they increased and multiplied at a rate which fascinated and horrified the public and bolstered the tabloid

Life means Life For Gay Bondage Killer

Three bodies were found in the garden

REPEATED POLICE REQUESTS FOR help, sympathetic advice to homosexuals to be cautious about strangers, and televised broadcasting of a Charing Cross Station security video fuzzily showing a man in a dark anorak walking through the crowd were a feature of 1993. A killer was stalking the London gay bars, seeking men who enjoyed bondage and masochistic games, strangling or suffocating them without mercy once they were tied up and in his power.

Between March and June, victims were:

- Peter Walker, 45, theatre director of Battersea
- Christopher Dunn, 37, librarian of Wealdstone
- Perry Bradley, 35, sales director of Sulphur Springs, Texas
- Andrew Collier, 33, hostel warden of Dalston
- Emanuel Spiteri, 41, Maltese chef from Hither Green.

Maximum publicity did not start until almost all victims were killed, for at first it looked as though many might be accidental victims of erotic auto-asphyxiation.

But once the publicity began, the case was quickly solved. For 39-year-old Colin Ireland suffered the serial killer's frequent hunger for recognition. Most of his earlier attempts to bring himself to the attention of police or press had been dismissed as attention-seeking lies. But once he called in a solicitor to "defend" him against the "similarity" of the video image (which nobody else had recognised) he was not to enjoy much more freedom.

And this year he heard a judge bleakly pronounce that he would go to prison for life, and in his case that should mean life.

---

press. It was most dreadful that both Wests should be charged with the murder of their daughter Heather. But it was more satisfactory to the salacious that Mrs West should have charges of rape and assisting at rape laid against her.

The case promised to be an instant classic for crime buffs. True crime writers were hastening to acquire contracts to write the book of the case, even though nothing could be said very positively until fair trials had shown whether the Wests really were responsible for the accumulation of corpses wherever Fred had lived. And that meant a decent interval before substantial books could be published, since the trial was not expected before September 1995.

But Fred West did not live to see it. He survived 1994, although complaining of threats from other prisoners. He fired one solicitor who prematurely negotiated the sale of his story, but was said to be writing his own life in the privacy of his cell.

And there, on New Year's Day 1995 he was found hanging; a disaster for Home Secretary Michael Howard, who had spent much of 1994 huffily protesting that he was not responsible for an ever-increasing sequence of prison security scandals.

Twelve-Year-Old Cases Cleared up by Child-Killer's Conviction

THE SEARCHES FOR SUSAN MAXWELL (11), Caroline Hogg (5) and Sarah Harper (10) in 1982, 1983 and 1986 respectively were among the most high-profile investigations of the 1980's. Especially as all three children's bodies were subsequently found, and definite murder hunts were on.

But since Susan had been abducted from the Scottish Borders, and later dumped over 200 miles away between Uttoxeter and Stafford; Caroline was kidnapped from Edinburgh, and her body abandoned in Leicestershire; Sarah was last seen alive in Leeds, and found in Nottingham, it was not at first at all certain that one and the same man might be responsible. Police, however, were impressed by the kidnapping of two kiddies from Scotland both of whom were deposited in the Midlands.

In 1990 they struck lucky. A man in a blue van tried to abduct a child in the Scottish borders. But she ran away, and not realising there were adults who had seen him, he drove back through her village, leading to his own arrest.

The police found they had a 43-year-old poster delivery man on their hands. Robert Black lodged in Stamford Hill where he had a substantial collection of paediophiliac pornography. But he travelled all over the country. He was quickly convicted of the attempted abduction. But he wasn't admitting anything about the earlier murders.

It took four years of painful policing to put together the case against him. And then his credit card vouchers for petrol purchases, bed and breakfast bills, and delivery dates showed that Robert Black had undoubtedly been on the spot for not only the three highlighted killings of the 1980's, but other less well-recalled cases, like that of April Fabb from East Anglia or Pauline Hale from Devonshire.

In 1994 Black was sentenced to very long minimum terms of imprisonment for the murders of Sarah, Caroline and Susan. And police settled to the slow and heartbreaking work of trying to prove that he was also responsible for at least 17 other child murders, a couple possibly on the continent.

IN BRIEF

The cases of Robert Black and Fred West may suggest shocking detective inefficiency, with unsolved crimes from twenty years back suddenly being cleared up as chance or surprise informers deliver the right clues. But before sighing for "the good old days" of the 1950's and earlier remember that the population was smaller then, and far less people owned cars. The mobile mass murderer of today benefits from our huge anonymous population and our ability to move freely and without question very great distances in very short spaces of time.

INDEX

INDEX

ACKNOWLEDGEMENTS

The publishers would like to thank the following sources for their kind permission to reproduce the pictures in this book:

Associated News; Deseret News/Tom Smart; Hulton Deutsch Collection; Mirror Syndication International; Peter Newark's Pictures; Popperfoto; Range/Bettmann; Rex Features.

Every effort has been made to acknowledge correctly and contact the source and/or copyright holder of each picture, and Carlton Books Limited apologises for any unintentional errors or omissions, which will be corrected in future editions of this book.